"In the field of international human rights, the lure of law entices both lawyers and non-lawyers alike. Making rights legal promises precision, predictability and enforceability, in an area crying out for all three. And there are sound reasons to have faith in the law, for sometimes it delivers on these promises. At other times, however, it fails to deliver, or delivers inadequately. The essays in this timely volume spell out the positives and negatives for human rights of relying on the law, using live case studies from around the world, and in ways that are trenchant, practical and forward-looking."

—David Kinley, *The University of Sydney*

"This exciting new volume will be of interest to scholars of international relations and law. Taken together, the contributions from a range of interdisciplinary scholars offer cogent arguments for the importance of law and norms in global governance, tempered with a healthy recognition of their limitations."

—Chandra Lekha Sriram, *University of London, School of Oriental and African Studies*

The Politics of the Globalization of Law

How does the globalization of law enhance or evade the fulfillment of international human rights? Alison Brysk's edited volume aims to assess the institutional and political factors that determine the influence of the globalization of law on the realization of justice.

The globalization of law has the potential to move the international human rights regime from the generation of norms to the fulfillment of rights, through direct enforcement, reshaping state policy, granting access to civil society, and global governance of transnational forces. In this volume, an international and interdisciplinary team of scholars explores the development of new norms, mechanisms, and practices of international legal accountability for human rights abuse, and tests their power in a series of "hard cases." The studies find that new norms and mechanisms have been surprisingly effective globally, in terms of treaty adherence, international courts, universal jurisdiction, and the diffusion of citizenship rights—but this effect is conditioned by regional and domestic structures of influence and access. Thus, while the globalization of law has shaped greater rights responsiveness in hard cases in the United States, Europe, and Latin America, law has a more mixed impact on abuses in Mexico, Israel-Palestine, and India. Brysk concludes that the globalization of law is transforming sovereignty and fostering the shift from norms to fulfillment, but that peripheral states and domains often remain beyond the reach of this transformation.

Theoretically framed, but comprising empirical case material, this edited volume will be useful for both graduate students and academics in law, political science, human rights, international relations, global and international studies, and law and society.

Alison Brysk is the Mellichamp Professor of Global Governance in the Global and International Studies Program at the University of California, Santa Barbara. She has authored or edited eight books on international human rights. She has been a visiting scholar in Argentina, Ecuador, France, Spain, Sweden, the Netherlands, South Africa, and Japan, and held the Fulbright Distinguished Visiting Chair in Global Governance at Canada's Centre for International Governance Innovation. In 2011, she served as the Fulbright Senior Specialist at Ravenshaw University in Orissa, India. Her new study of communication politics and human rights campaigns, *Speaking Rights to Power*, will be published by Oxford University Press.

Routledge Advances in International Relations and Global Politics

For a full list of titles in this series, please visit www.routledge.com

The Politics of the Globalization of Law

Getting from Rights to Justice

Edited by Alison Brysk

Routledge
Taylor & Francis Group

NEW YORK AND LONDON

First published 2013
by Routledge
711 Third Avenue, New York, NY 10017

Simultaneously published in the UK
by Routledge
2 Park Square, Milton Park, Abingdon, Oxon OX14 4RN

*Routledge is an imprint of the Taylor & Francis Group,
an informa business*

© 2013 Taylor & Francis

Library of Congress Cataloging-in-Publication Data

The politics of the globalization of law : getting from rights to justice / edited
   by Alison Brysk.
      pages cm.
   1. International law and human rights.   2. Law and globalization.
I. Brysk, Alison, 1960– editor of compilation.
   KZ1266.P65 2013
   341—dc23
   2012044979

ISBN: 978-0-415-81488-1 (hbk)
ISBN: 978-0-415-83202-1 (pbk)
ISBN: 978-0-203-06668-3 (ebk)

Typeset in Sabon
by Apex CoVantage, LLC

Contents

Part II
Hard Cases: From Rights to Justice?

Figures and Tables

Acknowledgments

This project grew from a set of workshops at the University of California, Santa Barbara (UCSB) in the spring and fall of 2011, generously funded by the Duncan and Suzanne Mellichamp Endowed Chair of Global Governance. Its humane vision has supported all of my work at UCSB, including this project, and I am immensely grateful. The first workshop also benefited from critical seed funding and logistical assistance from the Orfalea Center of UCSB, with special thanks to Victor Faessel.

I would like to express my appreciation for the participation of several colleagues, beyond those represented in these pages, whose perspectives were influential during the workshops. They include Paul Amar, Eve Darian-Smith, Hilal Elver, Richard Falk, and Lisa Hajjar from UCSB. The workshops also received valuable contributions from Asli Bali (University of California, Los Angeles); Jamie Mayerfeld (University of Washington); Peter Spiro (Temple University); and Kamala Visweswaran (University of Texas).

The chapter authors included in this project have displayed a range of editorial virtues that deserve commendation above and beyond the scholarly prowess apparent in their contributions. Wayne Sandholtz, Tony Smith, and Arturo Jimenez endured multiple workshops and made multiple collegial contributions to the development of the collective enterprise. Meanwhile Claire Wright, Jinee Lokaneeta, Mark Berlin, and Gershon Shafir crafted independent contributions on tight deadlines without the benefit of workshops. Alejandro Anaya and Ludwig Beckman braved taxing international journeys and communications. Rachel Cichowski, Tony Smith, and Jinee Lokaneeta revised their work extensively, ably, quickly—and cheerfully.

UCSB doctoral candidate Natasha Bennett provided an extraordinary range of much-appreciated logistical and editorial assistance over several years of the project. UCSB Master's student Ashley Brown also gave very valuable support for the first workshop. Antonio Gonzalez of UCSB, then University of California, Irvine, and currently University of California, San Diego, also participated in numerous research support capacities as he grew from undergraduate to graduate work. Routledge quickly provided a home for the project, constructive anonymous reviews, and timely and professional editorial support. We have all been inspired to think more deeply about the promise and pitfalls of the globalization of law by the decades of scholarship of Richard Falk.

Many of us are transnational citizens who experience globalization in our own lives and families, and all of us have dedicated our careers to the study of human rights. We came together from diverse nationalities, disciplines, and perspectives around our common pursuit of the pathway to the fulfillment of human rights. The findings of this project remind us of the agency needed to translate law into liberation: by principled judiciaries, persistent advocates, and visionary cosmopolitans who insist that the purpose of sovereignty is self-determination. It is to these agents of human rights—including many of our teachers, colleagues, families, and friends—that we dedicate this volume.

Contributors

Alejandro Anaya Muñoz is Professor-researcher at the Division of International Studies and Dean of the Central Region Campus of the Center for Research and Teaching in Economics (Centro de Investigación y Docencia Económicas, CIDE), in Mexico. He is also a member of Mexico's National System of Researchers.

He holds a PhD in Government and an MA in Theory and Practice of Human Rights from the University of Essex, England. He has been Mexico Public Policy Scholar at the Woodrow Wilson International Center for Scholars, in Washington, DC.

His publications on cultural diversity and human rights in Mexico include two books and articles in the *Human Rights Quarterly*, the *Journal of Latin American Studies*, the *Critical Review of International Social and Political Philosophy*, and the *International Journal of Human Rights*.

His most recent publication is *El país bajo presión. Debatiendo el papel del escrutinio internacional de derechos humanos sobre México* [The country under pressure. A debate on the role of international human rights scrutiny over Mexico] (Mexico, CIDE, 2012).

Ludvig Beckman is Professor of Political Science in the Department of Political Science, Stockholm University. His recent books include *The Frontiers of Democracy: The Right to Vote and Its Limits* (2009) and *The Territories of Citizenship* (2012) (edited with Eva Erman). He has published widely on democratic rights, intergenerational justice, integration and immigration, children's rights, privacy rights, and genetic testing. He is currently principal investigator in two research projects, Vice Head of Department, and Editor-in-Chief of *Scandinavian Political Studies* (together with Maritta Soininen).

Mark Berlin is a PhD candidate in political science at the University of California, Irvine. His research focuses on the development and impact of international law and norms, with particular emphases on human rights, international justice, and criminal accountability.

Alison Brysk is the Mellichamp Professor of Global Governance in the Global and International Studies Program at the University of California, Santa Barbara. She has authored or edited eight books on international human rights. She has been a visiting scholar in Argentina, Ecuador, France, Spain, Sweden, the Netherlands, South Africa, and Japan, and held the Fulbright Distinguished Visiting Chair in Global Governance at Canada's Centre for International Governance Innovation. In 2011, she served as the Fulbright Senior Specialist at Ravenshaw University in Orissa, India. Her new study of communication politics and human rights campaigns, *Speaking Rights to Power*, will be published by Oxford University Press.

Rachel Cichowski is an Associate Professor in the Department of Political Science with a joint appointment in the Law, Societies and Justice Program and Director of the Comparative Law and Society Studies Center at the University of Washington. She has published books and articles on international law and organization, human rights, comparative judicial politics, and legal mobilization. She has held visiting research positions at the European University Institute, Florence, Italy, and the Max Planck Institute, Bonn, Germany.

Antonio Gonzalez received his BA from the University of California, Santa Barbara, and is a graduate student in International Relations and Pacific Studies at the University of California, San Diego.

Arturo Jimenez-Bacardi is a PhD candidate in the political science department at the University of California, Irvine. His dissertation looks at how international humanitarian and human rights law has affected the wartime policies of the United States and Israel concerning the treatment of POWs and the use of targeted killings.

Jinee Lokaneeta is an Associate Professor in Political Science at Drew University, New Jersey. Her areas of interest include Law and Violence, Political Theory, Public Law, Jurisprudence, and Cultural Studies. She is the author of *Transnational Torture: Law, Violence, and State Power in the United States and India* (New York University Press, 2011). She has published in journals such as *Studies in Law, Politics and Society*; *Economic and Political Weekly*; *Theory and Event*; and *Law, Culture, and Humanities*. Her current work focuses on the impulse of liberal states to explore "scientific truth telling" techniques such as narco analysis (truth serum), brain scanning (MRIs), and lie detectors. She is also studying the racial profiling of Muslims in the post-9/11 United States.

Wayne Sandholtz is the John A. McCone Professor of International Relations in the School of International Relations and Gould School of Law at the University of Southern California. His recent research focuses on the development, diffusion, and effects of international norms, including studies of corruption, women and globalization, wartime plundering, human rights, and the International Criminal Court. His articles have appeared in *World Politics*, the *International Studies Quarterly*, the *European Journal of International Relations*, and *International Organization*. Recent books include *International Norms and Cycles of Change* (Oxford, 2009, co-edited with Kendall Stiles) and *Prohibiting Plunder: How Norms Change* (Oxford, 2007).

Gershon Shafir is Professor in the Department of Sociology at the University of California, San Diego, and Director of its Institute for International, Comparative, and Area Studies, and the founding Director of its Human Rights Minor.

He received BAs in Political Science, Economics, Sociology, and Anthropology from Tel Aviv University, an MA in Sociology from the University of California, Los Angeles, and a PhD also in Sociology from the University of California, Berkeley.

He is the author or editor of eight books, among them: *Land, Labor, and the Origins of the Israeli-Palestinian Conflict, 1882–1914* (Cambridge University Press, 1989), co-author with Yoav Peled of *Being Israeli: The Dynamics of Multiple Citizenship* (Cambridge University Press), which won the Middle Eastern Studies Association's Albert Hourani Award in 2002, and co-editor with Mark Levine of *Struggle and Survival in Palestine/Israel* (University of California Press, 2012).

Charles Anthony Smith received his PhD from the University of California, San Diego (2004) and his JD from the University of Florida (1987). He is an Associate Professor at the University of California, Irvine. He is the author of *The Rise and Fall of War Crimes Trials: From Charles I to Bush II* (Cambridge University Press, 2012) and has published articles in *Law and Society Review*, the *Journal of Human Rights*, *Human Rights Review*, the *International Political Science Review*, *Journal of International Relations and Development*, *Judicature*, *Justice Systems Journal*, and the *Election Law Journal*, among others.

Claire Wright has a PhD in Political Science and a Master's degree in Latin American Studies from the University of Salamanca, where she is currently working as a research assistant for a project on natural resources, conflict, and indigenous peoples in Latin America. Claire's research focuses on emergency powers, conflict, and indigenous politics, and has been published in peer-reviewed journals including *Democratization* and *Latin American and Caribbean Ethnic Studies*.

1 The Politics of the Globalization of Law

Alison Brysk and
Arturo Jimenez-Bacardi

How does the globalization of law—the growth of legal norms, mechanisms, and jurisprudence across borders—affect the fulfillment of international human rights? While the past generation has seen tremendous growth in the international human rights regime, how much have new treaties, courts, and repertoires like universal jurisdiction actually improved the enforcement of core rights of the person? This volume examines the *political processes* that determine the capacity of law to produce justice, within and across nations. The globalization of law is a dialectical process whose outcome for human rights can range accordingly. As skeptics complain, the globalization of law can serve as a shield for administering economic displacement or reinforcing national security regimes—but law across borders can also be used as a weapon of the weak, a sword against the state, or a safety net for people out of place. Looking across a range of critical issues and "hard cases," we show that the key factors that make a difference include the relative autonomy of liberal legal institutions, the configuration of sovereignty for the rights at issue, and the empowerment of civil society to claim new rights within and across borders.

We seek to analyze the politics between the promise of global norms and the fulfillment of rights on the ground. David Kinley summarizes the utility of law for advancing human rights in an era of globalization as a combination of providing normative principles, a universal repertoire of definitions and boundaries, a link to state enforcement, predictable processes for conflict resolution, and a doctrine of equal standing (2009: 215). Through this range of functions, the globalization of law has the potential to increase states' enforcement of human rights for their own citizens; global regulation of interstate, transnational, or private power relations according to rights standards; and the standing or capacity of civil society actors to claim rights vis-à-vis their own states or international bodies.

We argue that norms are powerful and generate new possibilities, but norms are not enough. Global law and its institutions can fulfill its promise when it is matched by critical elements of democracy—independent liberal legal institutions, empowered and open civil societies, and some level of self-determination. When these elements of national and global democracy are present, they can move imperfect states along the spectrum towards enforcement, ungoverned spaces towards regulation, and enhance the counterhegemonic capacity of citizens within and across borders.

THE GLOBALIZATION OF LAW

The globalization of law refers to a linked ensemble of changes in the scale, scope, mode, and juridical forms: (1) the global diffusion of legal norms and processes; (2) multilayered legal pluralism including regional, indigenous, and family law; (3) new global legal institutions like the International Criminal Court (ICC); (4) transnational law governing private cross-border activities; (5) new repertoires of jurisprudence and practice, such as participation rights for noncitizens; (6) the growing salience of conventional interstate and comparative jurisprudence for domestic practice, such as universal jurisdiction for crimes against humanity. International human rights have become globalized in several overlapping senses. Human rights norms are increasingly universal via an "overlapping consensus" on core rights of the person. Human rights mechanisms are increasingly cosmopolitan, reaching above, below, and across state sovereignty. And human rights threats are increasingly globalized, either resulting directly from transnational nonstate actors or occurring in areas of limited sovereignty. Finally, globalization has shifted the repertoire of state responsiveness through the "citizenship gap" in which global power dynamics—from economic exchange to migration—may evade, transcend, or outsource the state's traditional provision of rights for members via citizenship.[1]

The intersection between the globalization of law and the globalization of rights is a question of global governance: in what ways and to what extent can and should law across borders regulate and enforce the protection of individuals from abuse of both global and local authority? Nonetheless, many argue that state power is still the ultimate enforcer of the rights of the individual, whether the addressee is one's own state, a transnational entity, or another state transgressing boundaries through war crimes, genocide, or illicit detention. The question is how the globalization of human rights legal norms, mechanisms, and practices affect the fulfillment of human rights on the ground. Fulfillment is broader than "compliance"—it will generally involve some combination of enforcement by a state, regulation of a state's practices, enhancement of citizen capacity to claim rights, or a reconstruction of claims and practices.

Since 1945, with the creation of the United Nations (UN) and the passage by the UN General Assembly of the Universal Declaration of Human Rights (UNDHR) three years thereafter, the world has experienced the proliferation of human rights law as well as enforcement mechanisms. Today, there are seven core international human rights treaties that have been ratified by at least 70% of the member states of the UN: 141 states have ratified the

Convention on the Prevention and Punishment of the Crime of Genocide; 174 states have ratified the International Convention on the Elimination of All Forms of Racial Discrimination (CERD); 160 states have ratified the International Covenant on Economic, Social, and Cultural Rights (ICESCR); 167 states have ratified the International Covenant on Civil and Political Rights (ICCPR); 187 have ratified the Convention on the Elimination of All Forms of Discrimination Against Women (CEDAW); 149 have ratified the Convention Against Torture and Other Cruel, Inhuman or Degrading Treatment or Punishment (CAT); and 193 have ratified the Convention on the Rights of the Child (CRC). Several of these core human rights treaties have been supplemented by optional protocols specifying further protections. There are also several regional human rights conventions, notably in Europe and the Americas, as well as many more international human rights treaties that have been drafted and begun the process of ratification. In terms of setting new laws on the books, the human rights regime has significantly evolved in recent decades.

With the emergence and expansion of international human rights law, legal processes and mechanisms have followed in an attempt to enforce such protections. Sikkink and Walling (2007) explain that since 1979 there has been an explosion of national truth commissions and national, foreign, and international human rights trials. Out of 84 new states and/or transitioning democracies from 1979 to 2004, 63 of them established either a truth commission or a human rights trial, illustrating the larger global phenomenon towards individual criminal responsibility and accountability for human rights. Similarly, in the last two decades there has also been a significant progression in international criminal tribunals. In the spring of 1993, the UN Security Council established the ad hoc International Criminal Tribunal for the former Yugoslavia (ICTY), the first international tribunal since the Nuremberg and Tokyo Trials. Eighteen months later, the UN also approved the establishment of the International Criminal Tribunal for Rwanda (ICTR). Since then, the international community has also approved several hybrid domestic-international trials, including the Special Panels for Serious Crimes in East Timor, the Special Court for Sierra Leone, the Extraordinary Chambers in the Courts of Cambodia, and the Special Tribunal for Lebanon. Finally, in 1998 with the adoption of the Rome Statute by 120 states, the international community moved to establish the International Criminal Court (ICC), the first permanent international court authorized to charge individuals with war crimes, crimes against humanity, and genocide. As a result of this increase in national, regional, and international human rights jurisprudence, Lutz and Reiger (2009) report that between 1990 and 2008 there have been 67 heads of state or government officials from 43 countries from around the world that have been formally charged or indicted with serious criminal offenses (half of which dealt with human rights violations, and the other half with corruption)—an impressive feat given less than a handful of such cases prior to 1990.

At the same time, international jurisprudence and practice have produced new or expanded repertoires for human rights accountability. These repertoires are neither particular human rights norms nor specific institutions, but rather the spread of new or increasingly legitimate strategies to use institutions to apply or expand norms. Important repertoires include the extension of universal jurisdiction for crimes against humanity, individual or nongovernmental standing in international human rights institutions, transnational litigation for corporate responsibility, use of civil as well as criminal law for human rights accountability, greater use of reparations and intergenerational justice, characterization of forced disappearance as an ongoing crime not subject to statues of limitation, and global shifts in legal protocols regarding sexual and domestic violence. Repertoires like universal jurisdiction interact tightly with the development of tribunals, with some effect on national jurisprudence. But transnational and civil litigation for corporate responsibility stands somewhat parallel to expanding treaties and courts as a spreading practice—a new strategy for a new human rights challenge, using existing institutions in a new way. The most structurally diverse new repertoire concerns the legal treatment of rape and sexual violence, which has generated norms, shaped institutions, and mobilized practice. Shifting definitions, characterization, evidentiary standards, and standing to litigate sexual violence have affected international treaties, domestic laws, international courts, domestic courts, legal strategies of human rights campaigns, and refugee standards.

What does existing literature tell us about where we stand in our understanding of the extent and meaning of these intersecting forms of the globalization of legal norms, institutions, and practices? There is a rough spectrum from pessimistic structural theories through more optimistic cosmopolitan reformist theories of norm change, with a distinctive critical position that describes a dialectical struggle over the terms and impact of global governance between hegemonic forces and challengers. We first review the linked debates on the norms and institutions of the globalization of law, and then outline our own version of a dialectical approach that combines critical and constructivist insights on the transformative potential of law across borders through political process.

NORMS: DO TREATIES MATTER—AND HOW?

The conventional wisdom of international relations realism asserted that international law was a reflection of the power relations of states, and that rights were an epiphenomenal projection of the norms of powerful democratic states at best—and sheer hypocrisy at worst (Waltz 1979; Krasner 1999). Further along the spectrum, liberal institutionalists in international relations (Keohane 1984; Keohane and Martin 1995; Goldstein and Keohane 1993) and game-theoretic legal theorists (Goodman and Jinks 2004;

Guzman 2008) believe that the globalization of law and rights is real and consequential—but limited in impact. For these skeptics, the construction of collaborative and multilevel institutions may occur when it is functional for the powerful—and may even take on a life of its own and construct new interests, as has clearly occurred in Europe. Nevertheless, for this school the scope of global law will be limited to coordination dilemmas and governance failures, and will be weakly tied to normative universalism.

Representative of the pessimism of structural theories, Eric Posner (2009: xv) has argued that "it is most definitely not my claim that international law does not exist or does not matter. The argument is instead that international law exists and matters when it serves nation-states' interests in international cooperation." Thus, individual states will engage in a cost-benefit calculation where they will weigh the potential gains from abiding with international legal standards against the potential costs of abrogating such agreements. The costs of not complying with international obligations can be high, Posner explains, so states do not violate such agreements lightly, but when and if the pay-offs from compliance change, then it becomes logical to expect a state to violate any given treaty (Ibid.). However, when it comes to human rights law, structural pessimists are quick to point out that human rights treaties lack the three key components that make the violation of other forms of international law costly: (1) coercion or the genuine threat of international enforcement; (2) mutual gains; and (3) the logic of reciprocity (Goldsmith and Posner 2005; Posner 2009; Goodman and Jinks 2004; Guzman 2008; Hathaway 2002; Hafner-Burton 2005).

Although Goldsmith and Posner acknowledge that powerful states—since at least the beginning of the modern state system—do on occasion coercively intervene in the affairs of other states for humanitarian reasons, such interventions remain rare. Furthermore, interventions on human rights grounds predate the establishment of multilateral human rights treaties. The impetus for human rights–inspired interventions arises from the concerns of citizens belonging to a powerful state (normally in relation to threats towards foreign coreligionists, co-ethnics, or co-nationals, though basic notions of human dignity can also inspire such campaigns) who then pressure their government to intervene in faraway lands (Goldsmith and Posner 2005). Examples include Britain's use of military force to ensure the elimination of the slave trade (Krasner 1999), or Britain, France, and Russia's 19th-century military interventions inside the Ottoman Empire to protect Christian minorities (Goldsmith and Posner 2005; Finnemore 2004), as well as more recent cases oftentimes referred to as "humanitarian interventions" (Wheeler 2002; Finnemore 2004). Such instances are quite unusual and thus rarely if ever deter or outweigh the domestic gains that political elites can incur from repressing segments of their population (i.e., maintaining the status quo). In addition to being rare, humanitarian interventions are also inconsistent, since the potential interveners might not always perceive another state's domestic repression as negative (i.e., repressive measures might crush an insurgency that is perceived as worse than the government in power) (Posner 2009). The costs of such interventions can also be high, which can deter a unilateral intervention, or cause a collective action problem that severely limits a multilateral response (Guzman 2008; Bagaric and Dimopoulos 2005). Ultimately, the human rights regime lacks a superior power with the authority or capability to ensure or compel compliance with human rights law (Hafner-Burton and Tsutsui 2005; Hathaway 2002), in contrast to much more institutionalized mechanisms that are present in other legal systems including the international trade regime.

Pessimists contend that human rights law also lacks the self-enforcing incentives that lead to cooperation and compliance (Goldsmith and Posner 2005; Hafner-Burton and Tsutsui 2005; Hathaway 2002; Simmons 2009). First, for the most part, multilateral human rights treaties do not provide material incentives or clear mutual gains in order to ensure self-compliance. What makes an agreement self-enforcing is that the parties need to perceive that abiding with an agreement will incur more gains than abrogating it (Guzman 2008; Hafner-Burton 2005; Simmons 2009). For example, the World Trade Organization's (WTO) market access rules are followed mainly due to the signatories' interest in maintaining their participation in and benefits from free trade (Simmons 2009). But no such clear benefits—certainly no clear material gains—result from complying with a multilateral human rights treaty (Hafner-Burton 2005, 2009). More important, a state can achieve its desired level of domestic rights protections without the need to cooperate with any other state (Simmons 2009). Second, the logic of reciprocity is also weak for human rights law. To continue with the example from trade law, a treaty partner is unlikely to violate an agreement for fear that the other parties to the treaty will also renege on their obligations threatening the benefits from future trade. With human rights treaties the same logic does not apply, after all, it is highly unlikely that a state will repress its own citizens in order to reciprocate for abuses elsewhere (Goldsmith and Posner 2005). Even reputational costs, which game-theoretic legal theorists and liberal institutionalists laud as a clear self-enforcing mechanism, do not seem to hold much sway with human rights law (Keohane 1984; Guzman 2008). Downs and Jones (2002) find that reputation costs help promote compliance with international trade and security agreements, but have little influence with environmental and human rights law. In other words, the main structural incentives (mutual gains) and disincentives (threat of coercion, reciprocity, reputational costs) that guide cooperation and compliance in several international legal regimes are either extremely weak or nonexistent in human rights law, making the international human rights treaty regime an "embarrassment," as Posner has put it (2009: 185–6). Instead, Goldsmith and Posner (2005: 134) contend that "most human rights practices are explained by coercion or coincidence of interest," not because a state has ratified a human rights treaty.

The empirical evidence with regards to the effects of human rights treaties on state behavior is quite mixed though. Consistent with several of the conclusions made by structural pessimists, several large-*n* studies have found that human rights treaties have had no independent effects on state behavior. Keith (1999) found that although countries that have ratified the ICCPR tend on average to respect civil and political rights more than nonparty states, she did not find any improvements in the behavior of ratifiers after they had adopted the treaty. In addition, when controlling for several factors (including democracy, economic development, population size, and engagement in civil or international wars) the impact of the treaty on state behavior completely disappeared. Keith concludes that the insignificance of the treaty is due to the weakness of the treaty's implementation mechanisms, which may lead some states to realize that, "with little to risk, they may gain a significant public relations tool in being a party to the covenant" (Keith 1999: 112). More alarming, Hathaway found that when controlling for several factors, treaty ratification for the Genocide Convention, CAT, and ICCPR (fair trial) are not only "not associated with better human rights practices than otherwise expected, but it is often associated with *worse* practices" (2002: 1989, emphasis added). Like Keith, Hathaway argues that since the monitoring mechanisms for human rights treaties are weak, noncompliance becomes costless, yet ratifying the treaty will garner "expressive" gains as the international community will acknowledge that state's acceptance of the norm regardless of the actual commitment to the treaty's principles (Hathaway 2002: 2006). Hafner-Burton and Tsutsui (2005: 1378) find that the international human rights law regime has created a "paradox of empty promises," where states with no intention of complying with the treaty nonetheless ratify it—at no cost—as a form of "window dressing" or "cheap talk" providing them with international legitimacy and shielding them from pressure to change their behavior (Bagarik and Dimopoulos 2005).

But paradoxically, the ratification of the treaty also provides legitimacy to the international norms of appropriate behavior, giving added leverage to human rights advocates in order to pressure repressive governments to comply with human rights norms (Hafner-Burton and Tsutsui 2005). By emphasizing the role of transnational advocacy networks, Hafner-Burton and Tsutsui delineate a point of departure between structural pessimist theories and cosmopolitan reformist theories of norm change. More liberal constructivist scholars of norms emphasize the "power of human rights" to promote change through changes in norms and the mobilization of nonstate actors in the international arena (Brysk 1993; Risse, Ropp, and Sikkink 1999; Lutz and Sikkink 2000; Simmons 2009). An additional break in the literature is that the more optimistic cosmopolitan reformist theories also stress the importance of domestic institutions in conditioning how governments respond to human rights law, an agenda we will take up in this study. Simmons argues that human rights treaties "have a singularly unusual property: They are negotiated internationally but create stakeholders almost exclusively domestically" (Simmons 2009: 126). Structural pessimists may be correct in asserting that human rights treaties lack the coercive and self-enforcing mechanisms necessary for them to have any significant effects on state behavior, but only insofar as state-to-state relations are concerned. Cosmopolitan optimists criticize structural pessimists for their interstate centric focus since it ignores the causal influence that international human rights law has on state-society relations (Simmons 2009; Moravcsik 2000; Biersteker, Spiro, Sriram, and Raffo 2007). Human rights treaties are meaningful because they empower transnational advocacy networks (Keck and Sikkink 1998), domestic political elites (Moravcsik 2000; Slaughter 2005), and other local groups or individuals (Santos and Rodriguez-Garavito 2005; Langer 2007). When a state commits itself to an international human rights instrument, it raises domestic actors' expectations; it helps set priorities, focus strategies and resources; it shapes meanings, identities, interests, and discourses, and strengthens the bargaining position of rights claimants (Simmons 2009; Santos and Rodriguez-Garavito 2005; Goodale and Merry 2007).

Several small-*n* studies have shown how human rights treaties are positively linked to improvements in state behavior, and have helped trace the causal mechanisms at work. Brysk (1993) found that during the last military dictatorship in Argentina (1976–83), the claims of domestic human rights groups were able to gain legitimacy—both at home and abroad—thanks to the resonance of their demands which gained international recognition as they tapped well-established international legal agreements. Consequently, the Argentine human rights movement was able to successfully connect with the international system and a transnational coalition began exerting pressure on the junta from above and below. Brysk concludes that without the linking of domestic demands with international human rights norms and advocates, the Argentine human rights groups would have been destroyed. Ultimately the transnational campaign was able to change the discourse of basic rights in Argentina, and empowered those rights groups to help shape the nature of Argentina's democratic transition. Lutz and Sikkink (2000) also found a positive relationship between the ratification of CAT and other regional instruments banning torture and improvements in state behavior in Uruguay and Paraguay. Thomas (1999) studied the effects of the 1975 Helsinki Accords, originally intended to ease tensions between the West and the Eastern bloc, but which also included pledges to respect human rights and abide by international human rights law. Local activists perceived the accords "not as a ratification of the status quo, as the Communist regimes were portraying it, but as a promising and unprecedented opportunity to challenge the repressiveness of those regimes" (Thomas 1999: 209). Local activists became empowered as their expectations and rights demands gained salience through the recognition and support they garnered from the international community helping reshape state-society relations. With varying degrees of success throughout Eastern European states, the human rights provisions within the Helsinki Accords empowered domestic activists to reshape the identities, interests, and behaviors of their respective states as they would all undergo radical transformations by the late 1980s. Similarly,

Ron (1997) shows how Israel's ratification of the CAT in 1991 significantly changed the way the Israeli government conducted interrogations against Palestinians, creating a much more regulated process and significantly limiting the use of intense physical force.

The diffusion of norms has also received increasing attention by more optimistic scholars focusing on the effects of international human rights law. Simmons, Dobbin, and Garrett (2006: 787) explain that international norms diffusion occurs when "government policy decisions in a given country are systematically conditioned by prior policy choices made in other countries," and can be further mediated by the role of nonstate actors. As with the larger literature on the effects of international law, scholars disagree as to which factors—ranging from coercion, competition, learning, and emulation—most influence the phenomenon of norm diffusion (Simmons, Dobbin, and Garrett 2006). Moreover, when tracing the mechanisms and agents at work, scholars also emphasize various actors and processes. For example, focusing on political elites instead of civil society, Moravcsik (2000) argues that European political leaders ratified human rights treaties in order to "lock-in" a certain level of political stability by constraining the actions of potential radical right/left-wing leaders. The European Convention on Human Rights, though, has seemingly taken a life of its own, and today, the European Court of Human Rights (ECHR) has proven to be as "effective as any domestic court" (Helfer and Slaughter 1997). Some have criticized these small-n studies as suffering from selection bias, as they tend to analyze well-publicized success stories and most of the cases either come from Europe or Latin America (Thoms, Ron, and Paris 2010).

Notwithstanding the critiques, more recent large-n studies have also found a positive relation between human rights treaty ratification and improved state behavior, with certain key intervening variables. Neumayer (2005) looks at the effects of CAT and the ICCPR (as well as several regional treaties) and finds that democratic states that ratify the treaties do indeed improve their behavior. There is also improved behavior in states where citizens participate in international nongovernmental organizations (NGOs). Landman (2005) finds a positive, though "limited" association with human rights treaty ratification and improvements in a state's respect for basic rights, while democracy, wealth, and interdependence each provide a significant boost to such protections. Following Keith's (2002) preliminary work, more studies need to test the importance of judicial independence in explaining adherence to human rights law (as Sandholtz does in this volume). Finally, Simmons (2009), after excluding false positives (states that ratify a human rights treaty without any intention of complying with its principles) and false negatives (states that support the principles of a treaty but do not ratify it due to domestic costs), finds that ratification of the ICCPR, CEDAW, CAT, and CRC *are* positively associated with improvements in human rights protections, but only when coupled with civil society activism, judicial enforcement, and transnational socialization.

The more recent phase in the globalization of law has been the expansion of several transnational legal mechanisms meant to close the accountability gap of the human rights regime. As with the debates surrounding the effectiveness of human rights treaties, liberal optimists and structural skeptics disagree about the normative desirability and usefulness of these new global legal mechanisms. We now turn to these debates.

THE GLOBALIZATION OF HUMAN RIGHTS MECHANISMS: CRIMINAL TRIBUNALS

With the proliferation of human rights treaties in the past 60 years, there has also been an impressive explosion of instruments and mechanisms that attempt to enforce accountability for gross human rights violations. Mechanisms include monitoring agencies; truth commissions; and domestic, foreign, regional, international, and hybrid courts.

The existence, design, and jurisprudence of human rights courts reflects global influences that generally seem to increase their impact. Slaughter (2005) has found a "transgovernmental" network of judges, regulators, and legislators that coordinate and learn from one another. Some of these networks have resulted in the expansion of human rights protections. For example, the South African Supreme Court found the death penalty unconstitutional in part by citing ECHR decisions. Also citing ECHR rulings, the Supreme Court of Zimbabwe ruled corporal punishment illegal. Tshosa (2001) illustrates how in Namibia and Botswana the ICCPR has helped guide and reshape their constitutional order and rights expectations and limited the types of punishments that the state can enact on convicted criminals, as well as increasing attempts at assuring fair trials. More recently, Langer (2007) has added to the literature by showing that norms can diffuse from peripheral or weak states to other peripheral and even core states. Focusing on the recent wave of reforms that have transformed the criminal procedure codes of 14 Latin American states from inquisitorial to accusatorial legal systems, Langer shows how a group of Latin American lawyers spearheaded the reforms as both the intellectual authors and key advocates for change in the legal process. From the drafting to the implementation of a new set of rules intended to increase transparency, efficiency, and due process protections—more consistent with legal standards—this "southern activist expert network" successfully convinced both local and international actors that the new codes needed to be adopted. As a result, a "diffusion from the periphery" began with these legal entrepreneurs, and once they had persuaded one state to adopt the new legal codes, a legal "code cascade effect" emerged generating "peer pressure" on others to follow suit (Langer 2007: 619). In other words, human rights norms can also transform the identities and interests of political and governmental elites—from both powerful and weak states—which in turn can change state behavior.

The debate on human rights trials following conflict or regime change is more contested. Cosmopolitan optimists argue that criminal prosecutions of gross human rights violations strengthen stability and peace by removing threats and deterring future abusers. They also foster national healing and reconciliation and improve human rights and democracy. Akhavan (2001: 9) asserts that the ICTY marginalized ultranationalist political elites, which opened the door for more moderate factions supportive of multi-ethnic co-existence to ascend to power, and discouraged violent reprisals by victim groups. In short, according to Akhavan, the ICTY helped the peace-building effort and allowed for a smoother transition from conflict towards sustainable peace. Looking at the 17 Latin American states that have had human rights trials, Sikkink and Walling (2007) found—in contrast to pessimists' claims—that democracy was not undermined in any case by the trials, nor was there any evidence that trials exacerbate violence. On the contrary, the evidence shows that "in 14 of the 17 cases of Latin American countries that have chosen trials, human rights seem to have improved" (Sikkink and Walling 2007: 442). In a much larger study that analyzes the effects of domestic and international human rights trials in 100 transitional countries, Kim and Sikkink (2010) once again find that states with human rights prosecutions show higher levels of respect for human rights than states with no prosecutions. In addition, states with more cumulative prosecutions also show higher respect for their citizens' basic rights than countries with less or no prosecutions. Kim and Sikkink argue that their findings help develop the theoretical claim that human rights prosecutions have a strong deterrent effect both within and beyond the borders of the prosecuting state. Human rights trials are more than just mechanisms of punishment or enforcement; they are also "high-profile symbolic events that communicate and dramatize norms" and increase the perception by state officials that the costs of repressing citizens are much higher than they were before (Kim and Sikkink 2010: 940). Finally, Olsen, Payne, and Reiter (2010) analyze the effects of a combination of human rights mechanisms in 91 transitions from 74 different states. Their results show that human rights trials on their own do not have any significant effects on state behavior. However, if human rights trials are coupled with amnesties then there are improvements in human rights and democracy. The logic is that the combination of trials and amnesties represent a balanced justice because demands for accountability as well as stability are respected.

Pessimists on the other hand claim that human rights trials—especially those with universal standards—can make matters worse, particularly when they fail to take political realities into consideration (Snyder and Vinjamuri 2003/2004). Goldsmith and Krasner (2003) argue that the prospects of human rights trials—especially if they are removed from power considerations—can lead heads of state or other armed groups to be wary of peace negotiations or end to hostilities for fear of prosecution. For example, they argue that "the threat of prosecution by the international tribunal in The

Hague made it practically impossible for NATO to reach an early deal with Milosevic, thereby lengthening the war and the suffering in the Balkans" (Goldsmith and Krasner 2003: 55). They also challenge the notion that the fear of prosecution can deter future leaders from taking repressive measures because gross human rights violators tend to be "motivated by their own sense of mission and justice. They have seen themselves as saviors, not sinners. They have been determined to cling to power and they believe, as all leaders with a mission do, that they can reshape the world in their own image" (Goldsmith and Krasner 2003: 55). Ultimately, the threat of prosecution will most likely prolong violence in entrenched conflicts, and could potentially spark another round of hostilities in dormant conflicts. Snyder and Vinjamuri (2003/2004) conducted a study with 32 cases of civil wars over a 14-year period starting in 1989. In terms of international tribunals they conclude that both the ICTY and ICTR failed to "deter subsequent atrocities or contribute to bringing peace in the region" (Snyder and Vinjamuri 2003/2004: 20). In Rwanda, for example, the Rwandan Patriotic Front engaged in severe revenge killings against Hutus within their state, and in the following years, Rwanda intervened in neighboring Democratic Republic of Congo, leading to massive death and destruction (Snyder and Vinjamuri 2003/2004: 25; Graubart 2010). For domestic tribunals, they find mixed results, with some cases showing marginal deterrence effects, and others worsening scenarios. Snyder and Vinjamuri conclude that amnesties, when properly implemented, are a much more effective mechanism for achieving peace and stability.

For both the effects of human rights law and its mechanisms there is significant variation across issue area (or right), and space (especially in terms of geographical regions). For example, East Asian and Pacific region states are much more reluctant to sign human rights treaties and are especially cautious not to ratify the CAT or ICCPR (Simmons 2009). Similarly, 54% of all truth commissions and human rights trials have taken place in the Americas (Sikkink and Walling 2007).

Lastly, with regards to cases involving universal jurisdiction, the debate—more normative than empirically based—follows along similar lines as those concerning the effects of international tribunals. Liberal optimists argue that universal jurisdiction increases international justice and stability by bringing criminals to trial, challenging impunity, deterring potential human rights abusers or war criminals, and setting a minimum global legal standard against gross human rights violations (Roth 2001; Roht-Arriaza 2005). Structural skeptics criticize the practice as a form of "lawfare"—a legal tool by the weak to humiliate or limit the actions of the powerful in the international arena, and for emphasizing irresponsible deontological as opposed to consequentialist ethics, potentially leading to judicial chaos and the further deterioration of conflicts (Kissinger 2001; Goldsmith and Krasner 2003).

The few empirical studies focused on the effects of universal jurisdiction present a more nuanced reality, where power dynamics have mediated against the hopes of optimists and the fears of skeptics. Roht-Arriaza (2005) finds that the initial euphoria of the Pinochet case was premature. With more than 120 states having some universal jurisdiction provisions in place, it appeared that this rediscovered legal mechanism was going to change transnational justice. Yet, of the more than 1,000 universal jurisdiction complaints filed, only 32 ever made it to trial (Langer 2011). More important, it quickly became clear that current heads of state or individuals with strong connections to the centers of power remain safe from prosecution. The decentralized and often haphazard way in which several of the complaints and prosecutions were managed "overloaded" the system and led to a combination of judicial decisions and legislative actions that gutted key components of the universal jurisdiction regime (Roht-Arriaza 2005). For example, prosecutions in Spain and Belgium, the two main forums for high-profile cases, resulted in the incorporation and diffusion of "link" (nationality tie) and "defendant's presence" requirements, effectively making "jurisdiction that is universal in name only" (Roht Arriaza 2005: 192).

Langer (2011) also shows that both proponents and skeptics have exaggerated their enthusiasm or concern over universal jurisdiction. Paying close attention to power considerations and domestic institutions, Langer emphasizes the incentive structure of universal jurisdiction (potentially high costs imposed by the defendant's state versus weak gains from domestic and human rights constituencies in favor of prosecution), and concludes that prosecuting states will most likely focus on defendants that pose low international relations costs. As such, most universal jurisdiction cases that have actually gone to trial have involved "low-cost" defendants from Rwanda (11), the former Yugoslavia (8), Nazi Germany (5), or Afghanistan (4), individuals whose state of origin refuses (or is unable) to defend them, and where the international community agrees that they should be prosecuted (Langer 2011: 8). Conversely, cases that involved "high-cost" defendants (i.e., *Belgium v George H. W. Bush*; *Germany v Jiang Zemin*) not only did not get much traction, but resulted in legislation strengthening executive discretion in the prosecuting state to make sure similar prosecutions are less likely to recur. Given the incentive structure, Langer concludes that universal jurisdiction,

> Will never establish a minimum international rule of law—that is, it will never substantially close the impunity gap regarding international crimes or be applied equally across defendants—since high-cost, most mid-cost, and many low-cost defendants are beyond the reach of the universal jurisdiction enforcement regime ... [In addition] several common criticisms of universal jurisdiction are unfounded, given that states have incentives to concentrate on defendants about whom there is broad agreement in the international community and whom their own state of nationality is not willing to defend. For these reasons, universal jurisdiction is unlikely to lead to unmanageable international tensions, judicial chaos, or interference with political solutions to mass atrocities. (Langer 2011: 2–3)

Thus, while the effects of universal jurisdiction have been modest, some positive effects can be attributed to this regime. As Roht-Arriaza explains, the Pinochet case did legitimize the transnational prosecution of gross human rights violators under certain circumstances. These cases also began to challenge the immunity of government officials by delegitimizing amnesty laws, and unfair trials, as such tools are now subject to outside scrutiny. More important, these transnational legal mechanisms created a sense of empowerment, providing legitimacy and agency to the victims and survivors of gross violations as they transformed into the driving forces behind new domestic prosecutions (Roht-Arriaza 2005).

Roht-Arriaza links the use of new mechanisms to expanding networks and repertoires of practice and finds a "two-track approach to international justice" (Roht-Arriaza 2005: 202). On the one hand are the growing global institutions of justice. Next to these is a burgeoning network of national courts, lawyers, activists, and rights-seekers demanding accountability through transnational prosecutions.

We turn now to examine the globalization of law through new bottom-up practices that are described and advocated by the critical cosmopolitan perspective.

GLOBAL REPERTOIRES OF ACCOUNTABILITY: A MULTITRACK CRITICAL APPROACH

In a different vein, subaltern cosmopolitan legalism proposes an alternative, critical cosmopolitanism of "counter-hegemonic globalization" (Santos and Rodriguez-Garavito 2005). This theoretical school systematically searches for the possibilities of subaltern reconstruction of global law as an emancipatory practice (Rajagopal 2003; Falk, Rajagopal, and Stevens 2008; Goodale and Merry 2007). Santos explains the focus of subaltern cosmopolitanism as "Instead of discarding cosmopolitanism as just one more variety of global hegemony, we propose to revise the concept by shifting the focus of attention to those who currently need it" (Santos 2002: 460). By emphasizing the "citizenship gap," or the "*discrimination* in the exercise of universal human rights," Brysk (2008: 56) shows how in Latin America, despite elections and theoretical improvements in the rule of law, universal human rights are far from being fulfilled, especially if the focus is on the most vulnerable members of society. Street children, the homeless, indigenous peoples, blacks, the poor, and women are effectively second-class citizens as their "language, illiteracy, and lack of economic resources systematically exclude them from access to the legal system and protection from its excesses" (Brysk 2008: 61). Multiple sources of violence and abuse—public, private, and transnational—as well as endemic impunity, massive inequality, and the demobilization of affected groups result in the "insufficient application of democracy to functional arenas of power outside the formal legal system that distort the juridical equality of citizenship" (Brysk 2008: 56). Given such (long-standing) challenges, subaltern cosmopolitans argue that the focus of analysis should then be on "whoever is a victim of local intolerance and discrimination needs cross-border tolerance and support; whoever lives in misery in a world of wealth needs cosmopolitan solidarity; whoever is a non- or second-class citizen of a country or the world needs an alternative conception of national and global citizenship. In short, the large majority of the world's populace, excluded from top-down cosmopolitan projects, needs a different type of cosmopolitanism" (Santos 2002: 460).

This kind of approach grapples with a wider range of transnational and "private" challenges, alongside the interstate and national regulation of civil and political rights of liberal cosmopolitanism. A leading area for expanding subaltern legal contestation encompasses the role that globalization has had in expanding the power of multinational corporations (MNCs), potentially at the expense of individuals across the globe, especially those in the global South. Critics of the current economic order point to an "accountability gap," or a lack of "corporate responsibility," and try to assess how actors are trying to resist this growing challenge. At the turn of the millennium, 51 out of the 100 largest economies in the world were MNCs (Sperling 2009). With hundreds of thousands of MNCs and their subsidiaries spread across the globe, these privately owned entities cast a heavy economic, environmental, and political shadow on people's daily lives. Under the deregulatory pressures of globalizations, states—especially weak states—are finding themselves not only unable to hold MNCs to account, but in many instances, the relationship is reversed, where states are the ones accountable to corporations' demands (Sperling 2009). As Human Rights First explains, with the rise of transnational corporate power, new challenges for the protection of human rights have also emerged,

> In the cold war ... the main issue was how do you hold governments accountable when they violate laws and norms. Today the emerging issue is how do you hold private companies accountable for the treatment of their workers at a time when government control is ebbing all over the world, or governments themselves are going into business and can't be expected to play the watchdog or protection role. (Quoted in Sperling 2009: 96)

Nonetheless, even as the influence of MNCs continues to grow, domestic and transnational actors have increased their pressure in hopes of attaining some form of corporate accountability and to strengthen the basic rights of victims of corporate abuse.

Most mechanisms for corporate accountability involve "soft" law, or voluntary commitments, as opposed to "hard" law, due in part to the larger deregulatory trend of the past three decades (Koenig-Archibugi 2004). In this regard, Graubart (2008) assessed the quasijudicial, nonbinding citizen petitions set up by the North American Free Trade Agreement (NAFTA)'s parallel accords on labor and environmental rights. Designed to partially alleviate discontent with the business-friendly, neoliberal orientation of NAFTA, the parallel accords enabled labor movements, environmentalists, and other activists to file complaints against any of the North American governments for alleged violations of labor or environmental laws (Graubart 2008: 3). While the quasijudicial bodies could make findings of rights violations and order further consultations among the member governments, they could not compel changes in behavior from the target government. Nevertheless, Graubart found that labor movements and environmental groups had success in incorporating these NAFTA petitions with ongoing political mobilization to shame both governments and private corporations into changing their behavior. In one petition, a coalition of Mexican and U.S. labor activists used a NAFTA labor petition to ratchet up political mobilization against both the Mexican government and U.S. companies in the *maquiladora* zone involved in systematic discrimination against pregnant workers. There, the petitioners successfully prodded the Mexican government to establish an outreach program to educate female workers and employers regarding constitutional prohibitions against discrimination against pregnant women and shamed several U.S. corporations to discontinue pregnancy screenings (Graubart 2008; Sperling 2009). This case shows that even "soft" law mechanisms, coupled with strong human rights advocacy campaigns, can force MNCs to improve the rights of their workers. To be sure, Graubart found that the success was often qualified with the powerful U.S. government being especially difficult to shame (Graubart 2008). Nonetheless, these quasilegal mechanisms have proven to be more effective than critics suggested (for early critiques, see Wallach and Naiman 1998; Fox 2002). Other attempts at establishing "soft" mechanisms of accountability for MNCs include naming and shaming campaigns such as the Fair Labor Association, involving U.S. apparel companies, universities, and human rights NGOs committed to setting and monitoring a code of conduct for the industry that respects worker's rights (Koenig-Archibugi 2004).

In addition to "soft" law mechanisms, another growing avenue for corporate responsibility has been the ascent of civil criminal accountability. Mainly through the use of the US Alien Tort Claims Act (ATCA), human rights victims from anywhere in the world can file civil lawsuits against MNCs for their involvement—direct or indirect—in breaching international human rights treaties (Herz 2008). Critics of corporate liability under the ATCA argue that such claims interfere with the sovereignty of other states; potentially weaken or limit incentives to develop their own legal systems; undermine U.S. foreign policy and attempts at "constructive engagement" meant to alleviate domestic human rights crises; and represent only a "second-best" response since sovereign immunity clauses often leave state violators free from prosecution. (Most of these arguments were advanced by the George W. Bush administration. See Nemeroff 2008; Herz 2008.) Proponents of the practice counter that ATCA claims help victims cope with past crimes, induce

MNCs to behave responsibly, and promote democracy and human rights by forcing MNCs to think twice before they partner up with brutal regimes (Herz 2008). This literature is more focused on the legal details and debates surrounding U.S. court decisions. Empirical studies are needed in order to assess the effects of ATCA claims on MNCs and foreign governments (both human rights violators and potential borrowers of the American model).

Subaltern cosmopolitans also expand their field of study by emphasizing the "citizenship gap," focusing on the rights of groups that have oftentimes gone unnoticed by the dominant human rights campaigns. For example, several studies have focused on the global shifts in the characterization and prosecution protocols regarding sexual violence. Copelon (2011) looks at the progress and remaining challenges towards accountability for violence against women in conflict zones. Legally, none of the major human rights treaties, including CEDAW, explicitly mention sexual violence as a crime. Similarly, the IV Geneva Conventions only "weakly prohibited rape" (Copelon 2011: 236). Consequently, prior to the advent of the women's human rights movement of the early 1990s, human rights NGOs "pursued an androcentric vision of human rights" (Copelon 2011: 238). The first wave of progress towards recognizing sexual violence as both forms of human rights violations and war crimes came in the 1990s. In 1992, the CEDAW Committee added a recommendation on violence against women, correcting the original treaty's omission of the crime (Edwards 2011). In 1995 the Inter-American Commission on Human Rights ruled that rape was a form of torture. Similarly, even though the legal language used to frame sexual violence for the ICTY and the ICTR was not as forceful as women's rights groups had been advocating, the establishment of a Gender Legal Advisor for the ICTY, and the constant monitoring by women's advocacy groups, led to "several early path-breaking Judgements: *Akayesu* in the ICTR and *Kunarac* in the ICTY. These Judgements grounded the jurisprudence that established accountability for crimes of gender and sexualized violence" (Copelon 2011: 244; Edwards 2011).

The Akayesu ruling established rape as an act of genocide. This ruling would not have been possible without the work of the Coalition for Women's Human Rights in Conflict Situations in conjunction with several Rwandan women's organizations that filed an *amicus curiae* brief to ensure that both the prosecutor and the judges not dismiss the testimony of several rape victims and reconsider the role of rape and sexual violence in the conflict. The Akayesu ruling significantly changed international law as it asserted that violence against women "was not marginal to but instead a critical part of genocide" (Copelon 2011: 245). The judgment also provided a broader definition of rape, and introduced the notion of noninvasive sexual violence (forced public nakedness, etc.). Finally, as a result of the Women's Caucus for Gender Justice, ICC codified rape and sexual violence as among the gravest of international human rights violations, although the provisions were added with ambiguous language, making their effects dependent on future prosecutorial discretion and the Court's interpretation (Copelon 2011). Copelon warns that while the expansion of the law is certainly a step in the right direction, these are merely a starting point, as treaties do not assure enforcement or deterrence. More research is necessary to assess the effects of this relatively nascent body of law.

With reference to domestic gendered human rights abuses, subaltern cosmopolitans emphasize social empowerment and counterhegemonic reconstruction (Santos 2002). For example, Merry (2006) looks at how global human rights treaties like CEDAW are actually put into practice at the local level. She argues that "in order for human rights ideas to be effective ... they need to be translated into local terms and situated within local contexts of power and meaning. In other words, to be remade in the vernacular" (Merry 2006: 1). Merry discovers a tension between transnational elites that present human rights in "universal" terms, and local activists and actors with distinct cultural preferences. Global human rights cultural concepts found in treaties like CEDAW, with their emphasis on autonomy, individualism, equality, secularism, and choice need to be "translated" or "vernacularized" by local activists to incorporate local visions of justice that correspond with their cultural understandings of kinship, religion, community, and so forth, without losing the core principles of the treaty (Merry 2006: 177–8). One of her case studies addressing violence against women in Delhi shows how during the mid-1990s, local activists have helped set up *nari adalats,* or women's (informal) courts, to help women deal with their legal problems. In the Vadodara district, these courts handled more than 1,200 cases since 1995 and successfully resolved a majority of them. Merry attributes part of the success of these informal courts to the fact that they use a dual strategy that incorporates two cultural modalities. First, "The women meet in government compounds close to police and local government offices, assert their status as part of the official MS program, use state symbols such as files, stamp paper, and seals, call on the police for protection, and cite formal laws to support their decisions as they were trained to do by urban activists," but at the same time, they also "reflect the communities they come from. They use humor and shaming to pressure litigants, adjust their meeting times to the rhythms of village life, and use their knowledge of local practices, customs, and social networks to gather evidence and negotiate agreements. They do not try to end marriages but emphasize the rights of the woman within marriage" (Merry 2006: 157). The program is still a work in progress as it continues to make stronger links with formal courts; nonetheless, it has brought significant relief to battered women.

Other groups that suffer from the "citizenship gap," but where legal mechanisms have helped address their basic grievances are indigenous communities. Arzey and McNamara (2011) have found that Aboriginal and Torres Strait Islander communities in Australia have begun to incorporate international human rights law in their campaigns to get their government to redress past grievances and enact legal reforms to address contemporary concerns. Given Australia's lack of a Bill of Rights or an equivalent legal form guaranteeing basic human rights or indigenous rights seemed to present a fruitful avenue for international law to disseminate the discourses, values, strategies, and instruments necessary for rights protections. In 2008, the Australian government apologized to the "Stolen Generation," and some family reunification measures were taken to redress past crimes (although reparations were refused). In addition, advances have been made in attaining equal standards to health, education, and other socioeconomic and individual rights. However, the emphasis on individual rights also allows the government to shun demands for collective rights. Equally problematic for claimants of indigenous rights is that international human rights law emphasizes a "state-centred international legal system that seeks remedies for human rights violations that legitimize and reinforce the structure of the nation-state" (Arzey and McNamara 2011: 746). By emphasizing individual rights and legitimizing the nation-state, human rights law creates serious limits to groups seeking more autonomy, collective rights, or self-determination, suggesting that a purely legal approach is insufficient.

Focusing on the successful challenge by the U'wa in protecting their communal rights to land against Occidental Petroleum and the Colombian government, Rodríguez-Garavito and Arenas (2005) also stress the limits of a law-centric approach in attaining indigenous rights. Instead they highlight a hybrid legal/extralegal counterhegemonic challenge, where transnational advocacy along with legal claims in regional, domestic, and quasi-courts is supplemented by civil-disobedience mechanisms including rallies, road blocks, occupations of contested sites, and even the threat of collective suicide in order to exert enough pressure to guarantee some form of victory. The campaign succeeded in getting Occidental Petroleum to withdraw its claims and explorations of U'wa lands. However, new challenges persist, as the Colombian state-owned oil company is now in charge of exploration efforts, potentially risking the survival and territory of the U'wa in the future.

Finally, emphasizing the gross power asymmetries in the international system, Graubart (2010) warns that the current global criminal justice system reflects a distorted morality, "marked by deep inequalities and weak global normative commitments enable great powers and influential local actors to enlist liberal legal structures for their own purposes. The result is a distorted brand of justice that renders law an instrument of power" (Graubart 2010: 411). Consistent with subaltern cosmopolitan legalism, he also stresses the local and bottom-up initiatives as the best alternatives for achieving justice. Here, global citizen tribunals, "like the Russell Tribunal of the late 1960s (addressing US aggression and war crimes in Indochina) and the recent World Tribunal on Iraq," represent trends towards a more desirable legality.

The promise of this subaltern cosmopolitanism lies in "reconnecting law and politics and reimagining legal institutions from below" (Santos and Rodriguez-Garavito 2005: 15). Subaltern cosmopolitans stress that both global law and global rights are necessary but not sufficient, operate at multiple scales, and are dialectically reconstructed by actors as diverse as Colombian indigenous people, Mexican maquila workers, and Indian advocates for knowledge rights.

An interesting indication of the potential fruitfulness of this mode of legal thought is the convergence of the most engaged constructivist international relations studies around a similar approach to the issue they label "compliance" (rather than enforcement or fulfillment). For both approaches, human rights treaties and new mechanisms affect state-society relations and with the appropriate domestic institutions, social learning of new practices, and transnational support networks, significant positive change can occur. We now turn to an outline of the rest of the volume that implements a synthesis of the liberal and counterhegemonic approaches to global law.

CRITICAL CONSTRUCTIVISM: A POLITICAL PROCESS APPROACH

Our approach to analyze and enhance the human rights impact of the globalization of law combines the liberal diffusion of norms and institutions with a critical dynamic of counterhegemony, through the political process identified by constructivist studies. Like its national counterpart, global law is not neutral and is embedded in power relations—but power relations are not inevitable or self-replicating, and can be transformed by a political process of multifaceted democratization. The democratization of law means establishing increasingly autonomous liberal legal institutions, protections for civil society participation at home and across borders, and self-determination for affected populations. In this view of the development of the international human rights regime, norms matter, but norms do not enforce themselves—the power of norms depends on enabling liberal institutions plus the critical construction of new repertoires and practices. Liberal institutions can strengthen norms, and are not simply an artifact of neoliberal hegemony—but their application depends on empowered civil society at the national and global level. We posit a politics in which a counterhegemonic increase in the fulfillment of human rights can operate through a combination of institutional enforcement, social empowerment, and the creation of new practices to expand repertoires of accountability.

In order to explore the pathways to human rights fulfillment, we analyze a series of cases that show the globalization of human rights norms, mechanisms, or practices. Sandholtz looks at the impact of treaties, and Wright of international limitations on "states of exception." Smith and Gonzalez and Cichowski examine the creation and functioning of international and regional courts, respectively. Berlin charts the emergence of the repertoire of universal jurisdiction, while Beckman and Jimenez-Bacardi investigate the impact of the globalization of law on both positive practices of democratic inclusion and negative repertoires of extralegal detention. We include "hard

cases" of chronic warfare in Israel-Palestine (Shafir), human rights violations by nonstate actors in Mexico (Anaya), and counterterror legislation
(Lookaneeta). Our cases are also diverse in geography and levels of hegemony, including Europe, the United States, and Latin America, as well as
understudied regions like India and the Mideast.

Most of our authors find that the globalization of law does contribute to
the fulfillment of human rights, although to different degrees and through
different political processes. Sandholtz's study of treaty enforcement continues to build the case for the positive potential of human rights norms, with
the assistance of domestic institutions; in this case, constitutions and autonomous judiciaries. Similarly, Wright shows that regional courts and international guidelines are taken on board by Latin American courts to constrain
Executives' abuse of states of emergency, and that such appeals and Ombudsman networks become a new repertoire. Berlin suggests the growth of a
cosmopolitan legal regime. Beckman also outlines a process of transnational
jurisprudence that builds national enforcement of the right to political participation. For Cichowski, the mobilization of domestic and transnational
civil society enhances rights fulfillment by the European Court. In a related
dynamic, Jimenez-Bacardi demonstrates the power of transnational legal
socialization to shift domestic power relations within the hegemonic state
to condition the practice of torture, disappearances, and to a lesser extent,
"extraordinary renditions." Smith and Gonzalez's study of the ICC suggests
that the Court provides both institutional autonomy to substitute for weak
states and support for repertoires of accountability.

For other authors, the outcome is more mixed—but similar dynamics of
political process account for the variance within or between cases. Shafir
compares the power of international human rights norms to constrain the
use of torture in Israel with the failure of international appeals against the
construction of the barrier wall that impinges Palestinians' rights to food
and health. The difference lies in the relative status of the legal institutions
and civil society actors involved, as well as the lower level of norm development for social rights. In a similar way, Anaya depicts varying levels
of human rights traction on violations by non-state actors in Mexico. He
shows how international human rights norms and networks have successfully pressured the Mexican state for regulation of private wrongs in the
border killings of women, but not drug-related violence. In this case again,
different norms, actors, and self-determination within the international
human rights regime help to explain the disparate impact of appeals to law.
In the most negative case of India, international diffusion of counter-terror
norms articulated with colonial and national security regimes to produce
a regression in protection against torture in the world's largest democracy.
This case fits a more critical perspective on the insufficiency of liberal institutions, and highlights the fragility of global law without the political
process of counter-hegemonic mobilization and socialization.

CONCLUSION

We find that new human rights norms and mechanisms have been surprisingly effective globally, in terms of treaty adherence, international courts, and the diffusion of citizenship rights. But this effect is conditioned by regional and domestic structures of influence and access. This domestic filter has enhanced the impact of law in zones of hegemony, including the United States and Europe. However, law has had a more mixed impact on abuses by non-state and transnational actors in less-developed countries such as Mexico and India, and in conflict zones like Israel-Palestine.

We conclude that the globalization of law is transforming sovereignty and fostering the shift from norms to fulfillment, but that peripheral states and domains often remain beyond the reach of this transformation. In the North, where legal institutions are more developed, political empowerment is needed but developing. However, in the global South and where the "citizenship gap" impedes access to such institutions, states tend to hegemonize law and use it to evade empowerment. A true globalization of law must be matched by a globalization of the critical tools for counter-hegemony, including self-determination at all levels: citizens, courts, and sovereignty.

NOTE

1. Although the notion of human rights has also expanded from physical integrity rights to cover a broad and interconnected set of social, economic, cultural, and collective entitlements, our initial discussion focuses on enforcement questions which are most clearly delineated in defense of core rights of the person from acute threats to life and liberty—such as genocide, torture, and forced disappearance.

WORKS CITED

Akhavan, Payam. (2001). "Beyond Impunity: Can International Criminal Justice Prevent Future Atrocities?" *American Journal of International Law* 95: 7–31.
Arzey, Sylvia, and Luke McNamara. (2011). "Invoking International Human Rights Law in a 'Rights-Free Zone': Indigenous Justice Campaigns in Australia." *Human Rights Quarterly* 3(33): 733–66.
Bagarik, Mirko, and Penny Dimopoulos. (2005). "International Human Rights Law: All Show, No Go." *Journal of Human Rights* 4: 3–21.
Biersteker, Thomas J., Peter J. Spiro, Chandra L. Sriram, and Veronica Raffo, eds. (2007). *International Law and International Relations: Bridging Theory and Practice*. New York: Routledge.
Brysk, Alison. (1993). "From Above and Below: Social Movements, the International System, and Human Rights in Argentina." *Comparative Political Studies* 26: 259–85.
——(2008). "Democratic Reform and Injustice in Latin America: The Citizenship Gap between Law and Society." *Whitehead Journal of Diplomacy and International Relations* Winter/Spring: 55–69.

Copelon, Rhonda. (2011). "Toward Accountability for Violence Against Women in War: Progress and Challenges." In *Sexual Violence in Conflict Zones: From the Ancient World to the Era of Human Rights,* edited by Elizabeth D. Heineman, 232–56. Philadelphia: University of Pennsylvania Press.

Downs, George W., and Michael A. Jones. (2002). "Reputation, Compliance, and International Law." *Journal of Legal Studies* 31: S95–114.

Edwards, Alice. (2011). *Violence Against Women Under International Human Rights Law.* New York: Cambridge University Press.

Falk, Richard, Balakrishnan Rajagopal, and Jacqueline Stevens, eds. (2008). *International Law and the Third World: Reshaping Justice.* New York: Routledge.

Finnemore, Martha. (2004). *The Purpose of Intervention: Changing Beliefs about the Use of Force.* Ithaca, NY: Cornell University Press.

Fox, Jonathan. (2002). "Lessons from Mexico-U.S. Civil Society Coalitions." In *Cross-Border Dialoues: U.S.-Mexico Social Movement Networking,* edited by David Brooks and Jonathan Fox, 341–418. San Diego: University of California, San Diego, Center for U.S.-Mexican Studies.

Goldsmith, Jack L., and Stephen D. Krasner. (2003). "The Pitfalls of Idealism." *Daedelus* 132: 47–64.

Goldsmith, Jack L., and Eric A. Posner. (2005). *The Limits of International Law.* Oxford: Oxford University Press.

Goldstein, Judith, and Robert O. Keohane. (1993). "Ideas and Foreign Policy: An Analytical Framework." In *Ideas and Foreign Policy: Beliefs, Institutions, and Political Change,* edited by Judith Goldstein and Robert O. Keohane, 3–30. Ithaca, NY: Cornell University Press.

Goodale, Mark, and Sally Engle Merry, eds. (2007). *The Practice of Human Rights: Tracking Law between the Global and the Local.* New York: Cambridge University Press.

Goodman, Ryan, and Derek Jinks. (2004). "How to Influence States: Socialization and International Human Rights Law." *Duke Law Journal* 54: 621–703.

Graubart, Jonathan. (2008). *Legalizing Transnational Activism: The Struggle to Gains Social Change from NAFTA's Citizen Petitions.* University Park: The Pennsylvania State University Press.

Graubart, Jonathan. (2010). "Rendering Global Criminal Law an Instrument of Power: Pragmatic Legalism and Global Tribunals." *Journal of Human Rights* 9: 409–26.

Guzman, Andrew T. (2008). *How International Law Works: A Rational Choice Theory.* Oxford: Oxford University Press.

Hafner-Burton, Emilie M. (2005). "Trading Human Rights: How Preferential Trade Arrangements Influence Government Repression." *International Organization* 59: 593–629.

Hafner-Burton, Emilie M. (2009). *Coercing Human Rights: Why Preferential Trade Agreements Regulate Repression.* Ithaca, NY: Cornell University Press.

Hafner-Burton, Emilie M., and Kiyo Tsutsui. (2005). "Human Rights Practices in a Globalizing World: The Paradox of Empty Promises." *American Journal of Sociology* 110(5): 1373–1411.

Hathaway, Oona A. (2002). "Do Treaties Make a Difference? Human Rights Treaties and the Problem of Compliance." *Yale Law Journal* 111: 1932–2042.

Helfer, Lawrence, and Anne-Marie Slaughter. (1997). "Toward a Theory of Effective Supranational Adjudication." *Yale Law Journal* 107: 273–391.

Herz, Richard. (2008). "Liberalizing Effects of Tort: How Corporate Complicity Liability under the Alien Tort Statute Advances." *Harvard Journal of Human Rights* 21(2): 207.

Keck, Margaret E., and Kathryn Sikkink. (1998). *Activists beyond Borders: Advocacy Networks in International Politics*. Ithaca, NY: Cornell University Press.

Keith, Linda Camp. (1999). "The United Nations International Covenant on Civil and Political Rights: Does It Make a Difference in Human Rights Behavior?" *Journal of Peace Research* 36: 95–118.

——(2002). "Judicial Independence and Human Rights Protection around the World." *Judicature* 85: 195–200.

Keohane, Robert O. (1984). *After Hegemony: Cooperation and Discord in the World Political Economy*. Princeton, NJ: Princeton University Press.

Keohane, Robert O., and Lisa L. Martin. (1995). "The Promise of Institutionalist Theory." *International Security* 20: 39–51.

Kim, Hunjoon, and Kathryn Sikkink. (2010). "Explaining the Deterrence Effect of Human Rights Prosecutions for Transitional Countries." *International Studies Quarterly* 54: 939–63.

Kinley, David. (2009). *Civilising Globalisation: Human Rights and the Global Economy*. New York: Cambridge University Press.

Kissinger, Henry A. (2001). "The Pitfalls of Universal Jurisdiction." *Foreign Affairs* 80 (July/August): 86–96.

Koenig-Archibugi, Mathias. (2004). "Transnational Corporations and Public Accountability." *Government and Opposition* 39(2): 234–59.

Krasner, Stephen D. (1999). *Sovereignty: Organized Hypocrisy*. Princeton, NJ: Princeton University Press.

Landman, Todd. (2005). *Protecting Human Rights: A Comparative Study*. Washington, DC: Georgetown University Press.

Langer, Maximo. (2007). "Revolution in Latin American Criminal Procedure: Diffusion of Legal Ideas from the Periphery." *American Journal of Comparative Law* 55: 617–76.

——(2011). "The Diplomacy of Universal Jurisdiction: The Political Branches and the Transnational Prosecution of International Crimes." *American Journal of International Law* 105(1): 1–49.

Lutz, Ellen L., and Caitlin Reiger, eds. (2009). *Prosecuting Heads of State*. New York: Cambridge University Press.

Lutz, Ellen L., and Kathryn Sikkink. (2000). "International Human Rights Law and Practice in Latin America." *International Organization* 54: 633–59.

Merry, Sally Engle. (2006). *Human Rights and Gender Violence: Translating International Law into Local Justice*. Chicago: University of Chicago Press.

Moravcsik, Andrew. (2000). "The Origins of Human Rights Regimes: Democratic Delegation in Postwar Europe." *International Organization* 54: 217–52.

Nemeroff, Teddy. (2008). "Untying the Khulumani Knot: Corporate Aiding and Abetting Liability under the Alien Tort Claims Act after Sosa." *Columbia Human Rights Law Review* 40(1): 231–86.

Neumayer, Eric. (2005). "Do International Human Rights Treaties Improve Respect for Human Rights?" *Journal of Conflict Resolution* 49: 925–53.

Olsen, Tricia D., Leigh A. Payne, and Andrew G. Reiter. (2010). "The Justice Balance: When Transitional Justice Improves Human Rights and Democracy." *Human Rights Quarterly* 32: 980–1007.

Posner, Eric A. (2009). *The Perils of Global Legalism*. Chicago: University of Chicago Press.

Rajagopal, Balakrishnan. (2003). *International Law from Below: Development, Social Movements and Third World Resistance*. New York: Cambridge University Press.

Risse, Thomas, Stephen C. Ropp, and Kathryn Sikkink, eds. (1999). *The Power of Human Rights: International Norms and Domestic Change*. New York: Cambridge University Press.

Rodriguez-Garavito, Cesar A., and Luis Carlos Arenas. (2005). "Indigenous Rights, Transnational Activism, and Legal Mobilization: The Struggle of the U'wa People in Colombia." In *Law and Globalization from Below: Towards a Cosmopolitan Legality,* edited by Boaventura de Sousa Santos and Cesar A. Rodriguez-Garavito, 241–66. New York: Cambridge University Press.

Roht-Arriaza, Naomi. (2005). *The Pinochet Effect: Transnational Justice in the Age of Human Rights.* Philadelphia: University of Pennsylvania Press.

Ron, James. (1997). "Varying Methods of State Violence." *International Organization* 51: 275–301.

Roth, Kenneth. (2001). "The Case for Universal Jurisdiction." *Foreign Affairs* 80 (September/October): 150–4.

Santos, Boaventura de Sousa. (2002). *Toward a New Legal Common Sense.* London: Butterworths.

Santos, Boaventura de Sousa, and Cesar A. Rodriguez-Garavito, eds. (2005). *Law and Globalization from Below: Towards a Cosmopolitan Legality.* New York: Cambridge University Press.

Sikkink, Kathryn, and Carrie Booth Walling. (2007). "The Impact of Human Rights Trials in Latin America." *Journal of Peace Research* 44: 427–45.

Simmons, Beth. (2009). *Mobilizing for Human Rights: International Law in Domestic Politics.* New York: Cambridge University Press.

Simmons, Beth, Frank Dobbin, and Geoff Garrett. (2006). "The International Diffusion of Liberalism." *International Organization* 60(4): 781–810.

Slaughter, Anne-Marie. (2005). *New World Order.* Princeton, NJ: Princeton University Press.

Snyder, Jack, and Leslie Vinjamuri. (2003/2004). "Principle and Pragmatism in Strategies of International Justice." *International Security* 28: 5–44.

Sperling, Valerie. (2009). *Altered States: The Globalization of Accountability.* New York: Cambridge University Press.

Thomas, Daniel C. (1999). "The Helsinki Accords and Political Change in Eastern Europe." In *The Power of Human Rights: International Norms and Domestic Change,* edited by Thomas Risse, Stephen C. Ropp, and Kathryn Sikkink, 205–33. New York: Cambridge University Press.

Thoms, Oskar N. T., James Ron, and Roland Paris. (2010). "State-Level Effects of Transitional Justice: What Do We Know?" *International Journal of Transitional Justice* 12: 1–26.

Tshosa, Onkemetse. (2001). *National Law and International Human Rights Law: Cases of Botswana, Namibia and Zimbabwe.* Aldershot, England: Ashgate.

Wallach, Lori, and Robert Naiman. (1998). "NAFTA: Four and a Half Years Later." *Ecologist* 28(3): 171–7.

Waltz, Kenneth N. (1979). *Theory of International Politics.* Reading, MA: Addison-Wesley.

Wheeler, Nicholas J. (2002). *Saving Strangers: Humanitarian Intervention in International Society.* Oxford: Oxford University Press.

Part I

The Globalization of Law and Human Rights

2 Treaties, Constitutions, and Courts
The Critical Combination

Wayne Sandholtz

The global human rights regime that developed after World War II has prop-agated an expanding array of rights among a growing list of countries. The primary mechanism for establishing international human rights norms has been the international treaty. Treaties create human rights obligations for states. Both human rights advocates and researchers have been concerned with the gap between human rights obligations at the international level and human rights practices at the domestic level. Hypocrisy is rampant: Some countries join human rights treaties with no intention of complying with their requirements. Yet human rights treaties do appear to improve human rights performance in at least some countries, under some conditions. This chapter argues that national legal institutions—in particular, constitutions and courts—can offer a bridge between international human rights treaties and the domestic fulfillment of human rights. Liberal domestic institutions may be crucial to realizing the cosmopolitan, rights-respecting society of states that Kant envisioned.

In terms of the framework developed by Brysk and Jimenez-Bacardi, the approach in this chapter begins with globalized human rights norms and examines mechanisms for connecting them to populations that might seek to claim or vindicate those rights. In other words, this study explores how "liberal legal institutions" can link the promise of human rights cosmo-politanism—in the form of core treaties—to those who would engage in the "critical construction of new repertoires and practices" (Chapter 1, 20). As Brysk and Jimenez-Bacardi note, the global human rights regime, built of treaties and judicial institutions, is not self-enforcing. For liberal cosmopoli-tans, the hope must be that treaties will provide one more tool to victims and their advocates, and to those who seek to expand the fulfillment of rights in their national and local communities.

I propose that the effects of treaties on human rights performance depend in part on how domestic legal institutions articulate with international law. Human rights law is almost certainly more effective when it bridges legal levels, national and international. The focus here is on two institutions: con-stitutions and courts. Constitutions can play the bridging role by incorporat-ing treaty law into domestic law. Courts are more able to apply international human rights norms against abusive governments when they are independent of the political powers. The chapter therefore focuses on the extent to which independent courts and constitutional provisions regarding treaty law affect domestic human rights performance. The argument is that constitutions can make a difference by acknowledging and connecting to international law. And treaties may have a greater effect on human rights practices in countries where independent courts can apply human rights rules for the benefit of claimants, even when they assert claims against their own governments. The links among treaties, constitutions, and courts—in terms of their interrelated effects on human rights fulfillment—are surprisingly understudied.

The basic proposition is that human rights treaties have a greater influence on rights in countries whose constitutions import treaty law and whose courts are independent of the political branches of government. The data analysis finds some support for that proposition, but the more decisive result is that liberal domestic institutions—liberal constitutions and independent courts—are more important for enhancing the fulfillment of human rights.

TREATIES, CONSTITUTIONS, AND COURTS

Human rights have gained prominence in both international law and constitutional law, especially since World War II. Research has investigated the effects of treaties and constitutions on human rights performance, with sometimes discouraging results.

Treaties

One way of charting the development of the global human rights regime is by counting the total number of countries that have joined human rights treaties. Figure 2.1 shows that development graphically. It depicts the total number of national ratifications of 18 human rights treaties over time (for a list of the treaties included, see the appendix). The slope of the line increases noticeably after about 1990, meaning that the expansion of the global human rights regime has been especially dramatic in the most recent decades, as newly independent countries ratified or acceded to the treaties almost universally.

One key question for researchers and practitioners alike has been whether the impressive expansion of international human rights norms has improved respect for human rights in practice. Broad studies of the relationship between treaties and human rights performance started on a rather pessimistic note with Keith's finding that ratification of human rights treaties was associated with less respect for human rights in practice (Keith, 1999). Hathaway essentially confirmed those findings in an analysis of treaties in five areas of human rights. She found that none of the treaties was consistently associated with better human rights performance and suggested that governments with no intention of respecting human rights might participate in human rights treaties as a form of international public relations (Hathaway, 2002).

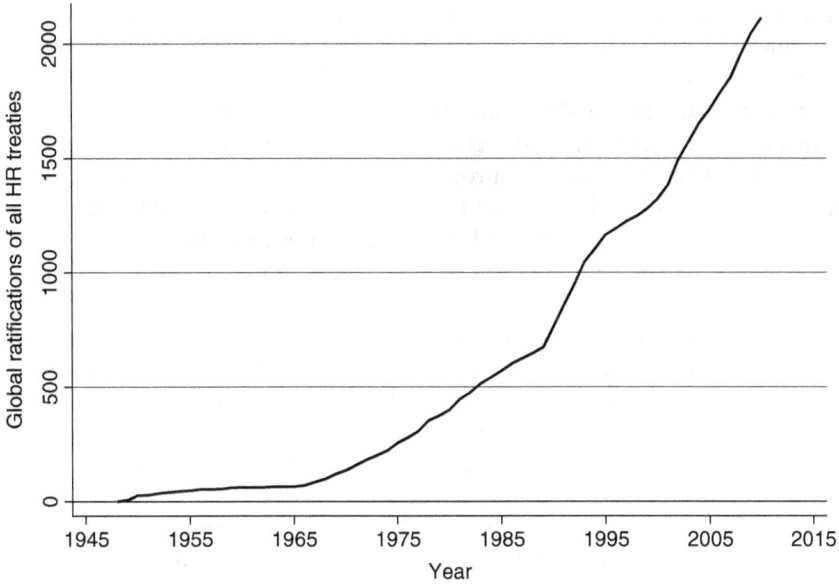

Figure 2.1   Growth of Global Human Rights Regimes

Gilligan and Nesbitt similarly found "no evidence that the spreading of the international norm against torture, measured by the percentage of countries in the world that have acceded to the United Nations Convention against Torture, has led to any reduction in torture" (Gilligan and Nesbitt, 2009, 445).

Other recent scholarship offers nuanced conclusions regarding the link between treaties and human rights in practice. Neumayer finds that human rights treaty ratification is related to better human rights performance "the more democratic the country or the more international nongovernmental organizations its citizens participate in" (Neumayer, 2005, 925). In nondemocratic countries with low levels of participation in international nongovernmental organizations (INGOs), treaty ratification has no effect or even a negative effect (Neumayer, 2005). Broader analyses, including multiple treaties and indicators of more specific rights, report significant effects of treaty ratification on human rights performance under certain conditions (Landman, 2005). In a wide-ranging study, Simmons finds that human rights treaties affect human rights performance via domestic linkages, by shaping elite policy agendas and empowering citizens who seek to vindicate their rights in the courts. Simplifying a diverse array of detailed findings, treaties have the greatest influence on human rights practices in countries that are neither full-blown autocracies nor well-established democracies (Simmons, 2009).

Constitutions

By the 21st century, constitutional protection of human rights had become the global standard. Essentially all modern constitutions, in both democratic and repressive states, enumerate specific individual rights (Alston, 1999; Kommers, 2002). Alston notes that of all national constitutions created between 1788 and 1948, 82 percent "contained some form of protection for human rights," and in the succeeding period (1949–1975), 93 percent did (Alston, 1999, 3). In the most recent period, with new constitutions proliferating in Central and Eastern Europe and in Africa after the end of the Cold War, "virtually all of these constitutions contain a major set of human rights provisions" (Alston, 1999). The list of rights varies from country to country, though a "core set" of rights has become nearly universal, including

> the right to life, freedom from torture, freedom from arbitrary arrest and detention, the right to be presumed innocent, the right to privacy, freedom of movement, the right to property, freedom of thought, conscience, and religion, freedom of expression, freedom of assembly and association, and the right to participate in government. (Alston, 1999, 2, 3)

Law and Versteeg find that, over past 60 years, constitutions show a trend toward "generic rights constitutionalism, wherein an increasing proportion of the world's constitutions shares an increasing number of rights in common" (Law and Versteeg, 2011, 1164).

Do rights on constitutional paper mean rights in practice? Research offers little reason for optimism on that score. Of the constitutional rights provisions enacted before 1990, Alston concludes that "many of them were tokenistic concessions to normative decency which bore no relationship to the realities of the society and were accompanied neither by the political will to take them seriously, nor accompanied by the institutional means which might have made them viable" (Alston, 1999, 3). Keith analyzes constitutional guarantees as predictors of rights performance and finds that only the right to a fair and public trial is associated with improved rights in practice. The majority of formal rights she evaluates do not correlate with better rights performance, and some constitutional rights are associated with higher levels of abuses, including torture (Keith, 2002a). In a later article, Keith and her co-authors report similarly "disappointing" results, though some constitutional provisions are associated with better rights protection (Keith, Tate, and Poe, 2009, 652). In fact, countries that regularly abuse human rights often boast the most elaborate lists of constitutional rights, including the more "esoteric" ones (Law and Versteeg, 2011, 1170).

Courts

Independent courts can, in principle, review the actions of other branches of government and resist the efforts of those other branches to influence judicial outcomes (Ackermann, 1989; Rosenthal, 1990). Indeed, a key part of the rise of "the new constitutionalism" has been the promotion of rights through independent courts and judicial review. Some empirical research has found that independent courts are associated with enhanced respect for human rights (Blasi and Cingranelli, 1996; Keith, 2002b; La Porta et al., 2004), though that result varies across different measures of judicial independence and different rights (Keith, Tate, and Poe, 2009).

With respect to torture, Powell and Staton estimate the joint probabilities of ratifying the Convention Against Torture (CAT) and committing torture, for varying levels of judicial independence and effectiveness. They find that independent and effective courts raise the costs both of ratifying the CAT and of committing torture. Where courts are independent, ratifying the CAT raises the possibility of government legal liability for torture—a potentially real cost (Powell and Staton, 2009). Simmons similarly argues that litigation is an important mechanism through which human rights treaties can affect domestic practices. Once rights are established in treaties, they can attract lawyers and NGOs, increasing rights litigation (Simmons 2009, chap. 4). Of course, for such litigation to make a difference, courts must have room for independent decision making. Reviewing empirical research on constitutions and rights practices, Law concludes that "the success of [constitutional rights] guarantees might be dependent upon somewhat demanding institutional and environmental conditions, such as the existence of judicial review by independent courts" (Law, 2010, 382–83).

Some research, reviewed above, suggests that treaties influence human rights practices in some kinds of countries, under some conditions. But previous studies have not taken into account fundamental ways in which treaty law articulates with domestic legal systems. I have suggested that treaties connect with domestic legal systems in two key ways, through constitutions and through independent courts. I argued that when constitutions make treaties equal or superior to domestic statute, the positive effects of human rights treaties should be greater. When treaties have this domestic legal status, they can provide one more tool for activists and advocates to use against rights-abusing governments. The argument is not that treaty status in itself is a major determinant of human rights performance, but rather that it enhances the effect of treaties on domestic human rights practices. The argument with respect to independent courts is similar. The proposition here is that independent courts are more able to invoke international human rights norms against national governments that violate those standards. So, independent courts should enhance the positive effect of treaties on human rights practices.

A variety of factors—political, economic, and social—powerfully affect the human rights behavior of governments. The size and character of domestic opposition; the degree to which regional, ethnic, or religious groups are excluded from governance; the level of domestic political violence; the extent of economic development—all of these influence the degree to which governments are likely to resort to repressive measures. Treaties, constitutions, and courts are thus likely to have an effect at the margin. Of course, when it comes to human rights, the margins are important and any source of improvement in respect for rights is welcome. The hypothesis leading into the data analysis is therefore that treaties, constitutions, and courts will together have a small but significant positive effect on human rights performance.

DATA AND ANALYSIS

To test the proposition that treaties, constitutions, and courts together can improve the level of respect for human rights in a country, I analyze data from about 150 countries, covering up to 36 years. The analysis focuses on the foundational treaty for basic rights, the International Covenant on Civil and Political Rights (ICCPR). I begin with a broad measure of civil rights (the Freedom House Civil Liberties score; Freedom House, 2010);[1] then shift to an indicator of the more specific right to be free from political violence, the Political Terror Scale (PTS). The PTS rates countries on the prevalence of political disappearances, imprisonment, torture, and murder (Gibney, Cornett, and Wood, 2010). Both rights measures are scaled so that higher scores indicate greater respect for human rights. In interpreting results, therefore, positive coefficients mean that a variable is associated with better human rights performance.

The primary variables of interest on the explanatory side concern treaty participation, constitutional recognition of international treaties, and judicial independence. Treaty participation appears in two variables. One indicates whether or not a country has ratified the International Covenant on Civil and Political Rights (ICCPR) and the other counts the number of human rights treaties to which a country is party in a given year, with a maximum of 19 (listed in table A1 in the appendix). Using data from the Comparative Constitutions Project, I have created a binary measure that codes as "1" if a country's constitution gives treaties a legal status equal or superior to ordinary legislation (Elkins, Ginsburg, and Melton, 2010).[2] Because this variable is new to analyses of the effects of treaties on human rights, it is worth looking at descriptively.

As of 2006, the constitutions of 45 countries gave to treaties a legal status equal to or superior to that of ordinary law (see table A2 in the appendix). These countries represent about one third of the countries that are included in the analyses, so the practice of granting domestic legal status to treaties is fairly common. Of the 45 countries, 12 are postcommunist (with constitutions created after 1990) and 16 are in Sub-Saharan Africa (with constitutions established since the 1950s). Another 6 of these countries are Latin American.

For the independence of courts, I create a set of variables based on the Cingranelli-Richards (CIRI) Human Rights Dataset's Independence of the Judiciary score (Cingranelli and Richards, 2010). One captures partial independence of the judiciary and a second captures general independence of the judiciary. A third variable captures whether a country has at least some degree of judicial independence (it has either partial or general judicial independence).

Finally, the analyses include a number of variables that previous studies have identified as affecting respect for human rights. These controls include measures of economic development (GDP/capita), population, population density, democratic governance, regime durability, and involvement in wars (civil and international). A country's level of international interactions can also influence its absorption of international norms (Sandholtz and Koetzle, 2000; Sandholtz and Gray, 2003). The analyses therefore control for trade dependence (trade/GDP), participation in INGOs, and membership in one of the three regional human rights systems (the African Charter on Human and People's Rights, the American Convention on Human Rights, and the European Convention on Human Rights [ECHR]).

Table 2.1 summarizes the results from models with Freedom House Civil Liberties as the outcome (detailed regression results are available in appendix table A3). Several of the stronger findings are not surprising: Wealthier countries and more democratic countries tend to respect civil liberties. Last year's level of civil liberties (FH civil liberties (*t*-1)) is strongly related to this year's. Turning to the main variables of interest, both treaty status (Treaties superior or equal) and judicial independence are consistently associated with better human rights performance. My argument also suggests that the

Table 2.1   The ICCPR and Civil Liberties

	1	2	3
FH civil liberties (t-1)	+++	+++	+++
ICCPR	n.s.	n.s.	n.s.
HR Treaties	n.s.	n.s.	n.s.
Treaties superior or equal	++	++	++
Judicial indep.: partial	+++		
Judicial indep.: general	+++		
Judicial indep.: dummy		+++	+++
ICCPR * Treaties sup. or eq.			n.s.
ICCPR * Judicial indep.			n.s.
Treaties sup. or eq. * Judicial indep.			n.s.
Treaties sup. or eq. * Judicial indep. * ICCPR			n.s.
GDP/cap (ln)	++	++	+++
Population (ln)	n.s.	n.s.	n.s.
Democracy	+++	+++	+++
Regime duration	- -	- -	- -
INGOs/population	n.s.	n.s.	n.s.
Civil war	- - -	- - -	- - -
ECHR	+	+	n.s.
ACHR	n.s.	n.s.	n.s.
ACHPR	+++	+++	+++
Observations	3094	3094	3094
Countries	144	144	144

Note: "+" indicates a positive relationship; more "+" signs indicate greater statistical significance.
"-" indicates a negative relationship; more "-" signs indicate greater statistical significance.
"n.s." means "not significant."
"*" indicates multiplicative interaction among variables (variables are multiplied).

interactions of treaty status and judicial independence with ratification of the ICCPR should also be associated with better human rights performance. That is, treaty status and independent courts should enhance the effect of ICCPR ratification on human rights. That proposition was not borne out, as none of the interaction terms (column 3) was significant.

With the multiple interaction terms, it is difficult to tell what the overall effects of the key variables are. Table 2.2 reports the marginal effects of the main variables of interest, taking into account all of their interactions. The most notable result is that both constitutional status for treaty law and judicial independence are strongly associated with better human rights performance. Ratification of the ICCPR is not significant.[3]

To test the robustness of these findings to other broad measures of human rights, I repeated the analyses using the Political Terror Scale as the outcome variable in place of the Freedom House Civil Liberties score. The PTS captures a narrower set of rights, focusing on the right to be free from political imprisonment, disappearances, torture, and political murder.[4] Table 2.3 displays the results (for more detailed results see appendix table A4). As with the Civil Liberties analysis, democracy, wealth, and the previous year's PTS score are consistently and positively related to rights as measured by the Political Terror Score. As for the main variables of interest, domestic legal status for treaties does not appear to affect human rights performance, but judicial independence does, showing significant coefficients by itself and in its interaction with ICCPR ratification. This latter finding is interesting, as it suggests that, as hypothesized, the combination of judicial independence and treaty ratification is associated with better respect for rights.

A look at the marginal effects (Table 2.4) gives a fuller picture. With respect to the Political Terror Scale, ICCPR ratification is associated with worse performance and judicial independence with better performance. The legal status of treaties has no significant effect.

Constitutional incorporation of treaty law (as superior or equal to statute) improves the broad Freedom House measure of civil liberties but has

Table 2.2   Average Marginal Effects of Key Variables on Freedom House Civil Liberties

	Marginal effect	Probability	95% Conf. interval	
ICCPR	−0.06	0.120	−0.13	0.02
Treaties superior or equal	0.08	0.012	0.02	0.15
Judicial independence	0.16	0.000	0.11	0.22

Note: Marginal effects are the average effect with all other variables held at their averages. Calculated from the model reported in column 3 of Table 2.1.

Table 2.3   The ICCPR and Political Terror

	1	2
PTS (t-1)	+++	+++
ICCPR	-	- -
HR treaties	++	n.s.
Treaties superior or equal	n.s.	n.s.
Judicial indep.: partially	+++	
Judicial indep.: generally	+++	
Judicial indep.: dummy		+
ICCPR * Treaties sup. or eq.		n.s.
ICCPR * Judicial indep.		+
Treaties sup. or eq. * Judicial indep.		n.s.
Treaties sup. or eq. * Judicial indep. * ICCPR		n.s.
GDP/cap (ln)	+++	+++
Population (ln)	++	+
Democracy	+++	+++
Regime duration	n.s.	n.s.
INGOs/population	++	+++
Civil war	- - -	- - -
ECHR	n.s.	n.s.
ACHR	+	++
ACHPR	++	++
Observations	3043	3043
Countries	144	144

+ = a positive relationship; more + signs indicate greater statistical significance.
- = a negative relationship; more - signs indicate greater statistical significance.
n.s. = not significant.

no significant effect on Political Terror scores. Judicial independence has a positive, and large, effect on both outcome variables with a high level of statistical significance. But only judicial independence appears to enhance the effect of ICCPR ratification on rights performance, and that relationship is significant only for personal security rights (PTS), not for civil liberties.

CONCLUSIONS

Scholars, activists, and victims of human rights abuses have long held to the hope that treaties could improve the protection of human rights. This chapter takes a first step toward assessing the combined effects of treaties, constitutions, and courts on human rights. It probes two main propositions: (1) that

Table 2.4   Average Marginal Effects of Key Variables on Political Terror Scale

	Marginal effect	Probability	95% Conf. interval	
ICCPR	−0.09	0.073	−0.18	0.01
Treaties superior or equal	0.01	0.763	−0.07	0.10
Judicial independence	0.17	0.000	0.10	0.24

Note: Marginal effects are the average effect on all observations with all other variables held at their means. Calculated from the model in column 2 of Table 2.3.

the constitutional status of treaty law and the independence of courts affect the level of human rights protections; and (2) that the constitutional status of treaties and independent courts modify (through interaction) the effect of treaty law on human rights performance. The analyses strongly support the first proposition but offer only limited evidence favoring the second.

In addition to the findings on the main questions, some additional results are worth taking note of. Civil wars, not surprisingly, consistently lead to human rights abuses. Countries that ratify more human rights treaties do not do a better job of protecting human rights in practice. Ratifying the ICCPR has no significant effect on civil liberties and is actually associated with greater abuse of physical integrity rights. These findings are consistent with prior research on the effects of treaties on human rights performance (Hathaway, 2002; Hafner-Burton and Tsutsui, 2005, 2007). Membership in the regional human rights regimes is sometimes associated with better human rights performance. The ECHR does not appear to improve human rights performance, but that result is understandable. Levels of wealth and democracy are both high, on average, in ECHR countries and both are strongly associated with greater respect for human rights. ECHR membership simply cannot do much additional work.

The finding that treaties do not have a direct positive effect on human rights may seem disappointing from the perspective of optimistic cosmopolitanism. But this study is consistent with other research that concludes that international norms work through domestic institutions to improve human rights (Simmons, 2009). International human rights norms provide one more tool for domestic and transnational activists and advocates to wield against governments that commit or tolerate human rights abuses. International standards can strengthen the hand of domestic actors in the political arena (mobilizing public pressure, persuading legislators, moving voters) and in the judicial.

The hope of the liberal cosmopolitans is, then, not empty. International human rights norms do make a difference. But they make a difference not because of some inherent force of their own, operating from the global heights, but rather through liberal domestic institutions—constitutions and courts. Global norms operating through liberal domestic institutions seems compatible with a Kantian liberal cosmopolitanism, in which international rule of law depends on republican government at the national level. And there may well be a meta-process that studies like this one cannot uncover, by which emerging global norms of democratic governance gradually nudge more countries toward representative democracy and its institutions, and thereby toward greater fulfillment of cosmopolitan human rights.

APPENDIX A

Table A1   Treaties Included in the Global Human Rights Regime Indicator

1	Genocide Convention
2	Convention Against Torture
3	Optional Protocol to the Convention Against Torture
4	Convention on the Elimination of All Forms of Discrimination against Women (CEDAW)
5	CEDAW Optional Protocol
6	International Convention on the Elimination of All Forms of Racial Discrimination (CERD)
7	International Convention for the Protection of All Persons from Enforced Disappearance (CPAPED)
8	Convention on the Rights of the Child (CRC)
9	Optional Protocol to the Convention on the Rights of the Child on the Involvement of Children in Armed Conflict
10	Optional Protocol to the Convention on the Rights of the Child on the sale of Children, Child Prostitution, and Child Pornography
11	Convention on the Rights of Persons with Disabilities (CRPD)
12	Optional Protocol to the Convention on the Rights of Persons with Disabilities
13	International Covenant on Civil and Political Rights (ICCPR)
14	Optional Protocol to the ICCPR
15	Second Optional Protocol to the ICCPR
16	International Covenant on Economic, Social, and Cultural Rights (ICESCR)
17	Optional Protocol to the ICESCR
18	International Convention on the Protection of the Rights of All Migrant Workers and Members of Their Families (ICRMW)

Table A2   Countries Giving Domestic Legal Status to Treaty Law, 2006

1 Albania	16 Czech Republic	31 Mali
2 Algeria	17 Djibouti	32 Moldova
3 Armenia	18 Egypt	33 Mozambique
4 Azerbaijan	19 El Salvador	34 Niger
5 Bahrain	20 Estonia	35 Paraguay
6 Benin	21 France	36 Peru
7 Bhutan	22 Ghana	37 Poland
8 Cameroon	23 Greece	38 Russian Federation
9 Central African Republic	24 Guinea	39 Rwanda
10 Colombia	25 Haiti	40 Senegal
11 Congo, Democratic Rep.	26 Italy	41 Spain
12 Congo, Republic	27 Kazakhstan	42 Tajikistan
13 Costa Rica	28 Korea, Republic of	43 Togo
14 Cote d'lvoire	29 Kyrgyz Republic	44 Ukraine
15 Croatia	30 Malawi	45 United States

Table A3   The ICCPR and civil liberties

	1	2	3	4	5
FH civil liberties (t-1)	0.65	0.65	0.62	0.63	0.62
	0.00	0.00	0.00	0.00	0.00
ICCPR	0.63	0.64	0.31	0.25	−0.09
	0.01	0.01	0.27	0.38	0.12
HR Treaties	−0.07	−0.08	−0.03	−0.02	0.01
	0.01	0.01	0.31	0.42	0.31
Treaties superior or equal		0.06	0.09	0.09	0.22
		0.06	0.01	0.01	0.01
Judicial indep.: partially			0.15		
			0.00		

(*Continued*)

Table A3   (Continued)

	1	2	3	4	5
Judicial indep.: generally			0.24		
			0.00		
Judicial indep.: dummy				0.16	0.17
				0.00	0.00
ICCPR * Treaties sup. or eq.					−0.03
					0.73
ICCPR * Judicial indep.					0.05
					0.35
Treaties sup. or eq. * Judicial indep.					−0.14
					0.12
Treaties sup. or eq. * Judicial indep. * ICCPR					−0.01
					0.94
GDP/cap (ln)	0.11	0.11	0.14	0.15	0.20
	0.01	0.01	0.02	0.01	0.00
Population (ln)	−0.29	−0.29	−0.13	−0.12	0.05
	0.02	0.02	0.53	0.53	0.68
Democracy	0.06	0.05	0.05	0.05	0.05
	0.00	0.00	0.00	0.00	0.00
Regime duration	0.00	0.00	−0.01	−0.01	−0.01
	0.00	0.00	0.00	0.00	0.00
INGOs/population	0.09	0.09	0.01	0.01	0.00
	0.00	0.00	0.56	0.57	0.92
Civil war	−0.25	−0.25	−0.21	−0.21	−0.21
	0.00	0.00	0.00	0.00	0.00
ECHR	0.20	0.19	0.17	0.15	0.09
	0.02	0.03	0.06	0.09	0.14
ACHR	0.00	0.00	−0.02	−0.03	−0.03
	1.00	0.94	0.80	0.76	0.69
ACHPR	0.12	0.11	0.20	0.20	0.24
	0.01	0.01	0.00	0.00	0.00
Observations	3912	3912	3094	3094	3094
Countries	146	146	144	144	144

Note: Dependent variable: Freedom House Civil Liberties score, reversed. Instrumental variable least squares regression, with country and year fixed effects. Unstandardized coefficients with probabilities below. Significant entries in boldface.

Table A4   The ICCPR and Political Terror

	Model 1	Model 2	Model 3
PTS (*t*-1)	0.47	0.43	0.45
	0.00	0.00	0.00
ICCPR	−0.22	−0.75	−0.18
	0.50	0.08	0.02
HR treaties	0.02	0.08	0.01
	0.52	0.07	0.20
Treaties superior or equal		0.03	0.07
		0.44	0.47
Judicial indep.: partially		0.14	
		0.00	
Judicial indep.: generally		0.22	
		0.00	
Judicial indep.: dummy			0.11
			0.06
ICCPR * Treaties sup. or eq.			0.03
			0.82
ICCPR * Judicial indep.			0.12
			0.10
Treaties sup. or eq. * Judicial indep.			−0.07
			0.54
Treaties sup. or eq. * Judicial indep. * ICCPR			−0.04
			0.76
GDP/cap (ln)	0.23	0.34	0.27
	0.00	0.00	0.00
Population (ln)	0.21	0.65	0.25
	0.30	0.02	0.10
Democracy	0.03	0.03	0.02
	0.00	0.00	0.00
Regime duration	0.00	−0.00	0.00
	0.11	0.63	0.69
INGOs/population	0.10	0.07	0.09
	0.00	0.04	0.00
Civil war	−0.53	−0.55	−0.55
	0.00	0.00	0.00

(*Continued*)

Table A4   (Continued)

	Model 1	Model 2	Model 3
ECHR	–0.00	–0.11	0.04
	0.97	0.38	0.66
ACHR	0.30	0.21	0.25
	0.00	0.06	**0.02**
ACHPR	0.06	0.18	0.12
	0.26	**0.01**	**0.02**
Observations	3450	3043	3043
Countries	145	144	144

Note: Unstandardized coefficients with *p*-values below. Dependent variable: Political Terror
 Scale. Instrumental variable least squares. Country and year fixed effects. Significant
 entries in boldface.

NOTES ON THE MODELS

All models reported use ordinary least squares regression with country and
time fixed effects. The data analyses take into account the possibility of recip-
rocal causation. Countries with better human rights records may more readily ratify human rights treaties because the treaties are consistent with their
values. Both Landman (2005) and Simmons (2009) find empirical evidence
for this relationship. But ratified treaties may also have an effect on human
rights performance, and recent research finds evidence for that relationship
as well, at least for some kinds of countries under certain conditions (Neumayer 2005; Landman 2005; Simmons 2009). One way of controlling for
this form of endogeneity is to "instrument" for the endogenous explanatory
variable. Instrumental variables, ideally, are strongly correlated with the variable for which they stand in, but not directly correlated with the outcome
variable. To control for the dual causality between treaties and human rights
performance, some of the models in this study instrument for treaty ratification. This is the approach taken by both Landman (2005) and Simmons
(2009). Following Simmons, I instrument for ICCPR ratification with common law legal tradition, the difficulty of the treaty ratification process, and
the proportion of countries in the same region that have already ratified (Simmons 2009, 172). To eliminate any serial correlation among observations, I
include the lagged dependent variable. Finally, to account for idiosyncratic
characteristics of countries that are likely to produce correlations within
countries across time, the models include country fixed effects. To account
for contemporary correlations across countries, the models also include year
fixed effects.

NOTES

1. A second Freedom House measure, Political Rights, is not well suited for this analysis because it is strongly correlated with the measure of democracy used in this study (the Polity IV indicator of autocracy and democracy).
2. I am grateful to Tom Ginsburg, Zachary Elkins, and James Melton for generously sharing additional data.
3. The marginal effects and their statistical significance were computed using the "margins" command in Stata 11.2, with the "dy/dx" option. The p-value for the marginal effects is not reported in the regressions themselves, which produce separate p-values for the variables and their interactions but not an overall p-value for each variable with its interactions.
4. The PTS levels of political terror are as follows:

Level 5: Terror has expanded to the whole population. The leaders of these societies place no limits on the means or thoroughness with which they pursue personal or ideological goals.

Level 4: Civil and political rights violations have expanded to large numbers of the population. Murders, disappearances, and torture are a common part of life. In spite of its generality, on this level terror affects those who interest themselves in politics or ideas.

Level 3: There is extensive political imprisonment, or a recent history of such imprisonment. Execution or other political murders and brutality may be common. Unlimited detention, with or without a trial, for political views is accepted.

Level 2: There is a limited amount of imprisonment for nonviolent political activity. However, few persons are affected, torture and beatings are exceptional. Political murder is rare.

Level 1: Countries under a secure rule of law, people are not imprisoned for their views, and torture is rare or exceptional. Political murders are extremely rare. (Gibney, Cornett, and Wood, 2010)

I reversed the scale so that higher numbers represent greater respect for human rights.

REFERENCES

Ackermann, L. W. H. (1989). "Constitutional Protection of Human Rights: Judicial Review." *Columbia Human Rights Law Review* 21: 59–71.

Alston, Philip. (1999). "Bills of Rights: An Analytical Framework." In *Promoting Human Rights through Bills of Rights: Comparative Perspectives*, edited by Philip Alston, 1–14. Oxford: Oxford University Press.

Blasi, Gerard J., and David L. Cingranelli. (1996). "Do Constitutions and Institutions Help Protect Human Rights?" In *Human Rights and Developing Countries*, edited by David L. Cingranelli, 223–237. Greenwich, CT: JAI Press.

Cingranelli, David L., and David L. Richards. (2010). *The Cingranelli-Richards Human Rights Dataset.* Version 15 August 2010. Available at http://www.humanrightsdata.org. Accessed 28 June 2011.

Elkins, Zachary, Tom Ginsburg, and James Melton (2010). *Characteristics of National Constitutions, Version 1.0.* Comparative Constitutions Project. Version 14

May 2010. Available at http://www.comparativeconstitutionsproject.org/index. htm. Accessed 28 June 2011.

Freedom House. (2010). *Freedom in the World Comparative and Historical Data.* Available at http://www.freedomhouse.org/template.cfm?page=439. Accessed 28 June 2011.

Gibney, Mark, Linda Cornett, and Reed Wood (2010). *Political Terror Scale 1976– 2008.* Available at http://www.politicalterrorscale.org/index.php. Accessed 28 June 2011.

Gilligan, Michael J., and Nathaniel H. Nesbitt. (2009). "Do Norms Reduce Torture?" *Journal of Legal Studies* 38(2): 445–470.

Hafner-Burton, Emilie M., and Kiyoteru Tsutsui. (2005). "Human Rights in a Globalizing World: The Paradox of Empty Promises." *American Journal of Sociology* 110(5): 1373–1411.

——(2007). "Justice Lost! The Failure of International Human Rights Law to Matter Where Needed Most." *Journal of Peace Research* 44(4): 407– 425.

Hathaway, Oona A. (2002). "Do Human Rights Treaties Make a Difference?" *Yale Law Journal* 111(8): 1935–2042.

Keith, Linda Camp. (1999). "The United Nations International Covenant on Civil and Political Rights: Does It Make a Difference in Human Rights Behavior?" *Journal of Peace Research* 36(1): 95–118.

—— (2002a). "Constitutional Provisions for Individual Human Rights (1977– 1996): Are They More than Mere 'Window Dressing'?" *Political Research Quarterly* 55(1): 111–143.

—— (2002b). "Judicial Independence and Human Rights Protection around the World." *Judicature* 85(4): 195–200.

Keith, Linda Camp, C. Neal Tate, and Steven C. Poe (2009). "Is the Law a Mere Parchment Barrier to Human Rights Abuse?" *Journal of Politics* 71(2): 644–660.

Kommers, Donald P. (2002). "Comparative Constitutional Law: Its Increasing Relevance." In *Defining the Field of Comparative Constitutional Law*, edited by Vicki C. Jackson and Mark Tushnet, 61–70. Westport, CT: Praeger.

La Porta, Rafael, Florencio López-de-Silanes, Cristian Pop-Eleches, and Andrei Shleifer (2004). "Judicial Checks and Balances." *Journal of Political Economy* 112(2): 445–470.

Landman, Todd. (2005). *Protecting Human Rights: A Comparative Study.* Washington, DC: Georgetown University Press.

Law, David S. (2010). "Constitutions." In *Oxford Handbook of Empirical Legal Research*, edited by Peter Cane and Herbert Kritzer, 376–398. Oxford: Oxford University Press.

Law, David S., and Mila Versteeg. (2011). "The Evolution and Ideology of Global Constitutionalism." *California Law Review* 99: 1163–1257.

Neumayer, E. (2005). "Do International Human Rights Treaties Improve Respect for Human Rights?" *Journal of Conflict Resolution* 49(6): 925–953.

Powell, Emilia Justyna, and Jeffrey K. Staton. (2009). "Domestic Judicial Institutions and Human Rights Treaty Violation." *International Studies Quarterly* 53(1): 149–174.

Rosenthal, Albert J. (1990). "Afterword." In *Constituitonalism and Human Rights: The Influence of the United States*, edited by Louis Henkin and Albert J. Rosenthal, 397–404. New York: Columbia University Press.

Sandholtz, Wayne, and Mark M. Gray. (2003). "International Integration and National Corruption." *International Organization* 57(4): 761–800.

Sandholtz, Wayne, and William Koetzle. (2000). "Accounting for Corruption: Economic Structure, Democracy, and Trade." *International Studies Quarterly* 44: 31–50.

Simmons, Beth A. (2009). *Mobilizing for Human Rights: International Law in Domestic Politics*. Cambridge: Cambridge University Press.

3 The International Criminal Court
Globalizing Peace or Justice?

Charles Anthony Smith and Antonio Gonzalez

INTRODUCTION: FROM SHOW TRIALS TO THE EXPANSION OF GLOBAL JURISPRUDENCE

The globalization of law, a multifaceted phenomenon with a range of causal pressures, goes well beyond the confines of the International Criminal Court (ICC). From broad international trends of judicialization, to local-level systemic adaptations of cosmopolitan norms, to the development of legal expectations and demands by individuals as citizens and stakeholders, the juridical and the global have begun to be intertwined and intermingled. Although the ICC is but one small facet of this complex emerging legal regime, the Court presents an opportunity to consider globalization more broadly, in particular with respect to the development and promotion of human rights. The Court provides an institutional constraint on egregious behavior for both states and quasi-states as well as for individuals. The Court also provides an administrative avenue for grievance resolution by those who are members of specific types of victim classes. Because the ICC embodies the global diffusion of norms and processes with respect to the development of a jurisprudence of criminal liability for bad acts committed on behalf of a state, it presents an ideal lens through which to consider legal globalization and the fulfillment of human rights.

The impact and evolution of the emerging global legal regime can be seen in the postconflict prosecutions of individuals who have acted on behalf of states during times of belligerence. Despite the best efforts of some of the architects of postconflict prosecutions, ultimately the search for justice through war crimes trials has been co-opted by concerns about political consolidation and the cessation of open conflict. Critics of these prosecutions suggest there has been a reversion to a show trial model, or victor's justice, that rivals the initial forays into political prosecutions. The rise and fall of the jurisprudence of war crimes has followed a path from the trial of Charles I of England through the so-called War on Terror (Smith 2012). Although over time, the trials have varied widely in their capacity to deliver on the promise of justice, the premise of holding individuals responsible for gross abuses of human rights, even when those actions are perpetrated on behalf of a state or some group with some claim against a state, has now been institutionalized through the creation of the International Criminal Court. This institutionalized assertion of individual responsibility for gross human rights violations represents a tangible developmental structure for the advancement of a global legal regime to promote and fulfill human rights. That is, the ICC is the embodiment of one dimension of the globalization of law and the movement from mere rights to actual justice.

At the outset, it is important to accept that the institution has been constructed with many flaws. The ICC has severe limitations on jurisdiction, including complementarity—which dictates the Court may only take jurisdiction where prosecution at the municipal level is not possible—and the multiplicity of Bilateral Immunity Agreements and Status of Forces Agreements which provide ubiquitous protections and immunity to the personnel and military forces of the most powerful countries. In practice, in the decade since its inception, the Court has only actually prosecuted actors from the weakest states, while the most powerful are virtually immune from prosecution. We discuss the role of the ICC in a globalized legal regime and then address the limitations of the Court as understood by the extant literature in the sections that follow. We then address the promise and peril of live indictments as a vehicle for universal jurisdiction.

THE ROLE OF THE ICC IN A REGIME OF GLOBALIZED LAW: THE DEVELOPMENT OF JURISPRUDENCE IN A BOUNDED INSTITUTION

The ICC embodies multiscalar legal pluralism. It was constructed through a long and broadly engaged negotiation which led to wide adoption of the Rome Statute. The participants in the conference that led to the Rome Statute included 160 states, 236 nongovernmental organizations, and 33 intergovernmental coalitions (Rome Statute 1998). Steven Roach identifies a globalized community as one constituted by the interests, beliefs, and values of a host of different agents including states, nonstates, and individuals, with a shared common desire of promoting global norms and rules (2009: 7, fn. 2).

The ICC is a clear example of an institution that results from coordination among the members of this sort of globalized community. The founders of the Court were able to overcome a host of barriers to the desired collective action, including the inherent conflict of laws issues raised by multistate prosecutions of crimes against humanity. Beyond a simple resolution of the challenges of harmonizing a prosecutorial regime among states and actors with broad variation in legal and cultural institutional norms, the Court faced an inherent barrier to creation because of the difficulties of transnational law governing cross-border activities. The basic challenge of an international court to the concept of state sovereignty as well as the jurisdictional impingement upon the privilege of regional involvement enjoyed by the most powerful states could well have subverted the effort entirely. The proponents of the Court persevered perhaps in part because of the growing salience of conventional interstate and comparative jurisprudence for criminal liability for crimes during war or conflict. In other words, because domestic or municipal legal regimes had begun to accept cross-pollination of legal norms from other systems, the notion of a global institution may have proved more acceptable.

Although the extant literature suggests that the institution of the ICC will serve the needs of the most powerful states and prosecute only those actors from weak states with little or no international power (Smith and Smith 2006, 2009; Roach 2009), the creation of the Court—even the contemplation of the Court—moved the jurisprudence of the protection and fulfillment of some human rights forward (Smith 2012). The broad global implications for this evolving jurisprudence have contributed to peace and stability in a host of venues (Kaminski and Nalepa 2006; Rotberg and Thompson 2002; Waldorf 2006; Kirsch and Holmes 1999). Although the efficacy of the Court and even the wisdom of its existence have been controversial (Goldsmith 2003; Sadat-Wexler 1999; Schabas 2004; Scharf 2001, 2004; Scheffer 1999a, 1999b, 2001), the global expectation of some modicum of responsibility for war crimes and crimes against humanity has gained traction. The jurisdiction of the ICC is unlikely to extend so far as to reach the most powerful members of the international community. These powerful states have ensured that their agents will not be subjected to prosecution through a variety of institutional design structures. The ICC imposes the rule of law for relatively narrow purposes in relatively narrow circumstances. Article 17 of the Rome Statute inhibits the actions of the Court through a powerful jurisdictional limit. Specifically, the ICC operates under the constraint of complementarity. That is, the jurisdiction of the Court complements, but does not (and cannot) rival the jurisdiction of existing national or municipal courts.

Because the most powerful nations already have well-developed and functioning court systems, these states can shield themselves from ICC prosecution through nominal national investigations. In contrast, the weakest members of the international order are most susceptible to ICC proceedings because they seldom have a functioning judiciary or a court system capable of prosecuting political or military elites or their agents. By narrowly focusing on gross violations of human rights in failed states or weak countries that lack consolidated judicial systems, the ICC serves the overly narrow purpose of policing "uncivilized" countries that are unable to prevent mass atrocities. In other words, the Court has been designed to respond to a narrow set of circumstances but is incapable of directly promoting global justice in a broad or comprehensive way (Franceschet 2004).

Some scholars find the source of strong support for the Court by the European powers and strong opposition to it by the great military powers to be grounded in the idea that the Rome Statute was designed by the European powers to increase their relative influence through a structural restriction of the military capacity of the great powers (Goldsmith 2003). Others have critiqued the Court out of concerns about its potential efficacy. These critics contend one of the primary drawbacks of the Rome Statute is that it did not go far enough (Sadat-Wexler 1999). The critique centers on the idea that the extremely restrictive subject matter jurisdiction obstructs the ability of individuals to initiate investigations or prosecutions. The docket of the ICC is controlled by the prosecutor and limited by complementarity. Almost any state can render a case inadmissible through any perfunctory or casual investigation of the suspects or facts at issue. There can be no question that the jurisdiction of the ICC is subordinate to municipal courts.

Moreover, some argue that because individual perpetrators of violations from nonsignatory nations can only be prosecuted upon a referral from the UN Security Council, the Court will often be incapable of pursuing some of the worst violators of human rights (Goldsmith 2003). Of course even if the UN Security Council refers a matter to the prosecutor, the ICC lacks the resources or capacity to ensure custody of a defendant and there is no universal guarantee of extradition. The ability of the prosecutor to detain and prosecute a defendant is contingent on the willingness and ability of member states to exert economic, political, and military force on behalf of the institution. Accordingly, the efficacy of the ICC is inherently bounded by the political will and preferences of its members.

The approach taken by the United States to avoid any potential prosecution before the ICC is particularly instructive. Not only does the United States benefit from the structural prohibitions put in place by the signatory states, but it has also constructed a variety of individualized barriers to jurisdiction which add a redundant safeguard to the institutional barriers to prosecution that serve as pillars for the Court. In particular, the United States entered into Bilateral Immunity Treaties (BIAs) and Status of Forces Agreements (SOFAs) with virtually every other country that ratified the Rome Statute. As the name suggests, BIAs provide immunity to the personnel of the signing states while SOFAs explicitly prevent the extradition of any service personnel to the ICC and establish broad immunity from extradition for U.S. troops abroad. Despite the virtual lock on broad immunity and an absence of jurisdiction, the U.S. Senate did not ratify the Rome Statute and George W. Bush promptly unsigned it after he became president. Given the electoral logic of the Senate, it is unlikely that U.S. opposition to the Court will diminish in the near future (Smith and Smith 2006).

In addition to undermining the efficacy of the ICC through overt hostility, the United States has played an active role in restricting cooperation with the Court by withholding or threatening to withhold funding for military aid in part through the aggressive use of the BIAs with more than 100 countries (Nooruddin and Payton 2010). Economically weak states that were dependent on U.S. aid signed BIAs quickly, while the ICC signatory states took somewhat longer to comply with the U.S. demands (Nooruddin and Payton 2010).

One of the more controversial institutional features of the ICC, and one of its primary contributions to the expansion of a global human rights regime, is the capacity to assume jurisdiction over individuals from nonsignatory states. This moves beyond the Vienna Convention on the Law of Treaties, which restricts the mechanisms by which treaties can create obligations for nonparties (Morris 2001). This is a substantial movement toward establishing universal jurisdiction, albeit in narrow and specific circumstances. Hand in glove with this development in the scope of personal jurisdiction is the expansion of subject matter jurisdiction. Specifically, the ICC conceptually stands as a court of assessment of the appropriateness of military activities and state use of violence. Of course, this status as guardian of appropriate belligerence is seriously bounded by the institutional constraints, but nonetheless, that a conceptual review board for political violence exists at all is a dramatic step toward a globalized system for the fulfillment of human rights. The ICC is an embodiment of an expanding global norm that recognizes limits to immunity for state actions and enhances greater individual accountability for gross violations of rights (Wise 1999).

While we concede the ICC is far from perfect, even in the shadow of the institutional deficiencies, there is considerable evidence that the evolving concept of the global jurisprudence at stake has enhanced the prospects for peace and stability in a variety of ways. In short, even with its truncated capacities, the ICC has promoted justice, enhanced rights recognition, and improved global prosecutorial jurisprudence.

GLOBAL GOVERNANCE: RIGHTS RECOGNITION AND A GLOBAL PROSECUTORIAL REGIME

The ICC is an instrumental dimension of the evolution toward a globalized legal regime for the prosecution of the worst types of behaviors in conflict. The most obvious rights at issue in this developing jurisprudence are the broad spectrum of human rights affiliated with physical integrity. Specifically, the ability of an aggrieved individual to seek justice broadly defined through this established Court of last resort should not be dismissed as trivial merely because the Court has narrow jurisdiction and the ability to initiate an investigation is strictly delegated. That the violation of the human rights of individuals is the crux of the prosecutorial regime at the ICC is an impressive step toward a globalized legal regime. After all, Nuremberg was first and foremost a prosecution for an unlawful war, not a prosecution for discrete violations of the rights of individuals. The movement from individual accountability for acts of state against other states to individual accountability for acts committed against individuals *qua* individuals represents a substantial maturation of the jurisprudence.

These now institutionalized notions of a prosecutorial imperative for acts against individuals also imply or suggest a cluster of related rights that, without the foundational commitment of the ICC, may not have flourished. Specifically, the more nuanced rights at issue in this global jurisprudence regime include the rights to substantive due process and procedural due process for the suspect class and the rights to transitional justice by the victim class. The prosecutorial imperative is bounded by an expectation of fundamental fairness. That is, the jurisprudential regime has established that the predicate aspects of justice are substantive due process and procedural due process delivered for the purposes of providing deterrence and retribution (Smith 2012). Substantive due process encompasses issues regarding the range of crimes as well as the specific identities of the defendants. Issues of procedural due process are those concerned with the manner in which the prosecutions are conducted. These types of issues include whether a predetermined outcome exists, whether the defendant received a full and fair defense, and whether an appellate structure exists. Deterrence is the premise that those prosecuted, as well as other prospective wrongdoers who are similarly situated, are put on notice of the consequences of future comparable bad behavior. This notice is presumed to dissuade recidivism and replication of the criminal behavior at issue. Retribution occurs to the extent those convicted face punitive sanctions and the manner in which the victim class, at the individual and at the society or collective level, are made whole. The establishment of the ICC has moved this aspect of the jurisprudence of human rights protection forward through not only an acknowledgment of the right to transitional justice for the victims, but also through the creation or acknowledgment that the global community is a stakeholder in the outcome of these types of prosecutions.

The creation and perseverance of the ICC is a globalizing phenomenon in both practice and concept. The legal regime and jurisprudence driven by the creation of the ICC create a criminal global governance schematic at least for the narrow substantive jurisdiction contemplated by the Court.

PROSECUTIONS, INDICTMENTS, AND GLOBALIZED LAW DURING CONFLICTS

The ICC provides an institutional venue to assert demands for rights from virtually every layer of political actor. The global community and states make claims about the right to prosecute bad actors and individuals assert claims of the right to seek retribution and punishment for gross violations of human rights. Additionally, members of the accused class assert claims for fair treatment and some semblance of full procedural due process and substantive due process.

The rights came about through an evolution of war crimes jurisprudence (Smith 2012). A consideration of prosecutions and indictments over the past five years suggests the ICC has become an important part of a globalized legal regime despite a limited capacity to prosecute representatives from the powerful states. That is, the ICC has been an avenue for delivery of significant elements of, in the language of Kathryn Sikkink (2011), a cascade of justice. Sikkink argues that, from the mid-1970s forward, the steady drumbeat of prosecutions of top officials for violations of human rights during their various reigns has altered the political landscape for human rights in both a municipal and international context (Sikkink 2011). As an illustration of one piece of this puzzle of a cascade, we turn to a discussion of live indictments and the ICC. A "live indictment" is a criminal indictment of someone still in power. The issue of live indictments presents a narrow but significant challenge to the realization of human rights and the implementation of an international criminal law regime that addresses the actions of states and those acting on behalf of states. As Jack Snyder and Leslie Vinjamuri noted, international justice must walk a "path of political expediency" (2003: 7) and that the perils of that path are revealed in the light cast by live indictments.

The challenge of live indictments is straightforward. A prohibition on live indictments presents a stricture on justice that creates a differentiation of criminal conduct based on the status of the perpetrator. Such a prohibition might very well further what Peter Stoett has referred to as a "culture of impunity" (2010: 4). That those in power could avoid indictment regardless of the crime cannot be squared with a notion of justice largely understood. Alternatively, if live indictments are embraced as a norm of justice dispassionately applied, then there is at least some risk that the use of live indictments will prolong conflict or increase the levels of violence as the indicted turn to any means necessary to avoid detention as well as loss of power. On the one side, a ban on live indictments would further limit the jurisdictional reach of the already bounded ICC. On the other, the use of live indictments may exacerbate gross violations of human rights. Live indictments land at the crossroads between the mandates of the ICC—to seek justice and to seek peace. Here, we suggest that live indictments should be an available but rarely used prosecutorial tool.

Our analysis is inherently limited, since the ICC has only taken a few preliminary steps toward fulfillment of its mission. Still, our understanding at this juncture of the implications of the choices we make now may help us toward a better outcome later. In the first and, so far, only case of a live indictment at the ICC of a sitting head of state, the ICC formally issued a warrant for the arrest of Omar al-Bashir of the Sudan on March 4, 2009.[1] The charges against Omar al-Bashir included five counts of crimes against humanity and two counts of war crimes for his alleged involvement in the Darfur conflict. On July 12, 2010, a second warrant was issued, which incorporated three new charges of genocide. The charges represent a landmark moment in global jurisprudence not only because al-Bashir is a sitting head of state, but also because Sudan is not a signatory of the Rome Statute.

In his remarks following the issuance of the first warrant against al-Bashir, prosecutor Luis Moreno Ocampo asserted, "there is no immunity for heads of state before the International Criminal Court. As soon as Omar al-Bashir travels through international air space, he can be arrested. Like Slobodan Milošević or Charles Taylor, Omar al Bashir's destiny is to face justice" (http://www.huffingtonpost.com/2009/03/04/albashir-arrest-warrant-i_n_171703.html Office of the Prosecutor 2009). Despite this assertion by the prosecutor, to date, al-Bashir has traveled abroad extensively and his warrant remains to be executed. The lack of progress in the prosecution of al-Bashir may be due in part to a backlash from African nations toward the ICC after the warrant was issued. At a summit of African leaders, African Union president Bingu wa Mutharika strongly criticized the warrant, stating, "There is a general concern in Africa that the issuance of a warrant of arrest for ... al-Bashir, a duly elected president, is a violation of the principles of sovereignty guaranteed under the United Nations and under the African Union charter." At the same summit, 53 African leaders drafted a resolution that included a paragraph advising states not to arrest al-Bashir regardless of whether they signed the Rome Statute. Although the paragraph regarding al-Bashir was deleted before adoption of the resolution, the sentiment seems to have persuaded states to ignore the obligations of the ICC (AlJazeera.com 2010). To date, al-Bashir has traveled without incident to Djibouti, Chad, Kenya, and Malawi, which are all ICC signatories. The efforts by the ICC to have al-Bashir arrested and detained by these states have been ineffective. The states have refused under a rationale that the maintenance of peace with Sudan is more important than obedience to the ICC and an assertion that the responsibility of the host states stops far short of an arrest of al-Bashir (BBC.co.uk 2011a; Guardian.co.uk 2010a, 2010b).

In anticipation of the announcement of the warrant for his arrest, al-Bashir smiled and danced for thousands of supporters, and taunted that the ICC could "eat" its arrest warrant (Telegraph.co.uk 2009c). Al-Bashir dismissed the indictment against him as worthless and stated, "Any decision by the International Criminal Court has no value for us, it will not be worth the ink it is written with" (Telegraph.co.uk 2009a). Al-Bashir repeated familiar critiques of the ICC as a tool of the dominant Western powers and referred to the indictment as a "conspiracy" by the West (Telegraph.co.uk 2009a). He pronounced the ICC a tool of neocolonialism and a "tool to terrorize countries that the West thinks are disobedient" (PBS 2009 http://www.pbs.org/newshour/extra/video/blog/2009/08/wanted_sudanese_president_deni.html). The nature and content of al-Bashir's objections are to be expected given the consequences for the target of compliance with a live indictment. Al-Bashir responded to the warrant by abruptly expelling 10 aid groups from

Darfur (Telegraph.co.uk 2009b). In the short term, the ICC warrant may have exacerbated some human suffering because of the retaliation directed at the providers of aid.

In the longer view, the impact of the ICC live indictment of al-Bashir may have provided positive leverage and nuanced pressure to move the region toward peace. In 2010, al-Bashir was reelected through a process rife with fraud. Despite the failure to meet even the modest international standards of election administration, the international community recognized the election as legitimate. International acceptance of these flawed elections was apparently the result of a desire to ensure that the expected referendum on the independence of South Sudan would proceed without interference from al-Bashir. To further dissuade al-Bashir from tampering with the referendum, the United States offered to review sanctions against Sudan and to remove it from the state sponsors of terror list (BBC.co.uk 2010a). In accordance with the terms of the 2005 Comprehensive Peace Agreement, which ended the 22-year civil war between Sudan and South Sudan, between January 9 and January 15, South Sudan held the referendum on a split from the north (U.S. Department of State 2011). As the global community, including the United States, coalesced around policies that promoted the referendum, the likelihood that al-Bashir would actually be arrested diminished considerably (Guardian.co.uk 2009a). The international acceptance of the reelection of al-Bashir gave his regime a veneer of legitimacy. Following al-Bashir's reelection, one senior Sudanese government official was quoted as stating: "This is a message to the whole world: the president is legal and the representative of the whole people. Any accusation now is an accusation against all the [Sudanese] people" (BBC.co.uk 2010d). The international acceptance of the reelection of al-Bashir could be interpreted as a rebuke of the ICC by the international community. If the live indictment is seen as part of a broad global strategy for the improvement of conditions in Sudan—that is, if the live indictment is but a portion of a strategic push toward fulfilling human rights, then whether the live indictment resulted in arrest is not the metric for success.

Rather, if the live indictment provided the framework for a worst-case scenario that the powerful states could diplomatically present as a less desirable option than the referendum, then the live indictment serves a useful and efficacious function even short of actual arrest. While consolidating power in northern Sudan, al-Bashir at first actively urged the south to vote in favor of unity at all costs (BBC.co.uk 2010e). In October, he accused SPLM leaders in the south of violating the terms of the peace agreement by publicly supporting southern secession. In addition, al-Bashir charged that conflict between the north and south would be more likely should the south split (BBC.co.uk 2010f). Government attacks on tribes loyal to the south in the contested region of Abyei were reported, indicating that the regime still hoped to influence the outcome of the referendum by whatever means necessary (BBC.co.uk 2010a). On the eve of the referendum, al-Bashir's public position took a significant turn. Al-Bashir granted his blessing to whatever the outcome was to be, and even offered the south logistical and technical support in the event the vote favored succession (BBC.co.uk 2011a). While al-Bashir's support was welcomed internationally, it may have been little more than an embrace of the referendum's expected outcome (Sudan Tribune 2011b). The vote on the referendum was held without major disruptions or incident and soon after, the Sudanese government requested the UN Security Council reward Sudan by "reconsidering the position vis-a-vis the hero of peace, al-President Bashir" (BBC. co.uk 2011b).

Although the future of South Sudan remains uncertain, the actions of al-Bashir demonstrate a broader point about the ICC. Following his indictment, al-Bashir chose to allow the referendum to occur with minimal direct interference in order to curry favor from previously hostile Western powers. By gaining their favor, al-Bashir hoped to undermine support for his ICC indictment and to ease international sanctions. Meanwhile, in anticipation of the referendum, al-Bashir consolidated power in northern Sudan. By silencing opposition and increasing violence in Darfur al-Bashir suppressed potential threats to his regime. He also held "free" elections in order to consolidate and legitimize his rule as a democratically elected leader. While al-Bashir's motives are transparent, the fact remains that the ICC indictment motivated him to consent to, and in the end support, a peaceful referendum process. Accordingly, the interests of justice have been served, albeit indirectly. While al-Bashir has not been directly held responsible for the acts that led to his indictment, the indictment spurred behavior that led to substantial progress toward self-determination in the south. The threat of criminal liability helped spur democratic processes. In the short term, the failure to execute the warrant may seem like justice delayed, but in the long run, the live indictment moved the status quo closer to a fulfillment of human rights, as Sudan has systematically moved to contract al-Bashir's scope of authority.[2]

We have one actual live indictment from which to draw conclusions. Whether the indictment of a sitting head of state furthers or inhibits a political transition, ameliorates or exacerbates extant violence, or makes custody and trial more or less likely is simply not yet resolvable. If, however, the concept of a live indictment is seen as part of the cascade of justice identified by Sikkink (2011), then this extension of international criminal authority may prove to be a vital tool for the fulfillment of human rights, as it is a significant movement toward accountability—even for those still in power. As discussed below, even if we arrive at a point where we accept that live indictments should be used as a regular tool of prosecution for the ICC, the concept of live indictments reveals a global governance gap, a profound challenge to sovereignty, and will invariably present some very hard cases.

CONCLUSION: "HARD CASES"
AND THE "GLOBAL GOVERNANCE GAP"

The ICC provides two critical functions that promote global human rights law. First, it is a venue through which the global discourse that promotes the protection of human rights has progressed in a formal and institutionalized manner. Second, the ICC provides an extranational venue for repertoires of accountability for some specific challenges to the fulfillment of human rights—and the prospects of a live indictment can be utilized effectively from a diplomatic standpoint. The premise of live indictments represents movement toward a universal jurisdiction for the most serious crimes, even if that particular tool will rarely be used. The modest step of one live indictment pushes the jurisprudence of universal jurisdiction forward in a nuanced, cautious, but substantial way.

"Hard cases" refers to two problematic dimensions of a global governance gap that are revealed by the reality of the ICC. First, powerful states seem immune from prosecution in the context of a global court while the weakest among the global actors face prosecution for similar acts to those committed by the powerful on occasion. If live indictments become routine, this disparate treatment between the powerful and the weak may become even more stark. Second, because the ICC essentially has no control over or access to mechanisms for enforcement, at times those who might appear before it can treat the court with complete impunity. There may be substantial erosion of the perceptions of the legitimacy of the Court if a string of live indictments results in a string of defiance where those indicted remain in power and act with impunity. Failure to detain or prosecute those who have been indicted may be a survivable flaw in the ICC prosecutorial regime, so long as it is a rare occurrence. Incapacity to prosecute its targets might fatally undermine the credibility of the Court if deterrence, or even prosecution, became roundly disregarded as empty threats.

Despite these two substantial gaps in global governance, the ICC provides a formative acid wash of homogenization of expectations regarding transitional justice, and live indictments serve as a critical foundation for those expectations. The ICC can be seen as more efficacious if considered as one moving part in a larger global effort at fulfillment of human rights. The Court represents the intersection of global institutions and individual empowerment, even while strengthening the hand of the dominant powers.

While peace may necessarily have to come before justice more often than not, the notion that a sitting head of state no longer has a shield of immunity is a critical step in the development of a global realization of a human rights regime. The development of live indictments, however flawed or rare, supports the diffusion of norms that promote the protection of human rights and fosters a global "race to the top" or "best practices" regime of human rights protections. The ICC has provided an important avenue for norm diffusion from the top down and a structure for rights claims in the most severe conflicts worldwide.

NOTES

1. Of course, the International Criminal Tribunal for the former Yugoslavia issued an indictment for Slobodan Milošević in 1999 but he was out of power before he was charged with additional crimes and extradited finally in 2001. The ICTY case is different as well because the court was constructed specifically to address that particular roster of violence.
2. On June 27, the ICC issued an arrest warrant for Libyan President Muammar el-Gadaffi, his son Saif-Al Islam, and Intelligence chief Abdullah al-Sanussi charging them with murder and with political persecution (BBC.co.uk 2011a). The warrant was the second "live indictment" issued by the ICC. That is, this was the second instance where the ICC indicted a sitting head of state. The Libyan government quickly rejected the warrants, and the justice minister was quoted as stating that the court was a "Tool of the Western world to prosecute leaders in the third world" (BBC.co.uk 2011b). Without the capacity to execute its own warrants, the court was forced to rely upon those engaged in the rebellion to arrest Gadhafi and the others. The effort to prosecute Gadhafi was derailed by his death at the hands of his captors (BBC 2011c). The Gadhafi case is distinguishable from the al-Bashir case because Gadhafi had lost control of the state and was a sitting head of state at the time of indictment in name only.

BIBLIOGRAPHY

AlJazeera.com. 2010. "A curious carrot for Khartoum." November 11. http://www.aljazeera.com/news/africa/2010/11/20101110145738844982.html

Blakesley, Christopher. 1999. "Association of American Law School Panel on the International Criminal Court." *American Criminal Law Review* 36: 223.

BBC.co.uk. 2008. "South Sudan 'on the Brink of War.'" May 27. http://news.bbc.co.uk/2/hi/africa/7421221.stm.

BBC.co.uk. 2008. "Armies 'head for central Sudan.'" June 4. http://news.bbc.co.uk/2/hi/africa/7435012.stm.

BBC.co.uk. 2008. "Court to rule on Sudan border row." June 22. http://news.bbc.co.uk/2/hi/africa/7467670.stm.

BBC.co.uk. 2008. "Sudan 'crimes charges' worry UN." July 11. http://news.bbc.co.uk/2/hi/africa/7501066.stm

BBC.co.uk. 2008. "Sudan braces for ICC charges' impact." July 14. http://news.bbc.co.uk/2/hi/africa/7504682.stm

BBC.co.uk. 2009. "Militia fights South Sudan army." February 24. http://news.bbc.co.uk/2/hi/africa/7908693.stm

BBC.co.uk. 2009. "Warrant issued for Sudan's leader." March 4. http://news.bbc.co.uk/2/hi/7923102.stm

BBC.co.uk. 2009. "South Sudan cattle raid crackdown." May 14. http://news.bbc.co.uk/2/hi/8050222.stm

BBC.co.uk. 2009. "Sudan denies sowing south dissent." June 16. http://news.bbc.co.uk/2/hi/africa/8104098.stm

BBC.co.uk. 2009. "Khartoum 'arming Sudan militias.'" August 4. http://news.bbc.co.uk/2/hi/africa/8183368.stm

BBC.co.uk. 2009. "Terms for Sudan referendum agreed." October 16. http://news.bbc.co.uk/2/hi/africa/8310928.stm

BBC.co.uk. 2009. "Obama offers Sudan 'incentives.'" October 19. http://news.bbc.co.uk/2/hi/africa/8314817.stm

BBC.co.uk 2010a. "Abyei killings 'intended to upset Sudan referendum.'" July 7. http://www.bbc.co.uk/news/10536510

BBC.co.uk. 2010b. "Dream election result for Sudan's President Bashir." April 27. http://news.bbc.co.uk/2/hi/africa/8645661.stm

BBC.co.uk.2010c. "Sharia law to be tightened if Sudan splits—president." December 19. http://www.bbc.co.uk/news/world-africa-12033185

BBC.co.uk.2010d. "South Sudan 'reneging on peace deal'—President Bashir." October 10. http://www.bbc.co.uk/news/world-africa-11510109

BBC.co.uk. 2010e. "Sudan opposition claims video shows election fraud." April 20. http://news.bbc.co.uk/2/hi/8633162.stm

BBC.co.uk. 2010f. "Tunisian President says job riots 'not acceptable.'" December 28. http://www.bbc.co.uk/news/world-africa-12087596

BBC.co.uk.2010g. "U.S. offers to remove Sudan early from state terror list." November 7. http://www.bbc.co.uk/news/world-africa-11707555

BBC.co.uk. 2010h. "Will Bashir let the south go?" January 20. http://news.bbc.co.uk/2/hi/africa/8470106.stm

BBC.co.uk. 2011a. "Libya: Muammar Gadaffi subject to ICC arrest warrant." June 27. http://www.bbc.co.uk/news/world-africa-13927208

BBC.co.uk. 2011b. "Libya rejects arrest warrant for Muammar Gaddafi." June 27. http://www.bbc.co.uk/news/world-africa-13937034

BBC.co.uk. 2011c. "Libya's col. Gaddafi killed in crossfire, says NTC." October 21. http://www.bbc.co.uk/news/world-africa-15397812

BBC. 2011. "Mexico updates four years of drug war deaths to 34,612." News Latin America & Caribbean, January 13. http://translate.google.com.mx/translate?hl=es&sl=en&tl=es&u=http%3A%2F%2Fwww.bbc.co.uk%2Fnews%2Fworld-latin-america-12177875&anno=2

BBC.co.uk. 2011d. "NATO assumes control of military operation." March 27. http://www.bbc.co.uk/news/world-africa-12876696

BBC.co.uk. 2011e. "South Sudan accuses President Bashir of plot." March 12. http://www.bbc.co.uk/news/world-africa-12723872

BBC.co.uk. 2011. "South Sudan independence: Bashir seeks Darfur 'reward.'" February 10. http://www.bbc.co.uk/news/world-africa-12414453

BBC.co.uk. 2011. "Sudan: Bashir threatens south over Abyei." April 28. http://www.bbc.co.uk/news/world-africa-13230498

BBC.co.uk.2011. "Sudan's Omar al-Bashir in Malawi: ICC wants answers." October 20. http://www.bbc.co.uk/news/world-africa-15384163

BBC.co.uk. 2011. "Syria army deserters 'kill 15 security personnel.'" November 2. http://www.bbc.co.uk/news/world-middle-east-15560324

BBC.co.uk. 2011. "Syria protests: 'armed insurrection won't be tolerated.'" April 19. http://www.bbc.co.uk/news/world-middle-east-13124591

BBC.co.uk. 2011. "Syria unrest: activist arrested on fifth day of protest." March 22. http://www.bbc.co.uk/news/world-middle-east-12824775

BBC.co.uk. 2011. "Syrian army 'attacks protest city of Deraa.'" April 25. http://www.bbc.co.uk/news/world-middle-east-13185185

BBC.co.uk. 2011. "Tunisia closes schools and universities following riots." January 10. http://www.bbc.co.uk/news/world-africa-12155670

BBC.co.uk. 2011. "Tunisia President Ben Ali 'will not seek new term.'" January 13. http://www.bbc.co.uk/news/world-africa-12187084

Businessday.co.za. 2011. "Syrian army's loyalty in doubt." October 28. http://www.businessday.co.za/articles/Content.aspx?id=157288

CBSNews.com. 2011. "Libya rebels in Tripoli, Gadhafi defenses collapse." August 21. http://www.cbsnews.com/stories/2011/08/21/ap/middleeast/main20095233.shtml

Franceschet, Antonio. 2004. "The Rule of Law, Inequality, and the International Criminal Court." *Alternatives: Global, Local, Political* 29(1): 23–42.

Goldsmith, Jack. 2003. "The Self-Defeating International Criminal Court." *University of Chicago Law Review* 70(1): 89–104.

Guardian.co.uk. 2011. "Explainer: Sudan's unresolved issues." June 30. http://www.guardian.co.uk/global-development/2011/jun/30/south-north-sudan-dispute-issues

Guardian.co.uk. 2011. "Is the Sudanese regime's star rising?" February 7. http://www.guardian.co.uk/commentisfree/2011/feb/07/sudan-omar-bashir-referendum?INTCMP=SRCH

Guardian.co.uk. 2010a. "Chad refuses to arrest Omar al-Bashir on genocide charges." July 22. http://www.guardian.co.uk/world/2010/jul/22/chad-refuses-arrest-omar-al-bashir

Guardian.co.uk. 2010b. "Kenya defends failure to arrest Sudan's President Omar al-Bashir in Nairobi." August 29. http://www.guardian.co.uk/world/2010/aug/29/kenya-omar-al-bashir-arrest-failure

Guardian.co.uk. 2009a. "Bashir slips out of court's grasp." June 11. http://www.guardian.co.uk/commentisfree/2009/jun/11/sudan-law?INTCMP=SRCH

Guardian.co.uk. 2009b. "Tensions soar in Sudan with violent clashes and political arrests." December 7. http://www.guardian.co.uk/world/2009/dec/07/sudan-splm-arrests-elections?INTCMP=SRCH

Kaminski, Marek M., and Monika Nalepa. 2006. "Judging Transitional Justice: A New Criterion for Evaluating Truth Revelation Procedures." *Journal of Conflict Resolution* 50(3): 383–408.

Kirsch, Philippe, and John Holmes. 1999. "Developments in International Criminal Law: The Rome Conference on an International Criminal Court: The Negotiating Process." *American Journal of International Law* 93(2): 332–338.

Morris, Madeline. 2001. "High Crimes and Misconceptions: The ICC and Non-Party States." *Law and Contemporary Problems* 64(1): 13–66.

MSNBC.com. 2009. "Sudan expels aid groups in response to warrant." March 4. http://www.msnbc.msn.com/id/29492637/ns/world_news-africa/t/sudan-expels-aid-groups-response-warrant/#.Tuj8wJifEfl

Nooruddin, Irfan, and Autumn L. Payton. 2010. "Dynamics of Influence in International Politics: The ICC, BIAs, and Economic Sanctions." *Journal of Peace Research* 47(6): 711–721.

NYTimes.com. 2010. "Bashir wins election as Sudan edges toward split." April 26. http://www.nytimes.com/2010/04/27/world/africa/27sudan.html

NYTimes.com. 2010. "Obama backs down on Sudan." April 21. http://www.nytimes.com/2010/04/22/opinion/22kristof.html, http://www.pbs.org/newshour/extra/video/blog/2009/08/wanted_sudanese_president_deni.html

Roach, Steven C., ed. 2009. *The Global Politics of the International Criminal Court: Global Governance in Context.* Oxford: Oxford University Press.

Rotberg, Robert, and Dennis Thompson, eds. 2002. *Truth v. Justice: The Morality of Truth Commissions.* Princeton, NJ: Princeton University Press.

Sadat-Wexler, Leila. 1999. "Association of American Law School Panel on the International Criminal Court." *American Criminal Law Review* 36: 223.

Schabas, William. 2004. "United States Hostility to the International Criminal Court: It's All about the Security Council." *European Journal of International Law* 15(4): 701–720.

Scharf, Michael. 2001. "The ICC's Jurisdiction over the Nationals of Non-Party States: A Critique of the US Position." *Law and Contemporary Problems* 64: 67.

Scharf, Michael. 2004. "Is It International Enough? A Critique of the Iraqi Special Tribunal in Light of the Goals of International Justice." *Journal of International Criminal Justice* 2: 330–337.

Scheffer, David. 1999a. "The United States and the International Criminal Court." *American Journal of International Law* 93: 12–22.

Scheffer, David. 1999b. "International Criminal: The Challenge of Jurisdiction." Speech to the American Society of International Law (March 26).

Scheffer, David. 2001. "Staying the Course with the International Criminal Court." *Cornell International Law Journal* 35: 47.

Sikkink, Kathryn. 2011. *The Justice Cascade: How Human Rights Prosecutions Are Changing World Politics.* New York: W. W. Norton.

Smith, Charles Anthony. 2012. *The Rise and Fall of War Crimes Trials: From Charles I to Bush II.* New York: Cambridge University Press.

Smith, Charles Anthony, and Heather Smith. 2006. "The Electoral Dis-Connection: Institutional Barriers to US Support for the ICC." *Eyes on the ICC* 3(I): 1–31.

Smith, Charles Anthony, and Heather Smith. 2009. "Embedded *Realpolitick*: Re-evaluating the U.S. Opposition to the ICC." In *The Global Politics of the International Criminal Court: Global Governance in Context*, edited by Steven C. Roach. Oxford: Oxford University Press.

Snyder, Jack, and Leslie Vinjamuri. 2003. "Trials and Errors: Principle and Pragmatism in Strategies of International Justice." *International Security* 28(3): 5–44.

Stoett, Peter. 2010. "A Question of Indictment: The International Criminal Court and Conflict Resolution." *Centre d'etude des politiques etrangeres de securite* (CEPES) Numero 36.

SudanTribune.com. 2011a. "U.S. denies reports on agreeing to defer Bashir's warrant." http://www.sudantribune.com/spip.php?iframe&page=imprimable&id_article=37923.

SudanTribune.com 2011b. "Why President Bashir made a sudden U-turn decision on south secession?" January 9. http://www.sudantribune.com/Why-President-Bashir-made-a-Sudden,37553

Telegraph.co.uk. 2009a. "Bashir calls ICC arrest warrant a 'conspiracy.'" March 5. http://www.telegraph.co.uk/news/worldnews/africaandindianocean/sudan/4942470/Sudan-President-Omar-al-Bashir-calls-ICC-arrest-warrant-a-conspiracy.html

Telegraph.co.uk. 2009b. "Sudan expels Oxfam and Médecins Sans Frontières from Darfur over war crimes threat to Omar al-Bashir." March 4. http://www.telegraph.co.uk/news/worldnews/africaandindianocean/sudan/4940315/Sudan-expels-Oxfam-and-Mdecins-Sans-Frontires-from-Darfur-over-war-crimes-threat-to-Omar-al-Bashir.html

Telegraph.co.uk. 2009c. "Sudan's Omar al-Bashir says ICC can 'eat' his arrest warrant." March 4. http://www.telegraph.co.uk/news/worldnews/africaandindianocean/sudan/4933329/Sudans-Omar-al-Bashir-says-ICC-can-eat-his-arrest-warrant.html

Tran, Chet J. 2004. "The Proliferation of Bilateral Non-Surrender Agreements among Non-Ratifiers of the Rome Statute of the International Criminal Court." *American University International Law Review* 19.

U.S. Department of State. 2011. "Sudan." 8 Apr. http://www.state.gov/r/pa/ei/bgn/5424.htm.

Van der Vyver, Johan D. 2001. "International Human Rights: American Exceptionalism: Human Rights, International Criminal Justice, and National Self-Righteousness." *Emory Law Journal* 50: 775.

Waldorf, Lars. 2006. "Mass Justice for Mass Atrocity: Rethinking Local Justice as Transitional Justice." *Temple Law Review* 79(1): 88.

Wise, Edward M. 1999. "Association of American Law School Panel on the International Criminal Court." *American Criminal Law Review* 36: 223.

4 Global Diffusion and the Role of Courts in Shaping the Human Right to Vote

Ludvig Beckman

The right to vote ranks among the human rights enumerated in the defining conventions and declarations of international law adopted since the Second World War. It figures already in the Universal Declaration of Human Rights, albeit expressed in general terms as "everyone's right to participation" (Article 12). More precise are the wordings of the International Covenant on Civil and Political Rights (ICCPR) where "the right to vote by all citizens" is affirmed (Article 25). The right to vote also figures in many if not all regional human rights conventions and instruments such as the American Convention on Human Rights and the Copenhagen document (Kirschner, 2003; Davis-Roberts and Carroll, 2010, 429). While the European Convention on Human Rights (ECHR) does not expressively refer to the right to vote, the Strasbourg court has subsequently affirmed the "solemnity" of voting rights under the Convention (Council of Europe, 1999, 202). Hence, the right to vote appears securely situated in contemporary human rights law (Fox, 1992, 541, n6; Joseph 2010).

The human right to vote predates the more recent appearance of the "right to democracy" and the imperative of democratic elections and rights (Franck, 1992; Boutros-Gali, 1996).[1] Yet, neither international legal conventions protecting the human right to vote, nor general proclamations of a right to democracy, implies the fulfillment of everyone's right to vote. The relevant provisions of human rights law were drafted with the intention to remain consistent with existing legal rules in the democratic world that effectively denied the vote to "marginal" groups (DeFeis, 2001, 324; Lardy, 2003, 126; Nowak, 2005, 576).[2] From this background, it is not surprising that the provisions of human rights law are largely indeterminate on the exact scope of the human right to vote and that the voting rights of marginalized groups are frequently contested.

However, the global diffusion of legal norms and practices do provide potential remedies to this "gap" in human rights law. The indeterminate human right to vote has been rendered more specific by the judgments of national and international courts offering new interpretations of the relevant sources of constitutional and international law. The tendency of courts to assume this power in relation to human rights is part of a more general shift in international law from state-centered norms to the protection of sub-jective rights, that is, rights claimable by individuals (Benhabib, 2009; Gard-baum, 2008, 762). As a result, the right to vote has evolved from "a right to elections" into a "subjective right to participation" (Mowbray, 2010, 285; Powers, 2006, 260).

This development is particularly visible in the case of prisoner voting rights. In the last decade, the voting rights of prisoners have been expanded as a direct result of judicial decisions. While parliaments have frequently been reluctant to expand suffrage to prisoners, the courts have ruled that restric-tions on their political rights are inconsistent with human rights law and basic constitutional principles.[3] It is tempting to infer from this observation that a new consensus on the importance of the right to vote is emerging among the courts. In fact, the point has been made that the case law on prisoner voting represents an "intriguing cross-section of judicial attitudes towards the na-ture of democracy" (Plaxton and Lardy, 2010, 139). In sum, the fulfillment of the human right to vote is propelled neither by democratic governments, nor by human rights law as such, but by the activism of national and inter-national courts—a positive aspect of the globalization of law discussed in the introduction to this volume.

But the final step to advance the reach of rights is to advance the juris-prudence that inspires and supports legal activism; the influence of courts is mediated through norms of reasoning and jurisprudence. These standards of reasoning constitute the legal method whereby judges offer substantive justifications for their judgments (Cohen-Eliya and Porat, 2011, 466). Is the reasoning produced by the courts indicative of a new emphasis on the inter-ests in democratic participation, as some people say, or are the rulings on the right to vote a mere byproduct of rigorously applied standards of rule of law? If the latter approach based on law, it would be mistaken to conclude that courts are acting as vanguards of democratic rights. Rather than acting as reforming "rationalists," probing how democratic rights are best justi-fied, the courts would act as conservative "Burkeans," seeking to maintain the legal order (Sunstein, 2009, chaps. 2 and 3). Rule of law–like standards mainly reflect a concern with arbitrary subjection to public power, whereas interest-balancing standards invite a judgment on the subjective importance of the right infringed by the government.

In this chapter, I argue that the globalization of law has produced a half-full glass for the right to vote, expanding the reach of the right to vote and the role of courts, but not yet offering jurisprudence to protect a broader right to democratic participation. In the first section below, I argue that there are essentially two distinct standards at work in the emerging global jurisprudence applied in recent voting rights cases. When courts engage in conflicts between participatory rights and government policy, they take re-course either to rule of law–like standards or to interest-balancing stan-dards. As will be shown in the second section, the courts are more likely to invoke standards of the first type: rule of law. This means that the rulings do not yet establish a duty to protect democratic participation interests. In the third, and last, section I elaborate on the implications of this finding for the future protection of rights to democratic participation.

TWO STANDARDS OF REASONING

Signatory states of human rights conventions are legally committed to comply with certain conditions in decisions restricting the right to vote. Two basic conditions are identified by the major legal convention regulating the right to vote, the ICCPR. The convention first of all prohibits all discrimination from the vote on the basis of the categories identified in Article 2, including class, sex, race, religious conviction, political opinion, and so on (General Comment No. 25 1996). In addition, the convention stipulates that the vote must not be subject to "unreasonable restrictions." The requirement that restrictions be "reasonable" is a unique feature of the right to vote (Article 25) and is not found elsewhere in the convention text (Macdonald, 2008, 1382).[4] The significance of this condition is far from obvious. Indeed, reasonableness has been characterized as an "extremely vague" legal standard (Endicott, 2001, 382). The legal conditions for restricting the right to vote consequently affirm the claim that the sections of human right law granting protection to democracy and political rights are considerably vaguer than other sections of human rights law (Steiner, 2008, 456).[5]

The vague character of the conditions for justified restrictions on the vote might have been less important if the practice established by democratic governments and the criteria developed by students of democracy had been more precise and more widely agreed upon. Yet, the practice that has developed, in contemporary democracies, is that universal suffrage exists as far as "no major groups" are excluded from the vote (e.g., Nohlen, 1995). If universal suffrage is understood as consistent with exclusions from the vote of "minor" groups it is evident why restrictions based on age, residence, citizenship, mental capacity, and criminal record are often considered unproblematic (e.g., Vanhanen, 2003; IDEA, 2002; Munck and Verkuilen, 2002). By implication, the claim that universal suffrage is a necessary feature of democracy does not automatically translate into the claim that each citizen enjoys a human right to vote. The porous notion of "universal suffrage" and the vague conditions for restricting the right to vote in human rights law both contribute to render the scope of the human right to vote ambiguous.

Although ambiguous, the norms protecting the vote are applied and interpreted by courts, international as well as domestic. At this point, signs are abundant of an emerging "global jurisprudence" or "constitutional cosmopolitanism," including growing cross-reference to cases adjudicated in other countries or at other levels in the international system (Slaughter, 2003, 193; Sunstein, 2009, 189). An implication of this development is that courts resolve conflicts between public policy and the legal entitlements of individuals by standards that are more uniform than they used to be. This is particularly clear in the case of the so-called proportionality principle that is increasingly seen as a global jurisprudential standard (Sweet and Mathews, 2008; Sweet, 2009, 3; Sottiaux and Van Der Schyff, 2011, 130). It is now considered an "undisputed fact" that the proportionality principle has achieved global if not universal recognition (Cohen-Eliya and Porat, 2011, 465; Letsas, 2007, 101). Proportionality is reportedly embraced by judges all over the world and constitutes a "common framework" whenever international and domestic courts face the task of adjudicating between public policy and individual rights (Beatty, 2004, 159; Barak, 2012, chap. 7).

The globalization of jurisprudential standards transforms the relationship between human rights law and democratic decision making in the nation-state in two ways. First, growing consensus on jurisprudential standards mitigates some of the fears associated with courts' activism. It has been noted that if human rights law is indeterminate, the courts will not merely apply human rights, they will "make human rights," as they add substance to the vague provisions of international conventions (Perry, 2007, 91).[6] The worry is consequently that courts will interfere arbitrarily with matters within the province of democratic decision making at the national level. Yet, the concern with the arbitrary character of the interference will be less justified if courts have adopted more standardized methods of legal reasoning.

Second, the globalization of jurisprudential standards offers a potential response to the claim that national legislation reflects a legitimate diversity in how to reconcile individual and public interests (Barak, 2010, 4). In Europe, certain deference to national legislation is institutionalized by the doctrine of a "margin of appreciation" that has grown out from the case law of the European Court of Human Rights (ECtHR). This doctrine in effect preserves the indeterminate and open-ended character of international norms and therefore constitutes a barrier to the development of a more precise and uniform account of human rights (Shany, 2005; Letsas, 2006). However, the rise of global constitutionalism and shared standards of legal reasoning reduces this barrier. As the norms applied in adjudication become more widely shared, the margin of appreciation is shrinking (Sweet, 2009, 5). The door is therefore opened for the courts to fill the "gaps" in the human right to vote.

In sum, in order to understand the nature of the human right to vote, we need to understand how courts apply the increasingly shared standards at work in interpreting restrictions on that right. Our analytical framework pictures adjudication on the right to vote as manifestations of either *rule of law–like* standards or of *interest-balancing* standards.[7] These standards are implied by the jurisprudence that has evolved out of the proportionality principle, but they are also implied by the condition of "reasonable" restrictions that is embedded in human rights law.

The distinction between these standards, as the underlying basis for proportionality and reasonableness, is not generally recognized. More often proportionality is depicted as a unified account of judicial reasoning, as a single "basic principle," defining a method for a very "focused factual inquiry" by the courts (e.g., Beatty, 2004, 160, 181). In a similar vein, Aharon Barak contends that standards of proportionality and reasonableness reflect the singular aspiration towards "balancing" conflicting legal principles (Barak, 2012, 378). However, these accounts obscure the difference in purpose served by distinct elements of the principle of proportionality. As I will argue below, the contrast between rule of law–like and interest-balancing standards is important since it sheds light on the nature of the claims produced in human rights law adjudication. After a brief explication of these notions, I proceed to explain why the distinction between them is vital in understanding recent adjudication on the human right to vote.

Rule of Law-Like Standards

The rule of law–like standard reflects a variety of more fundamental values associated with "legality," "rule of law," and "integrity" in law. The explication of these values is of course complex and is to some extent contested (McCubbins, Rodriguez, and Weingast, 2010, 1455–1471). Arguably, the shared purpose of these values is that of curbing arbitrary uses of public power (Waldron, 1989, 83; Waldron, 2010, 8). This ideal imbues human rights law no less than national legal instruments. The goal to protect individuals from arbitrary subjection of government power finds expression in the preamble of the Universal Declaration (Chesterman, 2008, 344). To the extent that human rights law reflects standards of adjudication concerned with the rule of law, it serves to protect individuals from arbitrary power and thereby contributes to the secure enjoyment of liberty and rights (Fox-Decent, 2008, 562).

In the documents specifying the conditions for restricting the right to vote, the rule of law–like qualities are paramount. As indicated above, the requirement that restrictions on the vote must be "reasonable" is affirmed by the ICCPR but figures also in the Universal Declaration and the American Convention (ICCPR 25b; Nowak, 2005, 576f.). The significance of this requirement is further emphasized in the Commentary of the Human Rights Committee that elaborates the jurisprudence related to Article 25 protecting the right to vote in the ICCPR (Human Rights Committee, 1996; Rich, 2001, 23; Joseph, Schultz, and Castan, 2004, 20).

Though "reasonable" restriction is bound to appear imprecise, its meaning can be rendered more determinate by looking at it as an expression of the ideal of rule of law. A reasonable restriction would signify a restriction that is not arbitrary. A legal restriction is not arbitrary if it can be demonstrated that it promotes some identifiable public aim (Corten, 1999). By this token, the requirement of reasonable restrictions is closely similar to the requirement of nondiscrimination. The Human Rights Committee defines discrimination as "differential treatment in similar cases without an objective and reasonable justification" (Vandenhole, 2005, 79). So understood, the condition that restrictions be reasonable, just as they must not be discriminatory, reveal a concern with arbitrary subjections to power. The notion that only reasonable restrictions on the vote are justified is consequently a manifestation of rule of law–like standards.

In addition, aspects of the proportionality principle are best understood as manifestations of the ideal of rule of law. The first steps in a proportionality analysis require a judgment on the connection between the reasons for the restriction of a right and the actual restriction. This account is regularly specified as the requirement that any restrictions on fundamental rights must be instrumental to some important public interest (Kumm, 2003, 580). This is also known as the "rational connection" or "suitability" test (Barak, 2012, 303; Sweet and Mathews, 2008, 75). The restriction is hence considered as "suitable" or "rational" if it constitutes an effective means towards the realization of the aims stated. In case it is not, the restriction is to be regarded as arbitrary.

Interest-Balancing Standards

Rule of law-like standards do offer some protections for the human right to vote. However, they do not clarify the importance of the substantive interests protected by this right in relation to competing interests. This is why rule of law-like standards are unable to prevent non-arbitrary restrictions on human rights. A method for weighing competing interests is needed in order to judge if the interests promoted by the restriction are important enough to justify the infringement of the interests protected by the right. Courts are occasionally forced to estimate the relative importance of the interests at stake and to produce a substantive justification of what they take to be the most significant interest (Cohen-Eliya and Porat, 2011, 472). It is in the performance of this "oracular function" that courts are able to close the "gaps" in the legal framework protecting human rights (Sweet, 2009, 5).

A model for balancing competing interests is offered by the third step of the proportionality principle.[8] This steps calls for a judgment on the proportionality of a restriction "in the strict sense" in relation to the interests protected. Following Alexy (2010, 28) a full-scale analysis of this sort requires a judgment of the severity of the restriction, the ends served by the restriction, and to what extent these ends justify the restriction. In the end, a balance must be struck between the costs in terms of individual interests and the benefits in terms of public interests, by which is understood that the severity of the restriction must be proportionate to the significance of interests served by it. This method is criticized for not recognizing that the individual interests at stake should be conceived of as *rights* (Tsakyrakis, 2009, 476). The "balance metaphor" is also said to be premised on a utilitarian approach to conflicts between individual and public interest (e.g., Waldron, 2003). But the method of proportionality does not entail any particular account of individual interests and their importance. The often-ignored point is that proportionality in the "strict sense" requires a judgment by the court on the significance and weight attached to the individual interests at stake. In other words, the "balance" to be struck requires a prior assessment of the principled importance of the interests protected by the right.

To summarize, it is here assumed that adjudication on voting rights restrictions will reflect either rule of law-like standards or interest-balancing standards. In the first case, the question asked by the court is if the restriction constitutes an arbitrary infringement. In the second case, the court is asking if the cost of the restriction in terms of the individual's interests is proportionate to the benefits in terms of public interests. Only in the second case do courts engage the value of democracy as they estimate the significance of the individual interests protected by democratic rights. By addressing the public importance of these interests, the court touches at the foundations of democracy. Each person's interest in the public acknowledgment of his or her moral personality is among the rationales for democratic institutions (Christiano, 2009, 93). The distinction between the two models of legal reasoning consequently permits us to determine to what extent the emerging "global jurisprudence" contributes to the human right to vote in the sense of shaping our understandings of democratic rights.

PRISONER VOTING AND THE COURTS

The question of prisoner voting has appeared before constitutional courts, domestic and international, a great number of times since the late 1990s. The political context is that 65 percent of the world's nations reportedly deny citizens sentenced to prison the right to vote (Uggen, Van Brakle, and McLaughlin, 2009, 60).[9] Meanwhile, policies of prisoner disenfranchisement have repeatedly been criticised by the Human Rights Commission (HRC) in several reports.[10] These reports indicate a growing consensus among human rights activists that depriving prisoners of the vote is inconsistent with the human right to vote.

However, while the HRC publishes recommendations, the courts are able to enforce legal norms and have done so in most such cases (Macdonald, 2008, 1387).[11] Constitutional courts in only five jurisdictions have invalidated policies of prisoner disenfranchisement since 1999. Moreover, it does not follow that they have done so on the basis of similar reasons. In order to explore the extent to which rule of law–like standards or interest-balance standards have been invoked to defend the right to vote by prisoners, we will now look further into these cases.

August and Another v. Electoral Commission and Others[12]

In 1999, the Constitutional Court of South Africa faced the question of whether imprisonment constitutes a reasonable restriction on the opportunity to make use of the right to vote. The issue was whether the government is bound by the constitution to take positive measures enabling prisoners to exercise this right. Previously, the Transvaal High Court had found no such obligation upon the state. The High Court had asserted that a person convicted for a crime and sentenced to prison had in effect deprived himself or herself of the opportunity to vote: "the predicament is of their own making" (§ 8).

The Constitutional Court found scant support for this view and made two important observations. First, it pointed out that the measures required to make the vote available to prisoners were not unreasonably burdensome. There was no evidence, the Court argued, that it would be "any more difficult" to provide opportunities for voting in prisons than to provide opportunities for voting in hospitals or abroad (§ 13). Since the government had already accepted the obligation to make voting possible in such circumstances, the refusal to make voting available in prisons appeared to be without basis. By not taking action the government was denying prisoners "their constitutionally protected right to register to vote" (§ 36). Second, the Court remarked that more than a third of the prisoners denied the vote were not convicted of any serious offence. Rather, they were imprisoned only because they were unable to "pay low amounts of bail or small fines" (§ 32).

Although the Court did not explicitly argue that denying prisoners effective opportunities to vote is equal to an arbitrary restriction, this conclusion appears to be implicitly affirmed by the Court. Not acting to provide this opportunity for prisoners constitutes an arbitrary restriction if the government has already accepted the obligation to provide such opportunities to others in relevantly similar situations. The judgment that the restriction is arbitrary is also suggested by the Court's indictment of the accidental nature of the circumstances deciding whether a convicted offender is imprisoned, thereby losing the vote, or merely fined and thereby able to continue voting.

The jurisprudential standard employed by the Constitutional Court of South Africa in this case is predominantly rule of law–like. The major argument of the Court is that the government is acting inconsistently and arbitrarily when it denies opportunities to vote for certain categories of eligible voters while it is at the same time providing such opportunities to other segments of the electorate. Yet, the Court also made a strong argument about the value of the right to vote. It pointed out that "universal adult suffrage" is one of the "foundational values" of the South African constitutional order. More important, the Court emphasized the value of the vote to "each and every citizen." This value is fundamental because the right to vote constitutes "a badge of dignity and personhood." The importance of the vote is not merely derived from the collective interest in a democratic political order that embodies the idea of universal suffrage. The Court is also keen to stress the importance of the vote as derived from the need to protect the "dignity" and "personhood" of the individual citizen. So construed, the margin for tolerating any exclusions from the vote is significantly reduced. The Court consequently saw a strong case for the principle that the franchise must be "interpreted in favor of enfranchisement rather than disenfranchisement" (§ 17).

Sauvé v. Canada[13]

The case of *Sauvé v. Canada* was resolved by the Supreme Court of Canada in 2002 and marked the end of a sequence of decisions by lower courts and the parliament. Despite attempts by the parliament to accommodate earlier court judgments, by amending the relevant sections of electoral regulations, the Supreme Court finally ruled that prisoner disenfranchisement was inconsistent with the Canadian Charter of Rights and Freedoms (adopted in 1982).

The Supreme Court majority (five out of nine judges) made clear that restrictions on the vote must be evaluated by rigorous standards. Hence, the Court adopted a strict proportionality analysis that included four steps. The court examined the legitimacy of the aims motivating the policy of denying prisoners the vote, the connection between the aims and the restrictions imposed on prisoners, the degree to which preventing prisoners to vote was truly necessary, and, last, if the benefits of achieving the aims of the policy were "proportionate" to the costs to the interests implied by the restriction on voting. In fact, the Court comes close to invalidating the law on all counts. While it did not reject conclusively the government's aims, the Court found them "suspect" (§ 24). In every other respect, the Court was emphatic that the law failed to stand up to scrutiny. The conclusion is remarkable in the sense that it would have been sufficient to establish that the law failed in just one respect.

In terms of the terminology adopted here, the Court's conclusion reflected both rule of law–like standards and balance of interest standards. The concern with the rule of law is visible in the argument that the government failed to establish a "rational connection" between denial of the vote and the objectives of the law. Supporting the argument, the Court observed that the policy of disenfranchisement hits any offender, serving two years or more, irrespective of his or her particular crime. The law is consequently "too broad," according to the Court, since it applies to many people who should not have been targeted. The law therefore cannot escape the requirement "absence of arbitrariness" (§ 48).

The Court also applied interest-balancing standards when it endeavored to ask about the benefits expected from the policy of depriving prisoners the vote. The benefits would be those identified by the government, namely, the enhancement of "civic responsibility" and respect for the law, as well as to impose additional punishment (§ 24, 25). Even if these benefits do constitute public interests, they provide a reason for restricting a constitutionally protected interest only if the benefit is substantial and compensates for the costs incurred to individual interests and other public interests. According to the Court, the costs caused by the policy are apparently considerable:

Denial of the right to vote to penitentiary inmates undermines the legitimacy of government, the effectiveness of government, and the rule of law. It curtails the personal rights of the citizen to political expression and participation in the political life of his or her country. It countermands the message that everyone is equally worthy and entitled to respect under the law. (§ 58)

Hence, in the Court's judgment, the negative effects of the law "greatly outweigh" the benefits that "might" ensue (§ 57). The negative effects are partly a result of the risk of undermining other public interests, such as the legitimacy of the government. But the individual interests at stake loom even larger in the Court's reasoning. They are individual interests in political participation and expression but also in the even more fundamental interest of preserving the principle of equal worth. The last remark in the passage quoted above is suggesting that the Court considers restrictions on the vote as violations of the very principle of equal human dignity. The connection between the vote and human dignity were in fact asserted twice before in the judgment. The Court had insisted that to deny any citizen the vote is to "run counter to our constitutional commitment to the inherent worth and dignity of every individual" (§ 35). Also, the Court had rejected the argument that prisoners deserve to be disenfranchised by pointing out that this claim is "inconsistent with the respect for the dignity of every person that lies at the heart of Canadian democracy" (§ 44).

The Sauvé judgment is significant in that the Court found prisoner disenfranchisement wanting both in terms of rule of law–like standards and in terms of interest-balancing standards. Indeed, the reason that the policy is arbitrary seems to be less significant compared to the reason that the interests protected by the right to vote are necessary for the preservation of equal huan dignity. Given the fundamental importance of human dignity, it is hard to see how any public interest could justify any deviation from this principle.

Hirst v. United Kingdom[14]

In 2005, the European Court of Human Rights ruled by 12 votes to 5 that United Kingdom, by denying the vote to prisoners, had violated Article 3 of Protocol No. 1 (right to free elections) of the European Convention on Human Rights. The decision affirmed the view of the vote as a fundamental right and rejected the view that the vote is a mere "privilege" that governments could regulate at will (Hill and Koch, 2011, 222).

The primary justification of the Court's ruling is to be found in its conclusion that the legislation introduced by the British parliament constituted an "arbitrary" and "disproportionate" restriction on the rights of individual prisoners. In order to reach this conclusion, the Court did not challenge the legitimacy of the aims proclaimed by the British government (Powers, 2006,

283).[15] Indeed, the Court saw "no reason in the circumstances of this application to exclude these aims as untenable" (*Hirst*, 75). The Court instead focused on the extent to which the aims identified by the government were served by the policy depriving all prisoners of the vote. There must be, the Court insisted, a "discernable and sufficient link" between the aim of the sanction and the circumstances of the individual prisoner (*Hirst*, 71).

Now, the link between the aims of the policy and the means it provides can be subject to scrutiny from various standpoints. In his concurring opinion, Judge Caflisch expressed doubts about the government's claim that a policy of prisoner disenfranchisement would ever promote "civic responsibility" (Concurring Opinion of Judge Caflisch, 5). But the Court did not essentially dispute the claim that the law could produce the desired effect. Instead, the Court struck down the application of the law to individual cases. Because the British law applied equally to every prisoner, it affected individuals to the same degree, irrespective of the length of the sentence or the gravity of the offence. The law provided no opportunity for British courts to contemplate the appropriateness of the additional punishment implied by disenfranchisement since the loss of the vote followed "automatically" from the prison sentence. This is what the European Court found inadmissible in light of the fundamental rights upheld by the Convention. By imposing a "blanket ban" on all prisoners, the convicted person is deprived of the vote without any consideration of the particular circumstances of his or her case. The Court accordingly concluded that the policy of prisoner disenfranchisement is "arbitrary" as there is no "logical link" between "the facts of any individual case and the removal of the right to vote" (*Hirst*, 75, 77; see also Powers, 2006, 282; Isphani, 2009, 41–44).

The *Hirst* judgment explicitly applied the first two steps of the proportionality principle, corresponding to what is here described as "rule of law-like" standards of reasoning. Thus, the Court "withdrew from a battle regarding the general principle without a fight" as it refrained from ever attempting to "balance" the conflicting interests against one another (Tsakyrakis, 2009, 486). In the absence of such an exercise, the Court did not have to produce an account of the individual interests protected by the right to vote. Accordingly, some commentators concluded that *Hirst* does *not* represent any "groundbreaking shift in the substantive right to vote" by the European Court (Powers, 2006, 287).

Nevertheless, the Court delivered a strong statement about the importance of the right to vote in a democratic society. It argued, "any departure from the principle of universal suffrage risks undermining the democratic validity of the legislature" (*Hirst*, 62). The Court also insisted that "the presumption in a democratic State must be in favor of inclusion" (*Hirst*, 59). This point reappears in the judgment of *Frodl v. Austria* in 2011. In this case, the Court insisted that the disenfranchisement of any prisoner must always be understood as an exception from the general rule (Briant, 2011, 279). These statements were not made in the context of attempting to identify the relative weight of the interests protected by the vote in the particular case. Instead, they provided a justification for the Court's position that it had the right to determine "in the last resort" whether the Convention is "complied with" in matters of voting rights (*Hirst*, 62). The Court's statements on the importance of universal suffrage should consequently not be read as a full-blown attempt to explicate the importance of the interests defended by the right to vote. Yet, they do reflect a radical understanding of universal suffrage as a concept that is not easily reconcilable with the "usual" restrictions. Following the Court's reasoning, universal suffrage is equivalent to the inclusion of all adult citizens.

Roach v. Electoral Commissioner[16]

In Australia, the case of prisoner disenfranchisement was brought before The High Court in 2006. The majority of the Court ruled in favor of the plaintiff and so invalidated the section of the Electoral Act providing for the disenfranchisement of "all prisoners serving a sentence for imprisonment for an offence against the law."[17] Yet, the case was seen as a "limited victory" by representatives of the civil rights movement (Orr, 2007). The sense of limitation follows from the Court's acquiescence to the basic aims of prisoner disenfranchisement. The Court accepted as within the prerogatives of the parliament to enforce a "symbolic separation" of the bond between imprisoned citizens and the community by means of disenfranchisement.

The Court nevertheless found the existing regime wanting and it did so by questioning the relation between the criteria of prisoner disenfranchisement and the implicit aims of these restrictions. According to the Court, temporary disenfranchisement of prisoners serves the purpose of marking "serious offending" as antisocial. The Court emphasized that only serious offenders could be understood as the intended target of the law. The reason for this interpretation is that the law would not debar from voting either persons in custody, who are not yet convicted, or persons receiving noncustodial sentences. The aim of the law is consequently to prevent serious offenders from voting.

Having identified the aims of the policy, the Court proceeded to inquire to what extent it justifies the criteria devised by the law. As has already been noted, the loss of the right to vote applies to anyone sentenced to imprisonment. Yet, the Court also makes the crucial observation that the provision applies to significant numbers of prisoners serving short-term sentences, for six months or less. This is where the Court finds the problem. It notes that Magistrates, who are charged with the imposition of short-term sentences, are in most cases required to investigate alternatives to imprisonment such as home detention, community service, or fines. However, the capacity to provide alternatives to short-time imprisonment is constrained by the recourses of the Magistrate as well as by the resources of the offender. For example, the alternatives are likely to be fewer for homeless or mentally unstable offenders. From these observations, it appears clear that people serving short-time sentences cannot generally be considered as "serious offenders." Indeed, the circumstances deciding whether an offender is serving a short-term sentence or not appear somewhat arbitrary. The Court accordingly concludes that the consistency of the government's policy "breaks down at the level of short-term prisoners." Because the criteria introduced by the Federal Parliament do not discriminate between serious and nonserious offenders, the right to vote becomes "arbitrary."

In *Roach*, The High Court made abundant reference to comparative law materials and to international law. The cases of *Sauvé* and *Hirst* were both explicitly discussed by the majority of the Court. Judge Kirby, siding with the majority in *Roach*, later wrote that the references to Canadian and European cases on prisoner disenfranchisement were part of the "ongoing judicial conversation" (Kirby, 2008, 170). At the same time, the dissenting minority of the Court criticized the Court for referring to legal material without standing in the Australian constitutional system.

Yet, in summarizing the reasoning employed in *Roach*, it is clear that the Court exclusively applied rule of law–like standards. The Court was not engaging the question whether the infringement of the individual's interest in voting was on balance justified by appeal to the public interests allegedly promoted by the law.

Chan Kin Sum v. Secretary for Justice[18]

The High Court of Hong Kong delivered its judgment on the disenfranchisement of prisoners in 2008. The law under scrutiny denied anyone sentenced to prison the right to register to vote. It further denied prisoners the right to register to vote even in the rare case that elections were held on the day of the person's release from prison. The Court found this minor point to be of principled importance, as it showed that the law applied even beyond the prison population.

In his judgment, the then Judge of First Instance Andrew Cheung (later to be Chief Judge of the High Court) declared that the vote is subject only to reasonable restrictions. This is because of the fact, "beyond argument," that the vote represents a fundamental right meriting constitutional protection on a par with other fundamental rights (§ 50). In defining the meaning of reasonable restrictions more precisely Judge Cheung made clear, with reference to international jurisprudence and human rights law, that restrictions must pass the proportionality test to be constitutionally valid (§ 70–77). The Court hence found itself positioned to examine whether the government's policy pursues a "legitimate aim." In contrast to the previous judgments reviewed here, the High Court of Hong Kong found the legitimacy of the government's policy hard to establish. However, the reason for this difficulty turned out to be merely formal as the Court could not detect "any clear statement from a responsible minister or official on the Government's reasons relied on to justify the relevant restrictions" (§ 46). In the end, upon submission of evidence from the government, the Court accepted that the existence of legitimate aims "are or can be" ascertained (§ 88, 97).

Recognizing the possibility of defensible aims served by a policy of prisoner disenfranchisement, the primary question for the Court turned out to be if there existed a "rational connection" between the pursuit of these aims and the measures that restrict the vote for prisoners. In considering this point, the Court gave extensive attention to previous judgments on prisoner voting in Canada, South Africa, and Australia and by the ECtHR (i.e., the cases discussed above). In fact, the Hong Kong High Court essentially draws on two different reasons that have been listed before. The first and undoubtedly most important reason invoked by the Court is the apparent arbitrariness of the restriction. This is inferred from the absence of individualized treatment in the decision to deprive a prisoner of the vote (§ 137). The "sweeping" character of the law (§ 112) in effect apportions the same punishment (loss of the vote) to any person, no matter the length of the prison sentence or the gravity of the offence. Also, the arbitrary nature of the law follows from the observation that fines or community service are sometimes substituted for short prison terms, depending on factors such as the family background of the convicted person. But since only persons sentenced to imprisonment are deprived of the vote, some people are thereby exempted from disenfranchisement due to "facts and circumstances that have no or little connection to the stated aims of imposing the voting restrictions." Recognizing the parallel to *Roach*, the Court concluded the restriction is for this reason "simply arbitrary" (§ 120).

The second reason offered by the Court is the lack of evidence substantiating the government's claim that restrictions on voting furthers the aims of the policy. The Court notes that the government has been unable to file any evidence to this effect and also that no other sources indicate the existence of such evidence (§ 145). The claim that disenfranchisement helps to prevent crime must thus be considered "an indefensible notion," according to the Court (§ 139).

Similar to the judgments in other places, The Hong Kong Court affirmed the fundamental nature of the right to vote. This is said by the Court to imply a "presumption" in favor of inclusion of all adult citizens in the vote (§ 106). At the same time, the Court did not provide a clear statement on the individual importance of the vote. What seemed more decisive to the final judgment were defects in the legal procedure applied in decisions restricting the vote of individual prisoners. While the Court did apply the proportionality principle in reviewing the electoral regulations, it did so exclusively with reference to the standards of rule of law.

FINAL DISCUSSION

Legal norms protecting the right to vote are an integrated part of human rights law. And yet, national governments frequently pursue policies that restrict opportunities for voting by marginalized groups. The consistency of such policies with the human right to vote remains possible due to the vague conditions for when restrictions are justified. While international conventions provide for the legal protection of the right to vote, the gaps of that framework make the protection less effective.

However, with the increasing activism of courts, in domestic and international settings, the legal situation is transformed. The courts are beginning to provide more substance to the relevant articles of human rights law. The courts are consequently decisive to the fulfillment of the human right to vote. The point stressed here, however, is that a vital condition for this development is the introduction of new jurisprudential standards. In a variety of places around the world, constitutional and international courts employ the "proportionality principle" in cases where the fundamental rights of citizens are at stake. The systematic comparison of individual and public interests envisaged by this principle allow courts to produce substantive judgments where the legal articles are either vague or ambiguous. This illustrates how the globalization of law is affecting outcomes by the diffusion of standards for legal reasoning.

Looking at this process critically, we have focused on how the reasoning of judges is shaping and defining the right to vote, and, ultimately, the very idea of democracy. The argument made here is that democratic rights will be differently construed depending on whether the courts approach them by rule of law–like standards or by interest-balancing standards. These standards reflect distinct aspects of the principle of proportionality and the doctrine of "reasonableness" that are embedded in human rights law and in constitutional law. The claim made here is that the distinction between rule of law–like standards and interest-balancing standards is significant in order to understand how democratic rights are shaped by the courts. Whereas the former gives priority to protections from arbitrary subjection to public power, the latter reflects substantive judgments on the relative importance of individual and public interests.

In most cases, where the disenfranchisement of prisoners has been invalidated by courts, the legal justification offered is rule of law–like. This implies that the courts do not per se reject the policy restricting voting rights, while insisting that such policies must satisfy higher legal standards of protection against arbitrary interference. The European Court exemplifies this stance most clearly. The European Court has referred to the "*Hirst* test" following its ruling in *Hirst v. United Kingdom*.[19] According to this test, restrictions on the right to vote of an individual citizen must be tried by a court in order not to be considered arbitrary.

The "*Hirst* test" reduces uncertainty in the legal entitlements of the individual by the requirement that restrictions are reviewed by judges. However, an alternative would be to place a higher premium on the existence of general and unambiguous legal rules that makes restrictions less likely. If the legal rules protecting the vote are general and precise, uncertainty about the legal status of the right is evidently reduced. Thus, an alternative to the "*Hirst* test" would be to submit that the democratic franchise should not be decided on a case-by-case basis.[20] The European Court did not pursue this route and therefore neglected the opportunity to make clear that the interests protected by the right to vote are of such importance as to preclude restrictions by reference to vague expectations of promoting the public interest.

However, in some cases, the courts have offered reasons based on the principled importance of the interests protected by the right to vote. The Supreme Court of Canada and the Constitutional Court of South Africa both picture the vote as a "badge of dignity" in a democratic society. From these and similar statements can be inferred a substantive appreciation of democratic rights and the interests protected by them that render both arbitrary and non-arbitrary restrictions on the vote hard to justify.

Yet, as can be readily observed from the survey of recent legal cases offered here, the courts are loath to offer substantive claims on the interest of prisoner voting. This means that there is not yet a general tendency towards a new understanding of the significance of democratic rights as such. With the advent of global standards of jurisprudence in the realm of human rights law, the legal protection of individual interests is improving. But more attention is needed to insure that the courts are acting to protect interests in democratic rights—not just rule of law.

NOTES

1. It remains contested if a human right to democracy can be defended as a basic moral entitlement. See Cohen (2006) and Christiano (2011) for the arguments for and against.
2. As frequently observed, the signatory states of the Universal Declaration never imagined it to be an instrument protecting democracy (Franck, 1992, 63; Steiner, 2008, 448). The most obvious concession to existing legal frameworks is that the vote, although framed as a "human right," does not apply to "humans" but only to "citizens."
3. The reluctance of elected representatives to enfranchise prisoners is further illustrated by recent events such as the refusal of the UK government to implement the European Court of Human Rights (ECtHR) judgment that prisoners must be granted the vote and the decision by the government of New Zealand (in 2010) to extend restrictions of that kind (The Electoral [Disqualification of Prisoners] Amendment Bill).
4. By "restriction" I henceforth refer to any formal condition for the enjoyment of a legal right, whether or not the condition is justified. Hence, a restriction is equal to what is also known as an "infringement." Infringements of legal rights do not imply the violation of legal rights, if the latter is defined as an unjustified infringement (Parent, 1980, 406).
5. Cf. Perry (2007, 91) arguing that human rights law in general is plagued by "indeterminacy."
6. The vagueness inherent in certain aspects of international law is not necessarily more serious than the vagueness of constitutional provisions generally. Indeed, it has been argued that international and constitutional law is

structurally similar exactly in terms of the "foundational uncertainty" and "contestation of meaning" (Goldsmith and Levinson, 2009, 1794).

7. See also McHarg (1999) and Souttiaux and Van Der Schyff (2011) for the contrast between rule-like decisions and balancing-like decisions in human rights adjudication, closely mirroring the distinction made here.

8. The proportionality principle is interchangeably described in terms of three or four steps. This is because the assessment of the legitimacy of the ends served by the policy is either perceived to be a preliminary step (leaving three steps for the subsequent application of the principle) or as part of the proportionality analysis itself (meaning there are four steps involved in its application).

9. In fact, the extent to which people sentenced for a criminal offence are permitted to vote is often a matter of degree. Disenfranchisement may apply exclusively to serious offenders, or to prisoners sentenced for particular offences only, such as electoral misconduct or treason.

10. The reports include criticism of Luxembourg (1993 and 2003), Hong Kong (1995), United Kingdom (2001), and the United States (2006). This is in line with the observation by Fox (1992, 63) that the HRC is increasingly making an independent interpretation of Article 25.

11. The only exception to my knowledge is the Supreme Court of India where a petition to enfranchise prisoners in 1997 was rejected. The decision was justified by the superior interest of securing "a healthy and clean democracy" (*A. C. Pradhan v. Union of India* [1997]).

12. *August and Another v. Electoral Commission and Others* (CCT8/99) [1999] ZACC 3.

13. *Sauvé v. Canada* (Chief Electoral Officer) [2002] 3 S.C.R. 519.

14. *Hirst v. United Kingdom* (No. 2) [2005] ECtHR 681.

15. The ECtHR rarely invalidates the legitimacy of government aims. Powers (2006, 264) depicts the Court's review of government aims as a "mere formality."

16. *Roach v. Electoral Commissioner* (2007) HCA 43.

17. The particular section had been introduced by the parliament only in 2006. Before that date, other constraints on prisoner voting had been variously in force since their first appearance in the 1918 Commonwealth Electoral Act.

18. *Chan Kin Sum v. Secretary for Justice*, HCAL 79/2008.

19. See *Frodl v. Austria* (201201/04 [2010] ECtHR 508) but also *Alajos Kiss v. Hungary* (38832/06 [2010] ECtHR 692), where the Court challenged restrictions on the vote for people under guardianship.

20. The argument here follows Sunstein's (2006) distinction between two conceptions of procedural fairness, the first emphasizing the value of general rules, the second emphasizing the value of individualized treatment.

REFERENCES

Alexy, Robert, 2010. "The Construction of Constitutional Rights," *Law and Ethics of Human Rights*, 4, 1, 20–32.

Barak, Aharon, 2010. "Proportionality and Principled Balancing," *Law and Ethics of Human Rights*, 4, 1.

Barak, Aharon, 2012. *Proportionality. Constitutional Rights and Their Limitations*, Cambridge: Cambridge University Press.

Beatty, David, 2004. *The Ultimate Rule of Law*, Oxford: Oxford University Press.

Benhabib, Seyla, 2009. "Claiming Rights across Borders: International Human Rights and Democratic Sovereignty," *American Political Science Review*, 103, 691–704.

Boutros-Ghali, Boutros, 1996. *An Agenda for Democratization*, New York: United Nations.

Briant, Sophie, 2011. "The Requirement of Prisoner Voting Rights: Mixed Messages from Strasbourg," *Cambridge Law Journal*, 70, 2.

Chesterman, Simon, 2008. "An International Rule of Law?", *American Journal of Comparative Law*, 56, 331.

Christiano, Thomas, 2009. *The Constitution of Equality*, Oxford: Oxford University Press.

Christiano, Thomas, 2011. "An Instrumental Argument for a Human Right to Democracy," *Philosophy and Public Affairs*, 39, 2, 142–176.

Cohen, Joshua, 2006. "Is There a Human Right to Democracy?", in Christine Sypnowich (ed.), *The Egalitarian Conscience—Essays in Honour of G.A. Cohen*, Oxford: Oxford University Press.

Cohen-Eliya, Moshe, and Iddo Porat, 2011. "Proportionality and the Culture of Justification," *American Journal of Comparative Law*, 59, 2, 463–490.

Corten, Olivier, 1999. "The Notion of 'Reasonable' in International Law: Legal Discourse, Reason and Contradictions," *International and Comparative Law Quarterly*, 48.

Council of Europe, 1999. *Yearbook of the European Convention on Human Rights*: Vol. 41a: Key Extracts from a Selection of Judgements of the European Court of Human Rights, Kluwer.

Davis-Roberts, Avery, and David J. Carroll, 2010. "Using International Law to Assess Elections," *Democratization*, 17, 3, 416–441.

DeFeis, Elisabeth, 2001. "Elections—A Global Right?", *Wisconsin International Law Journal*, 19, 321.

Endicott, Timothy, 2001. "Law Is Necessarily Vague," *Legal Theory*, 7, 379–385.

Fox, Gregory H., 1992. "The Right to Political Participation in International Law," *Yale Journal of International Law*, 17.

Fox-Decent, Evan, 2008. "Is the Rule of Law Really Indifferent to Human Rights?", *Law and Philosophy*, 27, 533–581.

Franck, Thomas M., 1992. "The Emerging Right to Democratic Governance," *American Journal of International Law*, 86, 1, 46–91.

Gardbaum, Stephen, 2008. "Human Rights as International Constitutional Rights," *European Journal of International Law*, 19.

Goldsmith, Jack and Daryl Levinson, 2009. "Law for States: International Law, Public Law, Constitutional Law," Harvard Law Review 122: 1791.

Hill, Lisa, and Koch, Cornelia, 2011. "The Voting Rights of Incarcerated Australian Citizens," *Australian Journal of Political Science*, 46, 3, 213–228.

*Human Rights Committee, 1996. *General Comment No. 25.* CPR/C/21/Rev.1/ Add.7.

*IDEA (International Institute for Democracy and Electoral Assistance), 2002. *Voter Turnout since 1945. A Global Report,* Stockholm: IDEA.

Isphani, Laleh, 2009. "Punishment and Social Exclusion: National Differences in Prisoner Disenfranchisement," in Alec C. Ewald and Brandon Rottinghaus (eds.), *Criminal Disenfranchisement in an International Perspective*, Cambridge: Cambridge University Press.

Joseph, Sarah, 2010. "Civil and Political Rights," in Mashood A. Baderin and Manisuli Ssenyonjo (eds.), *International Human Rights Law: Six Decades after the UDHR and Beyond*, Farnham: Ashgate.

Joseph, Sarah, Jenny Schultz, and Melissa Castan, 2004. *The International Covenant on Civil and Political Rights: Cases, Materials, and Commentary*, Oxford: Oxford University Press.

Kirby, Michael, 2008. "Domestic Courts and International Human Rights Law: The Ongoing Judicial Conversation," *Utrech Law Review*, 6, 1, 168–181.

Kirschner, Alexander, 2003. "The International Status of the Right to Vote," unpublished manuscript, Democracy Coalition Project, Open Society Institute and the Spanish foundation FRIDE.

Kumm, Mattias, 2003. "A Review Essay on 'A Theory of Constitutional Rights,'" *International Journal of Constitutional Law*, 2, 3, 574–596.

Lardy, Heather, 2003. "Translating Human Rights into Moral Demands on Government," *International Legal Theory*, 9, 123–134.

Letsas, George, 2006. "Two Concepts of the Margin of Appreciation," *Oxford Journal of Legal Studies*, 26, 4, 705.

Letsas, George, 2007. *A Theory of Interpretation of the European Convention on Human Rights*, Oxford: Oxford University Press.

Macdonald, Morgan, 2008. "Disproportionate Punishment: The Legality of Criminal Disenfranchisement under the International Covenant on Civil and Political Rights," *George Washington International Law Review*, 40, 1375–1408.

McCubbins, Mathew D., Daniel B. Rodriguez, and Barry R. Weingast, 2010. "The Rule of Law Unplugged," *Emory Law Journal*, 59, 6, 1455–1494.

McHarg, Aileen, 1999. "Reconciling Human Rights and the Public Interest: Conceptual Problems and Doctrinal Uncertainty in the Jurisprudence of the European Court of Human Rights," *Modern Law Review*, 62, 5, 671–696.

Mowbray, Alastair, 2010. "The European Convention on Human Rights," in Mashood A. Banderin and Manisuli Ssenyonjo (eds.), *International Human Rights Law: Six Decades after the UDHR and Beyond*, Farnham: Ashgate.

Munck, Geraldo, and Jay Verkuilen, 2002. "Conceptualizing and Measuring Democracy," *Comparative Political Studies*, 35, 1, 5–34.

Nohlen, Dieter, 1995. "Voting Rights," in S.M. Lipset (ed.), *Encyclopedia of Democracy*, Washington, DC: Congressional Quarterly Books.

Nowak, Manfred, 2005. *U.N. Covenant on Civil and Political Rights CCPR Commentary, 2nd revised edition*, Arlington: N.P. Engel.

Orr, Graeme, 2007. *Constitutionalising the Franchise and the Status Quo: The High Court on Prisoner Voting Rights*, Law School, University of Queensland Discussion Paper 19/07.

Parent, W.A., 1980. "Judith Thomson and the Logic of Rights," *Philosophical Studies*, 37, 4, 405–418.

Perry, Michael J., 2007. *Toward a Theory of Human Rights. Religion, Law, Courts*, Cambridge: Cambridge University Press.

Plaxton, Michael, and Heather Lardy, 2010. "Prisoner Disenfranchisement: Four Judicial Approaches," *Berkeley Journal of International Law*, 28, 101.

Powers, William Ashby, 2006. "*Hirst v. United Kingdom* (No. 2): A First Look at Prisoner Disenfranchisement by the European Court of Human Rights," *Connecticut Journal of International Law*, 21, 2, 243–295.

Rich, Roland, 2001. "Bringing Democracy into International Law," *Journal of Democracy*, 12, 3, 20–34.

Shany, Yuval, 2005. "Toward a General Margin of Appreciation Doctrine in International Law?," *European Journal of International Law*, 16, 907–940.

Slaughter, Anne-Marie, 2003. "A Global Community of Courts," *Harvard International Law Journal*, 44.

Sottiaux, Stefan, and Gerhard Van Der Schyff, 2011. "Methods of International Human Rights Adjudication: Towards a More Structured Decision-Making Process for the European Court of Human Rights," *Hastings International and Comparative Law Review*, 31, 1, 115–156.

Steiner, Henry, 2008. "Two Sides of the Same Coin? Democracy and International Human Rights," *Israeli Law Review*, 41, 445.

Sunstein, Cass, 2006. "Two Conceptions of Procedural Fairness," *Social Research*, 73, 2, 619–646.

Sunstein, Cass, 2009. *A Constitution of Many Minds*, Princeton, NJ: Princeton University Press.

Sweet, Alec Stone, 2009. "On the Constitutionalisation of the Convention: The European Court of Human Rights as a Constitutional Court," Faculty Scholarship Series. Paper 71.

Sweet, Alec Stone, and Jud Mathews, 2008. "Proportionality Balancing and Global Constitutionalism," *Columbia Journal of Transnational Law*, 47.

Tsakyrakis, Savros, 2009. "Proportionality: An Assault on Human Rights?" *International Journal of Constitutional Law*, 7, 3, 468–493.

Uggen, Christopher, Michelle Van Brakle, and Heather McLaughlin, 2009. "Punishment and Social Exclusion: National Differences in Prisoner Disenfranchisement," in Alec C. Ewald and Brandon Rottinghaus (eds.), *Criminal Disenfranchisement in an International Perspective*, Cambridge: Cambridge University Press.

Vandenhole, Wouter, 2005. *Non-discrimination and Equality in the View of the UN Human Rights Treaty Bodies*, Antwerpen: Intersentia.

Vanhanen, Tatu, 2003. *Democratization. A Comparative Analysis of 170 Countries*, London: Routledge.

Waldron, Jeremy, 1989. "The Rule of Law in Contemporary Liberal Theory," *Ratio Juris*, 2, 1, 79–96.

Waldron, Jeremy, 2003. "Security and Liberty: The Image of a Balance," *Journal of Political Philosophy*, 11.

Waldron, Jeremy, 2010. "The Rule of Law and the Importance of Procedure," New York University Public Law and Legal Theory Working Papers. Paper 234. http://lsr.nellco.org/nyu_plltwp/234

5   From Pirates to Pinochet
Universal Jurisdiction for Torture

Mark Berlin

On March 24, 1999, Great Britain's highest court ruled that former Chilean president Augusto Pinochet could be extradited to Spain to answer criminal charges of human rights violations committed under his rule. The decision capped a groundbreaking episode in the history of international justice: never before had a former head of state been subjected to criminal proceedings based on the principle of universal jurisdiction (Kaleck 2009, 928; Penrose 2000, 207). The principle allows the domestic courts of one state to prosecute other states' citizens regardless of where the crimes in question were committed or the nationality of the victims (Randall 1987). Six months earlier Pinochet had been arrested in a London hospital, where he had come to receive medical treatment. The arrest was initiated by an extradition request issued by a Spanish judge charging Pinochet with various human rights violations.[1] Pinochet's arrest led to a series of hearings that culminated in the unprecedented March 1999 decision affirming that Pinochet's status as a former head of state did not entitle him to the sort of official immunity traditionally recognized by international law, thus paving the way for his extradition to Spain ("Pinochet III" 1999).[2] The "Pinochet precedent" inspired a wave of mobilization and litigation by lawyers, judges, and civil society activists in Europe and elsewhere seeking accountability for past wrongs, as well as giving former leaders around the world new reason to fear traveling abroad (Robertson 2006, 362–363; Roht-Arriaza 2005).

How could this unprecedented decision have come about? In its final judgment authorizing Pinochet's extradition, Great Britain's House of Lords relied heavily on the 1984 United Nations Convention Against Torture—to which Chile, Spain, and the United Kingdom (UK) were all parties—as well as domestic legislation adopted in the UK to implement its obligations under the convention. In short, had it not been for the Torture Convention's universal jurisdiction provision, the Pinochet decision would have likely gone the other way.[3] But if the treaty's universal jurisdiction provision made such a decision possible, what then accounts for the existence of this clause in the first place? The notion of universal jurisdiction for human rights infringes on traditional, Westphalian conceptions of sovereignty, and its use has the potential to disrupt the everyday workings of international relations

(Kontorovich 2004, 188–189; Sriram 2003, 306). Accordingly, states have historically been resistant to expanding the purview of universal jurisdiction from its early associations with the laws of piracy to also include crimes committed by government officials. The U.S. representative during the drafting of 1948 Genocide Convention even called universal jurisdiction "one of the most dangerous and unacceptable of principles" (UN Doc. A/C.6/SR.100, 399). Yet three decades after the Genocide Convention, the Torture Convention marked a point of institutional change in the international human rights regime by becoming the first human rights treaty requiring states to either extradite or prosecute offenders found in their territories, regardless of nationality (Art. 7). Today many human rights lawyers, activists, and nongovernmental organizations (NGOs) consider universal jurisdiction an "essential" tool in the fight against impunity and advocate its use against suspected human rights abusers traveling abroad (Amnesty International 2010; Macedo 2004; Roth 2001). Accounting for the Torture Convention's universal jurisdiction provision is thus important for understanding the sources of institutional change and the emergence of new mechanisms for the protection of human rights.

This chapter argues that the inclusion of universal jurisdiction in the Torture Convention was made possible by a number of normative shifts in international law that unfolded over the three decades preceding the treaty. These shifts had the effect of fundamentally shaping the terms of the debate within the Torture Convention's drafting process and thus providing universal jurisdiction advocates with the ideational resources to persuade their opponents to accept the provision. These normative shifts were driven in large part by what this volume refers to as the "globalization of law," that is, "the growth of legal norms, mechanisms, and jurisprudence across borders." I argue that this growth helped alter intersubjective understandings regarding the limits of sovereignty, the place of the individual in international law, and the appropriateness of universal jurisdiction for human rights. These new understandings aided universal jurisdiction proponents in the Torture Convention by lending weight to their particular interpretations of the central normative debates over the provision. And as illustrated by the Pinochet case and its aftereffects, the normative innovation represented by the Torture Convention's universal jurisdiction provision would ultimately constitute a key contribution to the recent rise of criminal accountability for human rights, described by some scholars as the "justice cascade" (Lutz and Sikkink 2001; Sikkink 2011).

My argument thus supports two central claims made in this volume's introduction. First, the globalization of law, by producing new rules and new interpretations for existing rules, generates new possibilities for human rights advocates to establish new repertoires of accountability. This volume's contributions demonstrate that new human rights law can create new openings for citizens and activists to pursue the fulfillment of rights. But this chapter argues that *the expansion of international law in general*, by producing new intersubjective understandings, creates new possibilities for norm entrepreneurs and institutional architects to redefine the boundaries of more specific institutions, like international human rights law, thus providing new instruments for fulfillment. Second, the historical evolution of universal jurisdiction is consistent with the view that the globalization of law is a "dialectical process." While the 1948 Genocide Convention was a groundbreaking innovation in the development of modern international law, the normative structure of international law at the time of the Convention limited the abilities of universal jurisdiction advocates to pursue such an expansive enforcement regime. But the globalization of law over the next three decades redefined that normative framework. These changes empowered universal jurisdiction proponents by providing them with new ideational resources to legitimize their claims and delegitimize opponents' counterclaims.

This chapter proceeds as follows. First, I discuss existing rationalist and communicative theories of institutional design, arguing that neither adequately accounts for the different outcomes in enforcement provisions across the Genocide and Torture Conventions. I then extend communicative institutional design theory to account for the role of normative structures in mediating the type of persuasion dynamics central to this approach. The next section applies this insight to a comparison of the debates over universal jurisdiction in the two conventions, connecting their different communicative dynamics—and thus their outcomes—to changes in the normative structure of international law. I then survey how the Torture Convention's universal jurisdiction provision later contributed to both the Pinochet decision and the broader justice cascade. Finally, I conclude by summarizing my argument and discussing its implications in light of the hypotheses advanced in this volume's introduction.

WHY WAS UNIVERSAL JURISDICTION INCLUDED IN THE TORTURE CONVENTION?

Scholars working at the intersection of International Relations (IR) and international law have become increasingly interested in explaining variation in the design of international institutions (e.g., Goldstein et al. 2000; Koremenos, Lipson, and Snidal 2001). For example, why do some international agreements contain stronger enforcement mechanisms than others? Rationalist approaches to institutional design—what I refer to here as "rational design theory" (RDT)—follow in the tradition of neoliberal institutionalist IR theory (Koremenos, Lipson, and Snidal 2001, 763–768). From this perspective, rationally instrumental states design international institutions to solve collective action problems (Keohane 1984). Thus, explanations for variation in designs across institutions proceed from the assumption that states seek to maximize utility while minimizing sovereignty costs (Kahler 2000, 663).[4] Rationalist approaches hypothesize that, all things being equal, states will likely only accept "harder" agreements—that is, those with higher sovereignty costs—in exchange for increased benefits (Abbott and Snidal 2000).

We can examine how well this logic explains the outcome of universal jurisdiction in the Torture Convention by comparing it with the Genocide Convention. The two treaties are similar in that both are binding human rights agreements that establish criminal liability. But the treaties' different jurisdictional provisions mean that the Torture Convention exhibits what one RDT approach would call higher "delegation," that is, the degree of enforcement authority conferred on third parties (Abbott et al. 2000, 415–418). The Genocide Convention's enforcement regime is based on the principle of domestic jurisdiction, whereby states are the sole enforcers of human rights violations within their borders.[5] But the Torture Convention's enforcement provision goes much further. The treaty's universal jurisdiction provision—in the form of a so-called extradite or prosecute clause—not only authorizes any state to prosecute a violator in its territory, regardless of his nationality or where his crimes occurred (Art. 5), but in fact *requires* a state to do so should it not extradite the suspect (Art. 7). Thus, the Torture Convention's enforcement regime means that it establishes a harder agreement than the Genocide Convention.

According to the logic of rationalists, the Torture Convention should therefore offer states greater benefits than the Genocide Convention. But for at least two reasons, it appears that states would actually have more to lose and less to gain from a universal enforcement regime for torture than for genocide. First, genocide entails much higher spillover costs for neighboring states than does torture. Genocide, in contrast to torture, often leads to refugee flows, cross-border violence, and political destabilization. Therefore, genocide presents states with a more pressing collective action problem than does torture, suggesting a greater interest in enacting a stronger enforcement regime. Second, governments commit torture far more frequently than genocide. Therefore, a stronger enforcement regime against genocide is less risky for states concerned about the possibility of unilateral judicial action against their officials while abroad. This suggests states would have an interest in keeping the Torture Convention weaker than the Genocide Convention. In all, based on cost-benefit logic, RDT would predict that of the two treaties, the Genocide Convention would present states with greater benefits and lower risks, and thus be the more likely case for universal jurisdiction.

The failure of rationalists to account for the differences in these conventions stems from its assumption that states' preferences are a function of the *material* factors—in the forms of sovereignty costs and collective action gains—underlying design outcomes. In contrast, constructivist IR theory emphasizes the *ideational* factors that shape political behavior. Thus constructivist scholars have seized on this shortcoming of rationalists and attempted to show that negotiators' preferences are not necessarily fixed, but are open to modification through the deliberative process of treaty negotiations. Rationalist scholarship typically brackets this process of negotiations, assuming that design outcomes necessarily reflect maximally efficient equilibria given actors' deduced preferences (Thompson 2010, 272–273).[6] But constructivists have drawn on IR research that develops insights from Habermasian communicative action theory (Risse 2000) and framing theory (Keck and Sikkink 1998) to understand how "persuasion" works in institutional design negotiations (e.g., Deitelhoff 2009; Hawkins 2004). These communicative approaches argue that certain types of arguments, particularly those framed in terms of "preexisting" or "taken-for-granted understandings," will be more effective than others in changing other actors' bargaining positions (Hawkins 2004, 785). Whether genuinely or superficially, it can be difficult for actors in consensus-based environments, such as multilateral treaty negotiations, to resist assenting to claims that are grounded in such deep-seated shared understandings. Thus, it is possible for actors to back their opponents into a "rhetorical corner," forcing opponents to accept the validity of an argument despite their private beliefs to the contrary (Krebs and Jackson 2007, 42).

But as some scholars have pointed out, persuasion theory lacks clear scope conditions, predicting when norms matter (Payne 2001). In a study of the negotiations over the universal jurisdiction provision in the Torture Convention, Darren Hawkins (2004) argues that these types of appeals to widely subscribed norms allowed proponents of the provision to undermine opponents' efforts to defeat the provision. But as I discuss later, proponents in the Genocide Convention deployed very similar arguments as those in the Torture Convention, yet still failed to persuade their opponents. That is because appeals to widely held norms divorced from context are insufficient for persuasion—other factors must condition the persuasive power of these arguments.

One answer to the question of scope conditions begins from the insight that no norms exist on their own; instead, all norms exist as part of larger normative structures in which they are positioned in hierarchical relationships with other, associated norms.[7] Norms are shared standards of appropriate behavior (Finnemore and Sikkink 1998, 891), and contradictions among such deeply held imperatives are inevitable (Sandholtz 2008, 106). Thus, by imposing a relatively stable, yet malleable, order on competing norms, normative structures condition the relative weight of norms vis-à-vis one another. By defining, for example, who can act (say, states) and what kinds of actions are possible (e.g., as outlined in the UN Charter), international law makes much of its own normative structure explicit. Yet even specific rules require a stock of intersubjective background understandings to make sense of them (Kratochwil 2000, 40–41). Therefore even these explicit norms and their relations can be reinterpreted over time, either as new rules emerge or broader shared understandings change. And even so, universal norms, like the need to prevent bodily harm—emphasized by Hawkins as particularly potent—may at one time be deemed subordinate to other universal norms (like domestic jurisdiction for human rights) but at another point be perceived as more compelling. Similarly, the relative persuasiveness of competing interpretations of facts, such as whether a particular legal precedent applies to the matter at hand, will be conditioned by how those interpretations do or do not resonate with broader background understandings (Kratochwil 1989, 42; 2000, 51; Lowe 2000, 213).

Changes in normative structures themselves can be driven by various factors, such as exogenous shocks, brute force, or episodes of normative contestation. The globalization of law, by definition, also produces changes in normative structures. That is, by expanding rules, mechanisms, and jurisprudence, legal globalization necessarily redefines intersubjective understandings regarding hierarchies of norms, the relative desirability of goals, and the appropriate bounds of legal and political action. The interpretive community of international lawyers and diplomats who negotiate international agreements, given their shared educational and professional backgrounds and standards of legal reasoning and procedure, are especially attuned to these changes and thus are well suited to engage in persuasive discourse (Hawkins 2004, 784; Johnstone 2003).

THE GLOBALIZATION OF LAW AND UNIVERSAL JURISDICTION FOR TORTURE: 1946–1984

In this section, I trace how legal globalization in the twentieth century altered the normative structure of international law, and I make the case that these changes made the legalization of universal jurisdiction in the Torture Convention possible. In keeping with the framework outlined above, I adopt a comparative discourse analytic approach that focuses on the changes in delegates' arguments and their relative persuasiveness across the Genocide and Torture Conventions. I aim to show that the globalization of law fundamentally shifted the terms of the debate across the two conventions' drafting processes, making persuasion possible.

The Genocide Convention

The 1948 Genocide Convention was the first treaty that made a state's treatment of its own citizens a matter of individual criminal liability. The treaty's impetus came mostly from the efforts of one man, Polish American lawyer Ralph Lemkin (Cooper 2008). Lemkin coined the term *genocide* in his 1944 book *Axis Rule in Occupied Europe* and had long worked to see international law recognize what he saw as a yet-unnamed class of crime, that is, the destruction of "national groups." From the beginning, Lemkin urged that the crime of genocide be subject to universal jurisdiction. (Lemkin 1933, 1944, 93–94). Since international law already recognized universal jurisdiction for such crimes as piracy, slave trading, and drug trafficking, Lemkin argued, it would be "inconsistent with our concepts of civilization" not to do so for the crime of genocide (Lemkin 1946). But Lemkin's analogy belied the true ambitiousness of his proposal. These crimes in which universal jurisdiction found precedents were all acts that involved private actors working for private ends; international criminal law at the time did not recognize universal jurisdiction for crimes committed by state officials against their own populations (see Reydams 2003, 44–47). Lemkin authored the original UN General Assembly resolution calling on states to draft a treaty against genocide (Lemkin 1947) and participated in writing of the first draft of the convention (Cooper 2008, 89). Both times Lemkin inserted references to universal jurisdiction (UN Docs. A/BUR/50; E/447, Art. 7), and both times states' delegates voted them out. Despite its failure, the universal jurisdiction provision found support among some states—including Australia, Denmark, India, Iran, the Philippines, and Venezuela—who saw it as essential to the treaty's effectiveness. Nevertheless, the normative structure of international law at the time of the Genocide Convention was not amenable to the establishment of universal jurisdiction for human rights and thus worked against the efforts of these delegates.

Specifically, three interrelated sets of understandings militated against universal jurisdiction's prospects in the Genocide Convention. First, the norms of international law still remained strongly grounded in a Westphalian notion of sovereignty. Thus, in the words of Louis Henkin, "how a state behaved toward its own citizens in its own territory was a matter of domestic jurisdiction, i.e., not anyone else's business and therefore not any business for international law" (Henkin 1979, 228). While the horrors of World War II had helped put universal human rights onto the international agenda and make an antigenocide treaty possible, these emerging norms still remained subordinate to the prevailing, Westphalian view of sovereignty, which, as Henkin's characterization makes clear, privileged domestic jurisdiction for internal matters above universalist aims.

Second, international law at the time favored an accountability model that emphasized the responsibilities of states as actors, while conferring few duties on individuals (Sikkink 2011, 14–15). Traditionally, the only "subjects" of international law were states, and international law's purpose was to regulate conduct between them. Though customary international law had long recognized individual responsibility for certain international crimes, particularly piracy and slave trading, these crimes, as noted above, mostly pertained to private actors working for private ends, not government officials. The criminal tribunals at Nuremberg (1945–46) and Tokyo (1946–48) represented a "watershed" moment in the development of the idea of international criminal responsibility for political actors (Ratner, Abrams, and Bischoff 2009, 6). Yet, in keeping with existing international law, the charges against these defendants were defined so as to apply only within the context of armed conflict, and thus did not extend to crimes committed against their own citizens prior to the onset of war (Bassiouni 2011, 125). Thus the idea of international criminal responsibility for domestic acts—a central idea in the Genocide Convention—had little precedent prior to 1948. Indeed, this notion was seen in the Genocide Convention's debates as controversial in and of itself, universal jurisdiction or not (see Schabas 2009, chap. 9).

Finally, the notion of universal jurisdiction for government officials was itself antithetical to the prevailing norms of international law. Universal jurisdiction is the international legal principle that allows the domestic courts of one state to prosecute alleged perpetrators of particular crimes regardless of where the crimes took place, the nationality of the accused, or the nationality of the victims.[8] While the contemporary discourse around the exercise of universal jurisdiction has centered on the prosecution of accused war criminals and human rights violators (Amnesty International 2001; Kissinger 2001; Roth 2001), at the time of the Genocide Convention the principle was still mostly associated with the crime of piracy.[9] In fact, universal jurisdiction—both in custom and in statute—was originally developed to preclude the prosecution of political actors. Pirates were distinguished as "private" actors working for personal ends, as opposed to privateers, who were sponsored by states and not subject to the same laws (Brownlie 1998, 236). One purpose of this distinction was "to prevent universal jurisdiction over piracy from becoming a source or a tool of interstate conflict" (Morris 2007, 198). Needless to say, states had an interest in protecting their officials from unilateral third-party adjudication. But beyond practical political consequences, the principle that one state does not judge the actions of another (*par in parem non habet imperium*) has long been a fundamental norm of international law and goes to the heart of Westphalian notions of sovereignty and the sovereign equality of states (Brownlie 1998, 326–328). Thus, for both practical and principled reasons, it is unsurprising that governments have traditionally been wary of endorsing universal jurisdiction for acts committed by state officials.[10]

An examination of the discourse over universal jurisdiction in the Genocide Convention suggests that the prevailing normative context detailed above played a fundamental role in shaping the terms of the debate and thus the provision's prospects. First, universal jurisdiction opponents repeatedly invoked the related principles of sovereignty and domestic jurisdiction, appealing to prevailing understandings of international law that still deemed oversight of domestic human rights conditions to be the prerogative of sovereign states. In the words of one committee report, "[The delegations opposing universal jurisdiction] held that universal repression was against the traditional principles of international law and that permitting the courts of one State to punish crimes committed abroad by foreigners was against the sovereignty of the State" (UN Doc. E/794, 32). Thus, universal jurisdiction proponents were forced to frame their own arguments in terms of the implications for sovereignty, making the case that the important goal of eliminating genocide justified a reinterpretation of existing norms. For example, the Venezuelan delegate argued: "It was not impossible that the proposed convention might restrict that sovereignty to some extent, in order to ensure that the crime of genocide, so much more heinous than that of piracy, should be punished" (UN Doc. E/AC.25/SR.8, 6). Exceptions to sovereignty were necessary, because "governments had to cooperate for the purpose of suppressing international crime" (UN Doc. A/C.6/SR.100, 404). Nevertheless, despite proponents' appeals to the need to prevent bodily harm and the necessity of international cooperation—norms emphasized by Hawkins (2004) as particularly persuasive—opponents rejected these arguments with principled appeals to Westphalian norms. The French delegate, for example, responded to the Venezuelan representative by saying that he "could not possibly agree to any exception to the principle of territorial jurisdiction" (Hawkins 2004, 9).

Second, the prevailing normative context influenced the relative persuasiveness of opposing cost-benefit claims. Proponents argued that the benefit of a universal enforcement regime would be a more effective treaty. The Iranian delegate, for example, argued universal jurisdiction was necessary in situations where the accused was in a territory other than where the crimes occurred, and the offended state did not request his extradition. Thus, without universal jurisdiction the offender could escape punishment (UN Doc. A/C.6/SR.100, 395). In response, the provision's opponents argued that it was likely to be abused for political gain, often using the word *dangerous* to characterize the principle and its potential impact on international relations. The French delegate argued that universal jurisdiction (UJ) would "invite[] expressions of hostility on an international scale" and "insurmountable political difficulties" (UN Doc. E/AC.25/SR.8, 7, 11). As mentioned earlier, the U.S. delegate referred to UJ as "one of the most dangerous" of principles (UN Doc. A/C.6/SR.100, 399) and claimed the provision was "obviously liable to be abused" (UN Doc. A/401/Add.2, 9). The Iranian delegation thus proposed a qualified version of universal jurisdiction that would (1) not apply to "rulers" of states, and (2) only be activated in cases where the offended state had not requested extradition (also known as "subsidiary" universal jurisdiction). Despite this compromise offer, the Iranian amendment was defeated 29 to 6, with 10 abstentions (UN Doc. A/C.6/SR.100, 405–6). The prevailing norms of international law, which privileged sovereignty over human rights, validated a cost-benefit calculus that valued protection of officials from extraterritorial adjudication over a preference for the prosecution of human rights violators, even at the risk of enabling impunity.

Finally, the prevailing norms of international law influenced the relative weight of claims based on analogy and precedent.[11] Universal jurisdiction proponents, echoing Lemkin's earlier arguments, reasoned analogically that since genocide was "at least as outrageous" as piracy or drug trafficking, it was therefore unreasonable to endorse universal jurisdiction for the latter crimes, but not the former one (UN Doc. A/C.6/SR.100, 404). Also, proponents pointed to the precedent of universal jurisdiction for other international crimes to make the case that universal jurisdiction for genocide did not represent any more infringement on sovereignty than already existed under international law.[12] Notably, both these types of arguments would be used successfully by universal jurisdiction proponents later in the Torture Convention. Yet here these arguments met a majority coalition of unmoved delegates who countered with their own appeals to analogy and precedent. For example, these delegates challenged the analogy between the pirate and the genocidaire by pointing out that the two crimes were fundamentally different. Piracy, in contrast to genocide, "had no political character" (UN Doc. E/AC.25/SR.8, 9), an argument which invoked the traditional understanding of universal jurisdiction as limited to private actors. Also, some opponents challenged the piracy analogy on functional grounds. According to the Soviet delegate, unlike for genocide, universal jurisdiction "was justified in the cases of traffic in women or piracy by the fact that it was often extremely hard, if not impossible, to determine the place where the crime had been committed" (UN Doc. A/C.6/SR.100, 403). These delegations also questioned the relevance of existing international legal precedent. According to the Egyptian delegate, universal jurisdiction "had not yet been universally accepted, in spite of the examples which had been mentioned" (Ibid., 398). This debate demonstrates that appeals to analogy and precedent yielded no objective "correct" position on the appropriateness of universal jurisdiction for genocide. Therefore, the prevailing normative context played a role in resolving this indeterminacy by lending legitimacy to one interpretation over the other. The reluctance of universal jurisdiction opponents to interpret existing analogies and precedents in favor of universal jurisdiction for genocide was easily defensible in light of the prevailing, Westphalian notions of international law for which the idea of a universal criminal enforcement regime for human rights remained quite exotic.

1948–1978: The Changing Normative Structure of International Law

The three decades between the completion of the Genocide Convention and the first negotiations of the Torture Convention saw an unprecedented expansion of international legal norms, mechanisms, and jurisprudence in a variety of realms. First, the emergence and institutionalization of the new field of international human rights law helped redefine the place and meaning of sovereignty in the normative structure of international law. These new rules, institutionalized in a series of human rights treaties, expanded the purview of the international legal order from its original nineteenth-century purpose of upholding the rights and regulating the conduct between autonomous states to upholding the rights of individuals irrespective of sovereign authority, and regulating the conduct between governments and their populations (Gamble, Ku, and Strayer 2005; Held 1995, 101–107; Meron 2000; Teitel 2002). The new body of international human rights law contributed to this notion that sovereignty was not in opposition to the protection of human rights, but contingent upon it (Reus-Smit 2001). Thus, the perceived value of universally enforcing human rights increased in relation to the value of safeguarding a Westphalian notion of sovereignty. As a result, the norm of domestic jurisdiction—once considered a core feature of sovereignty—came to be viewed as a decreasingly legitimate defense against international concern and action over a state's domestic human rights performance.

Second, international law became more "individualized" (Slaughter and Burke-White 2002, 13–16). The rise of international human rights law described above placed new focus on individuals as *objects* of international law, that is, as bearers of rights which states are obligated to uphold. Meanwhile, the globalization of law produced new bases for individuals to be considered *subjects* of international law, that is, actors in their own right, with both responsibilities and capacities for positive legal action (Gamble, Ku, and Strayer 2005; Teitel 2002). As discussed above, the Nuremberg and Tokyo tribunals established new, if tentative, precedents for the notion of individual criminal accountability for international crimes. Over the next three decades the legitimacy of this model would be strengthened by a rapid increase in the number of international criminal treaties, including those pertaining to war crimes (1949 Geneva Conventions and its Additional Protocols of 1977), crimes against humanity (1968 Convention on Statutory Limitations), airline hijacking (1963 Tokyo, 1970 Hague, and 1971 Montreal Conventions), crimes against diplomats and other internationally protected persons (1973), and hostage-taking (1979). This increasing "criminalization of international law" (Meron 1998) contributed to a normative framework within which an individual criminal accountability model was increasingly deemed legitimate. Thus, for institutional designers, the site of normative contestation within treaty negotiations would shift from whether such a model was appropriate, to how best to enact it.

Finally, the globalization of law helped redefine understandings regarding the appropriate application of universal jurisdiction. In the years following the Genocide Convention, universal jurisdiction came to be incorporated in an increasing number of international criminal law treaties pertaining to transnational offenses, such as war crimes, airline hijacking, and attacks against diplomats. This expansion was especially rapid following the 1970 Hague Hijacking Convention, which was "the first of some twenty global and regional treaties concluded since 1970" that allowed for universal jurisdiction (Reydams 2003, 61). The reasons for this new emphasis on universal jurisdiction in international criminal law, according to Mitsue Inazumi (2005, 37–42), were an increase in the frequency of international crimes (particularly hijacking) as well as the realization that the "classical" enforcement regime, based on domestic jurisdiction, was ineffective. The 1970 Hague Convention was in part meant to address the weakness of the 1963 Tokyo Convention, in which a universal jurisdiction provision had been defeated (Abramovsky 1974, 389). This time, however, the desire for a more effective convention motivated the drafters to accept a universal jurisdiction provision (Art. 4; Abramovsky 1974, 397). Thus, following the Hague Convention, the expansion of universal jurisdiction in international criminal law contributed to an increasing association between the principle and the general notion of international criminal regime "effectiveness." In other words, after 1970 it became increasingly difficult to make the case that an effective international criminal treaty could be effective *without* universal jurisdiction.

This shift in attitudes was on display in a 1978 report by UN Special Rapporteur for Genocide, Nicodème Ruhashyankiko. Ruhashyankiko examined the question of enforcement of the Genocide Convention and concluded that establishing universal jurisdiction for genocide would make the Convention more effective (UN Doc. E/CN.4/Sub. 2/416, 56). Ruhashyankiko also made explicit reference to recent precedents of universal jurisdiction in treaties pertaining to hijacking, the protection of diplomats, and apartheid (UN Doc. E/CN.4/Sub. 2/416, 52). Though most states categorically rejected the inclusion of universal jurisdiction in the 1948 Genocide Convention, this time virtually all states who submitted comments either explicitly supported or expressed some willingness to consider Ruhashyankiko's recommendation (UN Doc. E/CN.4/Sub. 2/416, 52–55).[13] Canada even cited the Hague Convention as a model for such a provision (UN Doc. E/CN.4/Sub. 2/416, 70–71).

Changing attitudes toward universal jurisdiction can also be seen in the ways in which the general rationales for the principle changed over time. Mitsue Inazumi identifies two rationales for universal jurisdiction originating with its early associations with piracy: a functionalist rationale based on the inherent jurisdictional uncertainty entailed by piracy on the high seas, and a normative rationale based on the seriousness of the crime. Notably, over time the increasing legalization of universal jurisdiction came to rely decreasingly on both of these rationales, as the principle was recognized for less serious crimes that did not seem to entail jurisdictional uncertainty, such as drug trafficking (Inazumi 2005, 106–110).[14] Thus, not only did the years leading up to the Torture Convention witness an increasing relevance of universal jurisdiction in international criminal treaties, but also a shift in accepted views of its very *purpose*. Most important, the idea of universal jurisdiction went from being a mechanism explicitly cordoned off from use against official state actors to one widely deemed appropriate for specifically targeting such individuals for crimes against their own population, as indicated by the Ruhashyankiko report. This shift, in conjunction with the broader normative shifts outlined above, set the stage for universal jurisdiction to make its way into the Torture Convention.

The 1984 Torture Convention

In several ways, the 1948 Genocide and 1984 Torture Conventions followed similar paths. Both treaties were born of the efforts of nonstate norm entrepreneurs—Lemkin in the former case and Amnesty International in the latter—who raised awareness, lobbied governments, and organized support for their efforts.[15] Also, in both cases international lawyers who were experts on international criminal law contributed to these treaties' original drafts, and particularly, their universal jurisdiction provisions (Burgers and Danelius 1988, 26, 34–38; Sikkink 2011, 100–104). Thus, both treaties' original working draft texts also contained provisions for universal jurisdiction. Just as with the Genocide Convention, the universal jurisdiction provision in the Torture Convention proved highly controversial, and state delegates in favor of the provision were initially outnumbered by opponents (Hawkins 2004, 788–789). But over the seven years of negotiations (1978–1984) proponents of universal jurisdiction successfully defeated all challenges to either eliminate or modify the provision, ultimately persuading opponents to accept it.[16] Thus, despite their similarities, only the Torture Convention would include a universal jurisdiction provision in its final text.

An examination of the debates over universal jurisdiction in the drafting process of Torture Convention—and the contrasts with those in the Genocide Convention—suggest how the preceding three decades of legal globalization conditioned the very terms of the debate, and thus made persuasion possible in the first place. First, the most noticeable contrast with the Genocide Convention is the relatively low salience of appeals to Westphalian notions of sovereignty and domestic jurisdiction (Hawkins 2004, 790). Proponents in the Torture Convention, like their counterparts in the Genocide Convention, consistently framed the universal jurisdiction provision in terms of its contribution to the international community's common interests in combating torture and preventing impunity. In doing so proponents invoked a more cosmopolitan conception of international society that differed from the traditional Westphalian view. These delegates "emphasized over and over again that torture was a particularly horrible violation that deserved particularly strong measures" (Hawkins 2004, 791). The U.S. delegate, for example, argued that "[T]orture is an offence of special international concern and should have similarly broad jurisdictional bases" (UN Doc. E/CN.4/1314, 15). Yet even though the notion of extraterritorial jurisdiction challenges Westphalian conceptions of sovereignty, opponents rarely invoked this type of principled argument, which, in the Genocide Convention, had been so effective. Instead, opponents mostly focused on arguments about the provision's effectiveness or practical implications (see below). Hawkins argues that the widespread normative prohibition against torture made appeals to sovereignty in the Torture Convention "indefensible"; such an argument, he suggests, would have amounted to a claim that sovereignty granted states the right to use torture, a position with which no state was willing to be associated (Hawkins 2004, 790). But to examine the Torture Convention in isolation overlooks the fact that similar considerations did not prevent universal jurisdiction opponents in the Genocide Convention from invoking sovereignty to keep the treaty weak. This was possible because the normative structure of international law at the time of the Genocide Convention legitimated a conservative view of sovereignty. Thus there was little moral contradiction in appealing to the principle despite a clear normative prohibition against genocide. But the emergence and institutionalization of the international human rights regime in the intervening decades redefined these dominant understandings regarding the appropriate relationship between sovereign autonomy and universalist aims. By the time of the Torture Convention, the protection of human rights had become central to conceptions of legitimate statehood (Reus-Smit 2001), such that states could not deny the legitimacy of international enforcement.

Second, the normative changes brought about by the globalization of law altered the relative power of the same competing cost-benefit claims made in the Genocide Convention. This time, both sides of the universal jurisdiction debate largely framed their consequentialist claims in terms of the provision's potential impact on the treaty's effectiveness. This was in contrast to the Genocide Convention, in which appeals to effectiveness were mostly offered by the provisions' proponents, while opponents' cost-benefit arguments mostly focused on the potential for universal jurisdiction to cause political conflict. This suggests that changes in the normative structure of international law had increased the perceived value of effective criminal accountability for human rights violations in relation to the value of preventing politicization of the legal process. In other words, the "effectiveness" frame was more useful for opponents than the "politicization" frame. Thus, while universal jurisdiction proponents in the Torture Convention held up the provision as "the most effective weapon against torture which can be brought to bear" (UN Doc. E/1982/12/Add.l, 7), opponents, including Australia, France, the Soviet Union, and the UK, responded by pointing out several practical problems with the provision, such as its incompatibility with some domestic legal systems (Burgers and Danelius 1988, 40, 58). The Dutch delegate, for example, was concerned about the difficulties of gathering and presenting evidence for a crime that occurred abroad. Thus the Dutch representative opposed the draft's universal jurisdiction provision for fear that such problems would ultimately undermine prosecutions, making the treaty *less* effective (Baehr 1989, 40). The Brazilian delegate, who did emphasize that universal jurisdiction "could be exploited for political reasons" and "could result in trials on the basis of spurious accusations and fabricated evidence," nonetheless proposed modifying the provision to allow for a universal jurisdiction prosecution only after an extradition request had been denied (Burgers and Danelius 1988, 78). Interestingly, during the Genocide Convention, it was universal jurisdiction proponents who (unsuccessfully) offered to weaken the provision in order to improve its acceptability. This time, however, it was opponents who offered to make concessions, indicating that universal jurisdiction was no longer deemed categorically illegitimate as an institutional design choice, but could be negotiated over. In other words, the site of contestation over universal jurisdiction had shifted from whether it was legitimate at all to the conditions under which it should or could work.

Finally, the context of legal globalization provided proponents with legal precedents and analogies in other domains of international law to make their case that universal jurisdiction for human rights was appropriate. The universal jurisdiction provision in the Torture Convention was directly modeled after similar provisions in a number of other recently codified international criminal treaties (Burgers and Danelius 1988, 35, 58). These treaties pertained to issues such as airline hijacking, hostage-taking, and the protection of diplomats, and proponents consistently invoked these precedents to strengthen their case (Hawkins 2004, 791). Also, echoing Rafael Lemkin's analogical argument four decades earlier, proponents argued that torture was surely "no less horrifying or less important" than these other crimes for which universal jurisdiction had been recognized. Therefore, denying universal jurisdiction for torture was hard to justify in light of its acceptance for these other crimes (Hawkins 2004, 791).

Hawkins is correct that these appeals by proponents to existing international legal precedent, as well as taken-for-granted understandings regarding the necessity of international cooperation and the need to prevent bodily harm, were particularly effective in undermining opponents' challenges and persuading them to accept the universal jurisdiction provision (Hawkins 2004). Yet he does not go further to uncover the factors that mediate these arguments' power. Appeals to legal precedent and analogy are not persuasive on their own, because they do not lead to objectively determinate conclusions. As Kratochwil notes, instead these types of questions "turn more on the issue of whether a particular interpretation of a fact-pattern is acceptable rather than 'true'" (Kratochwil 1989, 42). Only those precedents and analogies that are consistent with the structure of high-order norms—like the particular relationship between sovereignty and human rights—will find traction with other actors. Universal jurisdiction opponents *could* have offered the same types of arguments used during the Genocide Convention to counter proponents' appeals to analogy and precedent. For example, torture (like genocide) differs from aircraft hijacking (and piracy before it) in that the former does not entail an inherent international dimension, and thus does not suggest a similar functional need for universal jurisdiction. The UK representative did make this argument (Burgers and Danelius 1988, 58), yet this time the point was not persuasive, despite its potency four decades earlier. Likewise, the argument in the Genocide Convention that universal jurisdiction "had not yet been universally accepted" (UN Doc. A/C.6/SR.100, 398) would still have applied at the time of the Torture Convention. That is, despite its inclusion in the above-mentioned treaties, there remained little precedent for the exercise of universal jurisdiction against public officials for human rights violations against their own populations.[17] Nevertheless, these precedents and analogies, however tenuous they may have been, were effective within a context of an international legal order that had become less grounded in Westphalian presumptions, more purposed toward individual accountability, and more accustomed to the notion of universal jurisdiction.

PINOCHET AND THE JUSTICE CASCADE

This section surveys the ways in which the successful inclusion of universal jurisdiction in the Torture Convention later contributed to what some scholars have described as the "justice cascade" (Lutz and Sikkink 2001; Sikkink 2011) or a "revolution in accountability" (Sriram 2003), that is, the surge in worldwide efforts beginning in the 1980s and 1990s to pursue criminal prosecutions for human rights violations.

While legal scholars point out that the House of Lords in its Pinochet decision did not actually rule on the question of universal jurisdiction's legality under international law (Bassiouni 2001, 125; Falk 2004; Reydams 2003, 207–209), it is clear that the Torture Convention's universal jurisdiction provision nonetheless helped make the judgment possible. The final House of Lords ruling turned on two main issues: double criminality and official immunity. First, British extradition law permits extradition only for crimes that were adjudicable by both the sending and receiving states at the time they were committed. For a Spanish warrant asserting universal jurisdiction, this meant that not only must the particular crimes have been defined in both Spanish and British law at the time they occurred, but also that both legal systems must have been competent to exercise universal jurisdiction. The Law Lords ruled that of the international crimes contained in the Spanish warrant, only torture met this requirement. This was because the UK passed legislation in 1988 to implement the Torture Convention (Criminal Justice Act 1988), and in keeping with the treaty's obligations, the statute also established universal jurisdiction. Thus, the Law Lords ruled that double criminality was satisfied for allegations of torture occurring after 1988. Second, the judges ruled that Pinochet did not enjoy immunity, because an international crime could not be considered an official act by a head of state. While the rationales on this point differed among the Law Lords, some relied on the Torture Convention's universal jurisdiction regime as evidence that preserving immunity for former heads of state would be contrary to the treaty's purpose. Thus, because Chile, Spain, and the UK were all parties to the Torture Convention, Pinochet could not claim official immunity for acts it prohibited ("Pinochet III" 1999).

The Pinochet case is often singled out as a "turning point" for the principle of universal jurisdiction (Lutz and Sikkink 2001, 15), as it "breath[ed] new life into the legitimacy and validity" of the principle (Roht-Arriaza 2009, 92). Following the case, universal jurisdiction prosecutions under the Torture Convention or its domestic implementing statutes have taken place in a number of European countries, including France, the Netherlands, and the UK (FIDH 2005, 2009; Laville 2005; Simons 2004). The United States exercised its own universal jurisdiction statute, adopted to implement the Torture Convention (18 USC § 2340 and 2340A), to prosecute Charles "Chuckie" Taylor Jr., the son of former Liberian president Charles Taylor (Gentile 2009; Keppler, Jean, and Marshall 2008). Meanwhile, many other cases have been initiated, if unsuccessfully, in even more European countries (Kaleck 2009 passim; REDRESS and FIDH 2010 passim).

But while the Pinochet case was ultimately narrowed to only cover charges of torture, it energized activists and jurists to revisit past abuses and pursue accountability for a variety of human rights violations, both extraterritorially as well as locally. That is, the landmark criminal proceedings against a former head of state, once thought to be beyond the reach of accountability, gave victims and justice advocates a new sense of what was legally and politically possible (Kaleck 2009; Roht-Arriaza 2005, chaps. 3–4; Sikkink 2011, 122–123, 175). Thus, back in Chile, the Pinochet case reinvigorated efforts to undo old amnesties and finally hold Pinochet and his collaborators accountable for their abuses (Roht-Arriaza 2005, chap. 3). Meanwhile, the episode in London sparked the creation of an entire international network of activists devoted to spreading, strengthening, and applying universal jurisdiction jurisprudence (Seroussi 2012). Due to their efforts, Europe has witnessed a steady, if modest, stream of new universal jurisdiction prosecutions for human rights violations and war crimes in the years since the Pinochet case (see REDRESS and FIDH 2010).

Nevertheless, political resistance to cases against more powerful actors, like American or Israeli officials, have led some observers to argue that universal jurisdiction will only ever be exercised against "low cost" defendants (Langer 2011). Efforts to target the so-called big fish have even sparked a backlash against permissive universal jurisdiction statues and the judges eager to exercise them. Thus, Belgium, Spain, and the UK have all amended their universal jurisdiction statutes in recent years to restrict their use (Reydams 2011). Yet, despite the uneven record of universal jurisdiction, the very existence of these contemporary controversies highlights how far international justice has come. As scholars of the justice cascade point out, new understandings of what is possible regarding international criminal accountability and the enforcement of human rights have fundamentally reshaped the discourse and practice of international politics (Lutz and Sikkink 2001; Sikkink 2011; Teitel 2011). And if the Pinochet case helped propel this justice cascade, then it was the Torture Convention that provided a crucial source from which the cascade drew its force.

CONCLUSION

In this chapter I have sought to show how the globalization of law provided activists and institutional designers with the normative resources with which to redefine the legal boundaries of the international human rights regime, and thus pursue further expansion of rules and mechanisms for the protection of human rights. The changing normative structure of international law gave universal jurisdiction advocates in the Torture Convention the rhetorical and normative bases from which to fashion arguments that would undermine opponents' claims and thus make institutional change possible. In keeping with the liberal constructivist argument advanced in this volume, my analysis demonstrates one way that norms can aid in the protection of human rights. That is, new norms make new types of action, like the creation of stronger rules—and thus institutional change—possible. The Torture Convention's normative innovation in the form of its enforcement regime, though largely unexercised for a decade after its establishment, proved to be a key contribution, both directly and indirectly, to later efforts to combat impunity for human rights violations. While this volume's contributions highlight the ways in which more human rights law can lead to better fulfillment of rights, this chapter goes one step back to demonstrate how *more international law in general can lead to more human rights law and thus new repertoires of accountability.*

Nevertheless, the story of universal jurisdiction's rise also speaks to the scope conditions this volume attaches to its central argument, that is, that norms exert their greatest impact when combined with liberal institutions. While the negotiations of international agreements are not necessarily analogous to domestic legislative processes, it is clear that the relative accessibility and consensus-based nature of the Torture Convention's deliberations—also characteristic of lawmaking in liberal polities—were favorable to universal jurisdiction advocates. First, empowered global civil society groups like Amnesty International and the International Association of Penal Law, by virtue of their expertise and advocacy, played important roles in legitimizing the idea of universal jurisdiction and putting sustained pressures on delegates to accept the provision. Second, consensus-based environments, like the treaty negotiations, where participants are united by a shared goal, are necessary for the type of communicative action that leads to persuasion (Risse 2000). Universal jurisdiction advocates in the Torture Convention were successful in their appeals to particular norms because opponents were already committed to the broader goal of an antitorture treaty. As a result, opponents were forced to negotiate from this premise, which enabled proponents to back them into a "rhetorical corner" (Krebs and Jackson 2007). Thus, liberal institutions may aid not only in the counterhegemonic enforcement of existing norms, but also in the counterhegemonic establishment of new norms.

NOTES

1. Though the initial warrant cited crimes only against Spanish citizens in Chile, and thus did not invoke universal jurisdiction, that warrant was superseded by a second one six days later that was based on universal jurisdiction. Both warrants are reprinted in Brody and Ratner (2000).
2. According to Lord Brown-Wilkinson, the ruling was the first time that "a local domestic court has refused to afford immunity to a head of state or former head of state on the grounds that there can be no immunity against prosecution for certain international crimes" ("Pinochet III" 1999, 268–269).

Pinochet would ultimately not be extradited on account of Home Secretary Jack Straw's determination that the 84-year-old Pinochet's health made him unfit to stand trial. See Roht-Arriaza (2005, 58–66).

3. For summaries of the Law Lords' reasoning, see Chinkin (1999) and Fox, Warbrick, and McGoldrick (1999). I discuss the role of the Torture Convention's universal jurisdiction provision in the House of Lords decision in a later section.

4. "Sovereignty costs are the costs of giving up decision-making autonomy" (Simmons and Danner 2010, 233). According to Abbott and Snidal (2000, 437) "[s]overeignty costs are at their highest when international arrangements impinge on the relations between a state and its citizens or territory, the traditional hallmarks of (Westphalian) sovereignty."

5. The Genocide Convention does allow for "international jurisdiction" to be exercised by an international criminal tribunal. See Article 6. However, the provision on international jurisdiction is weak and imprecise. For one, Article 6 requires signatories to separately recognize the competency of any subsequently established tribunal. According to the leading scholar on genocide and international law, William Schabas (2009, 454): "It seems clear enough from the text that article VI of the Convention does not make a State party automatically subject to the jurisdiction of a future international court." Another prominent genocide law scholar, Matthew Lippman (2002, 186), comments that the provision for an international tribunal "was intended as aspirational rather than obligatory." Indeed, many delegates seemed convinced that such a tribunal would never either exist or exert meaningful authority. For example, the UK delegate referred to the court provision as "harmless" and remarked that the Convention "put the court on a hypothetical, facultative basis and did not compel the parties to accept its jurisdiction" (UN Doc. A/C.6/SR.130, 676).

6. For recent attempts to apply RDT to the process of treaty negotiations, see Thompson (2010) and Grobe (2010).

7. Deitelhoff (2009) offers another approach to persuasion theory's scope conditions that focuses on the characteristics of particular negotiating environments and the degree to which they approximate ideal rational discourses.

8. For detailed legal and historical overviews of the theory and practice of universal jurisdiction, see Bassiouni (2001); Randall (1987); and Reydams (2003).

9. According to Bassiouni (2001, 110–111): "[U]niversal jurisdiction to prevent and suppress piracy has been widely recognized in customary international law as the international crime *par excellence* to which universality applies."

10. Before World War II, of about one hundred international criminal treaties that had entered into force, only two allowed for the exercise of universal jurisdiction (UJ). Notably, these treaties only pertained to offenses—counterfeiting and drug trafficking—committed by private individuals for personal ends and which "often involve[d] a transnational element" (Reydams 2003, 44–47).

11. Reasoning by precedent and analogy are fundamental not only to legal argumentation, which privileges such appeals, but to normative deliberation and contestation more generally (Sandholtz and Stone Sweet 2004, 243–244; Sandholtz 2008, 106–107).

12. Venezuela, Lebanon, and Iran made this argument. See UN Doc. A/C.6/SR.100.

13. These states included Bulgaria, Canada, Ecuador, Finland, Netherlands, Romania, and the UK.

14. The labels "functionalist" and "normative" are my own.

15. For more on Amnesty International's role in the origins of the Torture Convention, see Clark (2001, chap. 3).

16. For detailed accounts and discussions regarding the changes in delegates' positions on the universal jurisdiction provision, see Burgers and Danelius (1988); Hawkins (2004); Baehr (1989); and Burgers (1989).

17. The only case of such a treaty precedent at the time was the 1973 Apartheid Convention, which does permit (though, in contrast to the Torture Convention, does not require) the exercise of universal jurisdiction (see Art. 5). However, there is good reason to view the Apartheid Convention as an especially weak precedent. The Convention was designed to specifically target three states—Rhodesia, Namibia, and South Africa. As such, "states ha[d] little reason to fear reciprocity" and "it was obvious that the target regimes would never sign the Convention" (Reydams 2003, 59–60). It is unsurprising then that in the Torture Convention, the Apartheid Convention was not one of those precedents invoked by universal jurisdiction proponents.

REFERENCES

Abbott, Kenneth, Robert O. Keohane, Andrew Moravcsik, Anne-Marie Slaughter, and Duncan Snidal. 2000. "The Concept of Legalization." *International Organization* 54(3): 401–419.

Abbott, Kenneth, and Duncan Snidal. 2000. "Hard and Soft Law in International Governance." *International Organization* 54(3): 421–456.

Abramovsky, Abraham. 1974. "Multilateral Conventions for the Suppression of Unlawful Seizure and Interference with Aircraft Part I: The Hague Convention." *Columbia Journal of Transnational Law* 13: 381–405.

Amnesty International. 2001. *Universal Jurisdiction: The Duty of States to Enact and Implement Legislation*. London.

Amnesty International. 2010. *Universal Jurisdiction: UN General Assembly Should Support This Essential International Justice Tool*. London.

Baehr, Peter R. 1989. "The General Assembly: Negotiating the Convention on Torture." In *The United Nations in the World Political Economy: Essays in Honour of Leon Gordenker*, ed. David P. Forsythe. Houndmills: Macmillan, p. 36–53.

Bassiouni, M. Cherif. 2001. "Universal Jurisdiction for International Crimes: Historical Perspectives and Contemporary Practice." *Virginia Journal of International Law* 42: 81–162.

Bassiouni, M. Cherif. 2011. *Crimes Against Humanity: Historical Evolution and Contemporary Application*. Cambridge: Cambridge University Press.

Brody, Reed, and Michael Ratner, eds. 2000. *The Pinochet Papers: The Case of Augusto Pinochet in Spain and Britain*. The Hague: Kluwer Law International.

Brownlie, Ian. 1998. *Principles of Public International Law*. 5th ed. Oxford: Oxford University Press.

Burgers, J. Herman. 1989. "An Arduous Delivery: The United Nations Convention Against Torture (1984)." In *Effective Negotiation: Case Studies in Conference Diplomacy*, ed. Johan Kaufmann. Dordrecht: Martinus Nijhoff, p. 45–52.

Burgers, J. Herman, and Hans Danelius. 1988. *The United Nations Convention Against Torture: A Handbook on the Convention Against Torture and Other Cruel, Inhuman or Degrading Treatment or Punishment*. Dordrecht: Martinus Nijhoff.

Chinkin, Christine M. 1999. "United Kingdom House of Lords: *Regina v. Bow Street Stipendiary Magistrate ex parte Pinochet Ugarte* (No. 3)." *American Journal of International Law* 93(3): 703–711.

Clark, Ann Marie. 2001. *Diplomacy of Conscience: Amnesty International and Changing Human Rights Norms*. Princeton, NJ: Princeton University Press.

Cooper, John. 2008. *Raphael Lemkin and the Struggle for the Genocide Convention*. Houndmills: Palgrave Macmillan.

Deitelhoff, Nicole. 2009. "The Discursive Process of Legalization: Charting Islands of Persuasion in the ICC Case." *International Organization* 63(1): 33–65.

Falk, Richard A. 2004. "Assessing the Pinochet Litigation: Whither Universal Jurisdiction?" In *Universal Jurisdiction: National Courts and the Prosecution of Serious Crimes Under International Law*, ed. Stephen Macedo. Philadelphia: University of Pennsylvania Press, p. 97–120.

FIDH (Fédération Internationale des Ligues des Droits de l'Homme). 2005. *Groupe d'action Judiciaire de la FIDH, Mauritanie: Affaire Ely Ould Dah: Ely Ould Dah Condamné?!* http://www.fidh.org/IMG/pdf/GAJ_Ely_Ould_Dah_nov2005_OK.pdf (Accessed September 14, 2012).

FIDH (Fédération Internationale des Ligues des Droits de l'Homme). 2009. *L'affaire Khaled Ben Saïd Le Premier Procès en France d'un Fonctionnaire Tunisien Accusé de Torture.* http://www.fidh.org/IMG/pdf/Bensaid512fr2008_FINAL.pdf (Accessed September 14, 2012).

Finnemore, Martha, and Kathryn Sikkink. 1998. "International Norm Dynamics and Political Change." *International Organization* 52(4): 887–917.

Fox, Hazel, Colin Warbrick, and Dominic McGoldrick. 1999. "The Pinochet Case No. 3." *International and Comparative Law Quarterly* 48(3): 687–702.

Gamble, John King, Charlotte Ku, and Chris Strayer. 2005. "Human-Centric International Law: A Model and a Search for Empirical Indicators." *Tulane Journal of International and Comparative Law* 14: 61–80.

Gentile, Carmen. 2009. "Son of Ex-President of Liberia Gets 97 Years." *New York Times*: A14.

Goldstein, Judith O., Miles Kahler, Robert Keohane, and Anne-Marie Slaughter. 2000. "Introduction: Legalization and World Politics." *International Organization* 54(3): 385–399.

Grobe, Christian. 2010. "The Power of Words: Argumentative Persuasion in International Negotiations." *European Journal of International Relations* 16(1): 5–29.

Hawkins, Darren. 2004. "Explaining Costly International Institutions: Persuasion and Enforceable Human Rights Norms." *International Studies Quarterly* 48(4): 779–804.

Held, David. 1995. *Democracy and the Global Order: From the Modern State to Cosmopolitan Governance.* Cambridge: Polity Press.

Henkin, Louis. 1979. *How Nations Behave: Law and Foreign Policy.* 2nd ed. New York: Columbia University Press.

Inazumi, Mitsue. 2005. *Universal Jurisdiction in Modern International Law: Expansion of National Jurisdiction for Prosecuting Serious Crimes Under International Law.* Utrecht: Intersentia.

Johnstone, Ian. 2003. "Security Council Deliberations: The Power of the Better Argument." *European Journal of International Law* 14(3): 437–480.

Kahler, Miles. 2000. "Conclusion: The Causes and Consequences of Legalization." *International Organization* 54(3): 661–683.

Kaleck, Wolfgang. 2009. "From Pinochet to Rumsfeld: Universal Jurisdiction in Europe 1998–2008." *Michigan Journal of International Law* 30: 927–980.

Keck, Margaret E., and Kathryn Sikkink. 1998. *Activists Beyond Borders: Advocacy Networks in International Politics.* Ithaca, NY: Cornell University Press.

Keohane, Robert O. 1984. *After Hegemony: Cooperation and Discord in the World Political Economy.* Princeton, NJ: Princeton University Press.

Keppler, Elise, Shirley Jean, and J. Paxton Marshall. 2008. "First Prosecution in the United States for Torture Committed Abroad: The Trial of Charles 'Chuckie' Taylor, Jr." *Human Rights Brief* 15(3): 18–23.

Kissinger, Henry A. 2001. "The Pitfalls of Universal Jurisdiction." *Foreign Affairs* 80(4): 86–96.

Kontorovich, Eugene. 2004. "The Piracy Analogy: Modern Universal Jurisdiction's Hollow Foundation." *Harvard International Law Journal* 45: 183–238.

Koremenos, Barbara, Charles Lipson, and Duncan Snidal. 2001. "The Rational Design of International Institutions." *International Organization* 55(4): 761–799.

Kratochwil, Friedrich V. 1989. *Rules, Norms, and Decisions: On the Conditions of Practical and Legal Reasoning in International Relations and Domestic Affairs.* Cambridge: Cambridge University Press.

Kratochwil, Friedrich V. 2000. "How Do Norms Matter?" In *The Role of Law in International Politics: Essays in International Relations and International Law*, ed. Michael Byers. Oxford: Oxford University Press, p. 35–68.

Krebs, Ronald R., and Patrick Thaddeus Jackson. 2007. "Twisting Tongues and Twisting Arms: The Power of Political Rhetoric." *European Journal of International Relations* 13(1): 35–66.

Langer, Máximo. 2011. "The Diplomacy of Universal Jurisdiction: The Political Branches and the Transnational Prosecution of International Crimes." *American Journal of International Law* 105(1): 1–49.

Laville, Sandra. 2005. "UK Court Convicts Afghan Warlord." *The Guardian*. http://www.guardian.co.uk/uk/2005/jul/19/afghanistan.world (Accessed September 14, 2012).

Lemkin, Rafael. 1933. *Les Actes Constituant un Danger General (Interetatique) Consideres Comme Delits de Droit des Gens: Rapport spécial présenté à la V-me Conférence pour l'unification du droit pénal à Madrid (14-20.X.1933) (explications additionnelles)*, 1–8. Paris: A. Pedone.

Lemkin, Rafael. 1944. *Axis Rule in Occupied Europe: Laws of Occupation, Analysis of Government, Proposals for Redress.* Washington, DC: Carnegie Endowment for World Peace.

Lemkin, Rafael. 1946. "Genocide Before the U.N." *New York Times*: 22.

Lemkin, Rafael. 1947. "Genocide as a Crime Under International Law." *American Journal of International Law* 41(1): 145–151.

Lippman, Matthew. 2002. "A Road Map to the 1948 Convention on the Prevention and Punishment of the Crime of Genocide." *Journal of Genocide Research* 4(2): 177–195.

Lowe, Vaughan. 2000. "The Politics of Law-Making: Are the Method and Character of Norm Creation Changing?" In *The Role of Law in International Politics: Essays in International Relations and International Law*, ed. Michael Byers. Oxford: Oxford University Press, p. 207–226.

Lutz, Ellen L., and Kathryn Sikkink. 2001. "Justice Cascade: The Evolution and Impact of Foreign Human Rights Trials in Latin America." *Chicago Journal of International Law* 2: 1–34.

Macedo, Stephen, ed. 2004. *Universal Jurisdiction: National Courts and the Prosecution of Serious Crimes Under International Law.* Philadelphia: University of Pennsylvania Press.

Meron, Theodor. 1998. "Is International Law Moving Towards Criminalization?" *European Journal of International Law* 9(1): 18–31.

Meron, Theodor. 2000. "The Humanization of Humanitarian Law." *American Journal of International Law* 94(2): 239–278.

Morris, Madeline. 2007. "International Humanitarian Law: State Collusion and the Conundrum of Jurisdiction." In *International Law and International Relations: Bridging Theory and Practice*, eds. Thomas Biersteker, Peter J. Spiro, Chandra Lekha Sriram, and Veronica Raffo, 194–203. London: Routledge.

Payne, Rodger A. 2001. "Persuasion, Frames and Norm Construction." *European Journal of International Relations* 7(1): 37–61.

Penrose, Mary Margaret. 2000. "It's Good to Be the King: Prosecuting Heads of State and Former Heads of State Under International Law." *Columbia Journal of Transnational Law* 39: 193–220.

"Pinochet III." 1999. (*Regina v. Bow Street Metropolitan Stipendiary Magistrate, ex parte Pinochet Ugarte* [1999] 2 W.L.R. 827). Reprinted in *The Pinochet Papers: The Case of Augusto Pinochet in Spain and Britain*, ed. Reed Brody and Michael Ratner. The Hague: Kluwer Law International. 2000.

Randall, Kenneth C. 1987. "Universal Jurisdiction Under International Law." *Texas Law Review* 66: 785–842.

Ratner, Steven R., Jason S. Abrams, and James L. Bischoff. 2009. *Accountability for Human Rights Atrocities in International Law: Beyond the Nuremberg Legacy.* 3rd ed. Oxford: Oxford University Press.

REDRESS and FIDH (Fédération Internationale des Ligues des Droits de l'Homme). 2010. *Extraterritorial Jurisdiction in the European Union: A Study of the Laws and Practice in the 27 Member States of the European Union.* http://www.redress. org/downloads/publications/Extraterritorial_Jurisdiction_In_the_27_Member_ States_of_the_European_Union.pdf (Accessed September 14, 2012).

Reus-Smit, Christian. 2001. "Human Rights and the Social Construction of Sovereignty." *Review of International Studies* 27(4): 519–538.

Reydams, Luc. 2003. *Universal Jurisdiction: International and Municipal Legal Perspectives.* Oxford: Oxford University Press.

Reydams, Luc. 2011. "The Rise and Fall of Universal Jurisdiction." In *Routledge Handbook of International Criminal Law*, eds. William A. Schabas and Nadia Bernaz. London: Routledge, p. 337–354.

Risse, Thomas. 2000. " 'Let's Argue!': Communicative Action in World Politics." *International Organization* 54(1): 1–39.

Robertson, Geoffrey. 2006. *Crimes Against Humanity: The Struggle for Global Justice.* 3rd ed. New York: New Press.

Roht-Arriaza, Naomi. 2005. *The Pinochet Effect: Transnational Justice in the Age of Human Rights.* Philadelphia: University of Pennsylvania Press.

Roht-Arriaza, Naomi. 2009. "The Multiple Prosecutions of Augusto Pinochet." In *Prosecuting Heads of State*, eds. Ellen L. Lutz and Caitlin Reiger. Cambridge: Cambridge University Press, p. 77–94.

Roth, Kenneth. 2001. "The Case for Universal Jurisdiction." *Foreign Affairs* 80(5): 150–154.

Sandholtz, Wayne. 2008. "Dynamics of International Norm Change: Rules Against Wartime Plunder." *European Journal of International Relations* 14(1): 101–131.

Sandholtz, Wayne, and Alec Stone Sweet. 2004. "Law, Politics, and International Governance." In *The Politics of International Law*, ed. Christian Reus-Smit. Cambridge: Cambridge University Press, p. 238–271.

Schabas, William A. 2009. *Genocide in International Law: The Crime of Crimes.* 2nd ed. Cambridge: Cambridge University Press.

Seroussi, Julien. 2012. "The Cause of Universal Jurisdiction: The Rise and Fall of an International Mobilisation." In *Lawyers and the Construction of International Justice*, eds. Yves Dezalay and Bryant G. Garth. New York: Routledge, p. 48–59.

Sikkink, Kathryn. 2011. *The Justice Cascade: How Human Rights Prosecutions Are Changing World Politics.* New York: W. W. Norton.

Simmons, Beth, and Allison Danner. 2010. "Credible Commitments and the International Criminal Court." *International Organization* 64(2): 225–256.

Simons, Marlise. 2004. "Dutch Court Puts Former Congo Officer on Trial in Torture Case." *New York Times*: A13.

Slaughter, Anne-Marie, and William Burke-White. 2002. "An International Constitutional Moment." *Harvard International Law Journal* 43: 1–22.

Sriram, Chandra. 2003. "Revolutions in Accountability: New Approaches to Past Abuses." *American University International Law Review* 19(2): 301–429.

Teitel, Ruti G. 2002. "Humanity's Law: Rule of Law for the New Global Politics." *Cornell International Law Journal* 35: 355–387.

Teitel, Ruti G. 2011. *Humanity's Law*. Oxford: Oxford University Press.

Thompson, Alexander. 2010. "Rational Design in Motion: Uncertainty and Flexibility in the Global Climate Regime." *European Journal of International Relations* 16(2): 269–296.

6 Courts, Advocacy Groups, and Human Rights in Europe

Rachel A. Cichowski

In the last 50 years, international courts have incrementally transformed domestic and international governance. From war crimes to the adjudication of trade disputes, judicial organizations have both empowered and constrained nation-states. This global expansion means that individuals are now increasingly governed by a dense and binding set of international laws and norms. This volume critically examines how this global expansion of the law affects the fulfillment of human rights on the ground. In this chapter, I ask whether international courts may provide an avenue for enhancing the accessibility of the structures governing human rights law. In particular, this analysis examines increased opportunities for advocacy and interest group participation in the processes of law enforcement and the protection and development of rights. The research studies the role of an international court, the European Court of Human Rights (ECtHR), in rights protection and theorizes interest and advocacy group participation.

The research examines two key questions: (1) To what extent are interest and advocacy groups, from businesses to public interest activists, engaging international judicial institutions? (2) How and why does this action affect societal participation in law enforcement and rights protection and development? The chapter examines the ways in which increased nonstate actor access to international litigation can serve to expand the repertoires for human rights accountability.

Dominant theories of international politics as well as traditional understandings of international law begin with the assumption that powerful state executives control the nature and scope of international outcomes (e.g., Goldsmith and Posner 2006). This analysis proposes a set of expectations that moves beyond this general assumption and contributes to a more complex understanding of international law and politics as proposed in the Introduction, where societal groups, states, and international organizations play an important role in giving meaning to the law and at times transforming governance (e.g., Brysk and Jimenez-Bacardi, this volume; Kay 2011; Merry 2006; Simmons 2009; Sikkink 2011; Keohane, Macedo, and Moravcsik 2009; Cichowski 2007; Brysk 2009).

The chapter is organized as follows. First, I develop a framework elaborating how we can understand this dynamic interaction between international courts and societal participation. This conceptual framework suggests a set of general expectations that guide the empirical analysis. Second, the study turns to a historical analysis of ECtHR litigation to examine the factors that may condition how international courts serve as arenas for participation; in particular, the participation of advocacy and interest groups in law enforcement and rights development processes. I conclude by suggesting a set of broader lessons for scholars and practitioners concerned with the evolving role of international courts and advocacy and interest groups in the fulfillment of human rights.

CONCEPTUALIZING COURTS, PARTICIPATION, AND RIGHTS PROTECTION

A central goal of the analysis is a reconceptualization of participatory governance, which reflects a globalized world critically connected to international legal processes. Congruent with the liberal constructivist approach this democratization of the law entails making the judicial institutions protecting rights more accessible to societal groups—expanding who participates in the process of rights development and enforcement.

What factors characterize participatory governance? The analysis utilizes a key principle that the enhancement of participatory governance is defined as greater accountability, transparency, and societal participation in legal and political processes (e.g., Barber 1984). The analysis identifies two general participatory effects of widened access to international judicial organizations. First, expanding public access to courts can increase interest and advocacy group participation in the monitoring and enforcement of laws; we can observe this both domestically and internationally (e.g., Shapiro 1981; Cichowski and Stone Sweet 2003). Formal legislative processes are often quite closed, and with the exception of the United States, are often dominated by the executive, not the legislature. As the purview of government has expanded, including to the international level, judicial review may provide greater transparency and accountability. Thus, the analysis contributes to a body of socio-legal scholarship theorizing when and how courts can provide a more responsive institutional form of governance than traditional representative institutions (Zemans 1983; Graber 1993; Lovell 2003). These studies highlight the potential positive effects of legal processes for citizen access and involvement in law enforcement, yet this expansion in legal opportunities must also deepen long-standing debates over the tenuous relationship between courts (as countermajoritarian organizations) and representative democracy (e.g., Bickel 1962; Black 1960).

Second, the expansion of judicial power has gone hand in hand with the development of rights (e.g., Epp 1998; Stone Sweet 2004). Socio-legal scholars recognize the importance of litigation, both at the domestic and international levels, as an avenue for mobilization that can lead to the development and protection of rights (e.g., Barclay, Jones, and Marshall 2011; Bernstein, Marshall, and Barclay 2009; Cichowski 2007; Marshall 2006; McCann 1994; Osanloo 2009). And while scholars point to the increasingly integral role that advocacy groups play in developing and connecting local to global governance (Sikkink 2011; Tarrow 2005; Keck and Sikkink 1998), we know far less about their role in international litigation—a very powerful process at the global level that shapes both domestic and international law (see Alter 2011; Cichowski 2007).

How can we measure change in participatory governance through the changing functions and access to courts? This analysis focuses on two general institutional variables that may help us measure change: judicial enforceability of rules, and access to judicial institutions. Political scientists and legal scholars alike assert that the effective protection of international laws and rights is critically linked to their formalization and judicial enforceability (Abbott and Snidal 2000; Franck 1990; Fuller 1964). Greater precision through formal legal norms provides more certain codes of behavior that in the presence of independent judicial authority can then be enforced and protected. As the formality and enforceability of these rules and policies expand, we might expect the potential for participation to increase as this enhances an individual or group's ability to successfully initiate and pursue litigation. At the domestic and international level, legal mobilization scholars trace how human rights litigation alongside courts empowered with judicial review can at times serve as a powerful tool for policy reform (Epp 1998; Cichowski 2007; Barclay et al. 2011; Marshall 2006).

Alongside the judicial enforceability of rules and rights, the accessibility of judicial institutions is critically linked to change in participatory governance. Scholars observe that expanded public access points, as realized through such avenues as referenda, access to information, policy juries, and expanded access to justice, to name just a few, are becoming an increasingly common feature of advanced industrial democracies (e.g., Dalton, Scarrow, and Cain 2003; Scarrow 2001; Cichowski and Stone Sweet 2003). These access points are critical for participatory politics. Likewise, at the global level, the right to a hearing, transparency, and civil society participation beyond the interstate historic norm are increasingly an integral part of international institutions (Bignami 2005; Simmons 2009).

This analysis focuses specifically on access to international judicial institutions. International courts with individual access generally have higher caseloads (Keohane, Moravcsik, and Slaughter 2000, p. 475). This gives courts a greater opportunity to engage in important political issues through the strategy of incremental development of doctrine (e.g., Helfer and Slaughter 1997). Private parties, rather than states, may be more likely to utilize these courts for strategic policy reform (e.g., Cichowski 2007; Harlow and Rawlings 1992).

While these findings are significant, there is still an open question regarding the consequences of allowing nonstate access. We know that opening the "flood gates" does not always bring a flood when it comes to access to judicial institutions (Morag-Levine 2003). Studies on the use of international judicial institutions reveal that even when international courts provide the tools private actors can use to influence policy, domestic political and legal institutions and legal support structures can place limits on this access (Conant 2002; Alter 2012). There is also much to suggest that opening legal institutions to societal actors may empower groups differentially. Scholars observe that litigation strategies are often used most successfully by the "haves," those who may already be more socially, economically, or politically privileged (Galanter 1974). Yet we also know that even with losses in court, litigation can have powerful mobilizing effects for underrepresented individuals and groups (McCann 1994). And at the regional level, the accessibility or "permeability" of international organizations to nonstate actors is linked to the strength and success of democracy building (Hawkins 2008). In general, as citizen access is strengthened, we may expect individuals and societal groups to have increased opportunities to participate through rights claims, litigation, monitoring and implementing compliance, and expanding judicial protection for their access and mobilization. This chapter will assess some of these effects.

Data and Methods

To test these expectations, I created a series of datasets involving litigation before the European Court of Human Rights from 1960–2011. The Court, a judicial body of the Council of Europe (COE), is located in Strasbourg, France, and was established in 1959 by the then 13 member countries. Today membership in the COE includes 800 million Europeans from 47 countries. The Court rules on alleged violations of the European Convention on Human Rights (hereafter the Convention), an international treaty embodying a set of fundamental political and civil rights, and takes cases not only from COE citizens, but any individual living within a COE country.

The datasets were compiled from primary documents from the ECtHR including the Court's *Annual Survey of Activities* and *General Measures Adopted Report* (H/Exec (2006) 1) and the comprehensive full-text online judicial decision database, HUDOC.[1] The first dataset includes all ECtHR decisions from the first case, 1960 through 2011, a total of 14,854 decisions. These are coded by respondent state, decision year, decision outcome, and Convention rights invoked. A second dataset on decisions tracks third-party interventions (the Court granting a third party the right to submit a written brief in the case) from 1984 through 2011 for a total of 464 interventions.

A third dataset examines national implementation measures. In particular, the data include all national-level general measures taken to implement ECtHR decisions between 1966 and 2006. These general measures, which aim to prevent further violations in the future, reveal clearly the role of the

ECtHR in prospective policy making. Such measures have led to a host of significant national-level legislative and judicial reforms. The dataset includes 704 general measures taken, which are coded by year, respondent state, type(s) of general measure(s) taken, Convention rights violated, and interest and advocacy group participation (applicant, representing, or third-party intervention). Together, these datasets offer a comprehensive examination of the ECtHR decisions, their national effects, and societal group participation in this legal process.

ANALYSIS: THE ECTHR AND INTEREST AND ADVOCACY GROUPS

How has the globalization of the law affected the fulfillment of international human rights in Europe? In this section, I examine the judicial enforceability of European Convention rights and societal access to the ECtHR over time. If we find change in these two basic structures, we can feel confident that the levels of citizen participation in law enforcement and rights protection may also be changing.

Judicial Enforceability of Rules

The Convention system as a whole and the domestic incorporation (or transposition) of Convention rights into domestic law has greatly enhanced the type of rights available to individuals and societal groups, and the relative power they may gain in bringing claims against government action and acts. The Convention serves as a set of higher-order "quasi-constitutional" rules for contracting states throughout Europe. The degree to which Convention rights become more binding and enforceable is connected to the status these rights are given in domestic law.

Given the various legal traditions of monism and dualism, following ratification of the Convention, countries following a dualist tradition are given some degree of choice in how these new "constitutional" international human rights will be incorporated into the domestic legal order. Monist countries automatically incorporate international law upon ratification of international treaties. Incorporation, in some cases, has effectively created a quasi–bill of rights in countries that previously did not possess such a body of judicially enforceable rights. France, Sweden, and the United Kingdom are examples. These rights can serve as a powerful tool for individuals to engage public authorities and bring into question discriminatory state actions. Yet the level to which these rights can empower the individual vis á vis public authorities is critically linked to the actual domestic law status given to these international human rights. The Convention is given constitutional rank in some countries, including the Netherlands, Austria, Belgium, Cyprus, Czech Republic, France, Greece, Lithuania, Luxembourg, Malta, Portugal, Romania,

Spain, and Switzerland. Thus, when these international human rights come in conflict with domestic law they are given supremacy. This gives individuals considerable power to alter and in some cases quash discriminatory national practices that are in violation (e.g., *Sunday Times* Case, ECtHR 1979).

Other states relegate Convention rights to the level of national legislation. Germany and the United Kingdom followed this strategy when incorporating the Convention into the national legal system. In Germany, Article 59.2 of the Basic Law assigns the Convention federal law status. Thus, an individual cannot make a constitutional complaint based directly on these incorporated international human rights. This limits the ability of the individual to utilize the Convention in questioning the constitutionality of a public act or practice—an action that was possible in the above-discussed countries. That said, the German Federal Constitutional Court continues to state clearly in its case law that a constitutional complaint may (indirectly) invoke the Convention along with the individual's fundamental right to equality under Article 3.1 of the German Basic Law to argue for an arbitrary misapplication or nonapplication of the Convention rights.[2] Although the Convention is not given formal constitutional status, this case law gives individuals the opportunity to invoke Convention rights before the Constitutional Court in order to appeal a court's misapplication of the Convention, thus expanding the opportunities for participation through law enforcement and rights claiming.

The United Kingdom (UK) presents a similar dynamic, albeit more limited in terms of an individual's ability to alter public policy through litigation. After years of debate and 46 years after ratification, the European Convention was finally incorporated into the British legal system through the Human Rights Act of 1998. This made the UK the oldest signatory state to incorporate. Much of this delay centered on the issue of what status Convention rights would have, as the repercussions of constitutional status, both empowering individuals and national courts vis á vis Parliament, were not welcomed.[3] The Human Rights Act does not give supra-legislative status to Convention rights (and thus, allegedly maintains parliamentary sovereignty), yet it does state clearly that national courts are required to address these rights: "So far as it is possible to do so, primary legislation and subordinate legislation must be read and given effect to in a way which is compatible with Convention rights."[4] Further, under the Act, it is mandatory for all British courts and tribunals to take into account any judgment of the ECtHR.[5] While this may bode well for greater access to and opportunities for rights claims before British courts, individuals challenging the British government may continue to find direct action before the ECtHR a more successful route.

Beyond these transpositions of Convention provisions, courts are also an important agent for expanding the enforceability of these rights. We see this both at the domestic level and by the ECtHR. The Austrian Constitutional Court and the Swiss Federal Court, both of whom have a long history of engaging Convention rights, have intensified their tendency to expand rights protections, sometimes interpreting the rights beyond the practice of the ECtHR.[6] The dialogue between the ECtHR and national courts is also paramount to the work of courts in new democracies. ECtHR rulings have been integral to the work of the Spanish Constitutional Tribunal (SCT) since democratization in the 1970s, as the SCT routinely interprets the Spanish Constitution in light of Convention provisions (Polakiewicz 1996). The European Convention and ECtHR case law was also influential in the construction of the fundamental rights and freedoms included in the new constitutions in Central and Eastern Europe after the fall of communist regimes in the 1990s. For example, the Polish Constitutional Tribunal has taken a similar position as the Spanish and German Constitutional Courts by utilizing the Convention and ECtHR case law to interpret domestic constitutional provisions (Polakiewicz 1996).

ECtHR rulings have led to a host of national policy changes including administrative, legislative, judicial, and even constitutional reforms (Cichowski 2006, 2011; Helfer and Voeten 2012; Stone Sweet and Keller 2008; Anagnostou 2010). This reality is indicative of its comparatively remarkable compliance rate as an international court as well as its significant review powers (Polakiewicz 1996; Voeten 2008). In 1998 the Convention institutions underwent massive reform under Protocol 11 that significantly expanded the ECtHR's jurisdiction and power. Prior to 1998, Article 46, which governed the Court's jurisdiction, was optional—giving states the choice to have claims decided by an intergovernmental body rather than this independent court. The Court's jurisdiction then became compulsory for any state adopting and ratifying the Convention. These expanding judicial review powers laid the foundation for increased opportunities for participation in the processes of law enforcement and rights protection. Each of the ECtHR decisions represents a contracting state either indirectly (through inaction) or directly defending their national laws (or their interpretation of Convention provisions). Does the Court act to uphold these national practices or domestic interpretations of these rights? Or do we find these rulings leading to the enforcement of Convention rights in a way that expands their precision, enforceability, or scope, either through subsequent implementation for a contracting state that is in clear noncompliance or via a corrective interpretation of actions falling within the scope of the right?

We can look to the case law for an answer. The Court has rendered 14,854 judgments from 1960 to 2011. The violation rate is astounding with the ECtHR declaring a violation of the Convention in more than 83% of the cases. This quick snapshot reveals a Court that is not hesitant to overturn domestic interpretations of Convention rights and to enforce noncompliance. Italy, Turkey, Poland, and France were clearly the target of many of the claims, with over half (53%) of all ECtHR violation decisions involving these four legal systems. Taking a closer look at the domestic level, Table 6.1 examines the general measures adopted by national legal systems to ensure compliance and implementation of ECtHR decisions as reported to the

Table 6.1   General Measures Taken by the National Legal System to Ensure Compliance with ECtHR Judgments and Prevention of Future Violations, 1966–2006

General Measure Type Taken in the Domestic Legal System	Total # of Measures Taken	Measure Type Taken as a % of Total
Parliamentary Legislation	263	37%
Executive Action	102	14%
Change in National Jurisprudence	56	8%
Administrative Measures	46	7%
Publication of Judgment Requiring Nat'l Judges to Apply ECtHR Jurisprudence	156	22%
Practical Reform (e.g., recruit judges, build prisons)	21	3%
Dissemination	60	9%
Total	704	100%

Source: Data compiled by the author from Council of Europe (2006).

Council of Europe's Committee of Ministers between 1966 and 2006. The data includes information on the total number of each type of general measure taken including legislation, executive action, changes in jurisprudence, administrative action, publication of judgments with the expectation that national courts will directly apply the decision, practical measures, such as creation of prisons or recruitment of judges or dissemination of the ruling. Member states reported 704 measures adopted in the national legal systems during this time period. Interestingly, almost two-thirds (59%) of these measures involved new domestic legislation or publication of the ruling with the requirement that national courts apply the ECtHR ruling—demonstrating the real domestic policy effects of these international court judgments, which changed the rights available in the domestic legal system.

Elaborating these data, ECtHR rulings have led to a host of national policy changes including administrative, legislative, judicial, and even constitutional reforms (e.g., Stone Sweet and Keller 2008; Helfer and Voeten 2012; Cichowski 2011). Over time these legal reforms have expanded who can participate in rights claiming and law enforcement in the future. For example, ECtHR decisions resulted in the expansion of administrative review powers of courts in Sweden (*Pudas & Boden* Case, ECtHR 1987), and a new code of criminal procedure in Italy (*F.C.B.* Case, ECtHR 1971). Such decisions led the Austrian Constitutional Court to reverse its previous interpretations of "civil rights and obligations" (*Ringeisen* Case, ECtHR 1971); and even considered sensitive domestic issues such as the regulation of property—leading to changes in the administration of property tax codes (*Hentrich* Case, ECtHR 1994) and expanded access to judicial remedies in property disputes (*Holy Monasteries* Case, ECtHR 1994). The *Golder* Case (ECtHR 1975) led to the British Prison Rules of 1964 law to be reformed (Resolution (76) 35 of 22 June 1976); the *Airey* Case (ECtHR 1979) led to the establishment of a program to administer Civil Legal Aid and Advice in Ireland (Resolution DH (81) 8 of 22 May 1980); and the *De Haan* Case (ECtHR 1997) led to a Dutch law reforming the administrative courts procedures of appeal (Resolution DH (98) 9 of 18 February 1998).

Access to Litigation

We now turn to the mechanisms governing access to justice. Under the original Convention system, individual petitioners did not have direct access to the Court. Article 25 recognized the right of individuals to file an application, yet it was an optional not compulsory mechanism. The 1998 Protocol 11 reforms mentioned changed this, making individual access compulsory. Following these reforms, individuals were given both formal and practical access to the Court. These reforms also brought greater accessibility to groups and organizations. Today, the European Convention clearly provides the necessary rule or procedure for individuals and nongovernmental organizations (NGOs) to file an application before the Court (Article 34).

Over time, both individual social activists and advocacy and interest groups have increasingly gained access to the Court, and thus, have expanded the roles they play in ECtHR decision making. These roles include direct victim (applicant), representing an applicant, intervening as a third party (*amicus curiae*), and acting as a larger support structure, such as serving as educator to both the public, other groups, and lawyers, providing legal information and sponsoring litigation strategy workshops.

While the Convention today clearly provides the basis for nonstate actors to bring individual complaints, the access for groups is more limited. The group must prove that the organization has itself directly experienced a violation of Convention rights. This is laid out in the ECtHR's case law.[7] Nonetheless, the Court's jurisprudence also reveals the diversity of organizations and entities that have successfully brought claims, including church associations,[8] media groups,[9] trade unions,[10] human rights groups,[11] and many companies.[12] Interestingly, the Court has also incrementally developed an "indirect victim" approach that enables persons to bring a claim who were not directly affected, but who are close relatives and have a valid personal interest in having the violation confirmed.[13] While this evolving case law on "indirect victims" has not previously provided a clear standing for NGOs as an applicant representing a victim, one ECtHR judge suggests it may be an "indication of a possible evolution of the ECtHR's practice with regard to the role of representatives before the ECtHR" (Vajic 2005, p. 95).

Thus, in the future, there may be an expanded opening for greater NGO participation in filing an application, beyond its role as a direct victim.

Societal groups have also come to play an important role through third-party interventions. If we look over time, the ECtHR itself has largely been responsible for this expansion in access. The original Convention made no mention of third-party intervention, but instead it has evolved over time through the interaction of social activists and the Court[14] and then by state action to codify it in the Convention, Article 36§2 and the Rules of the Court, 44§2. Figure 6.1 includes all the third-party intervention requests from the time of this institutional reform, 1984 to 2011. During this time period, the Court has authorized 464 requests for third-party intervention (it refused 21 or 4%). From the mid-1990s interest and advocacy groups increasingly utilized this new access point to participate in the Court's law-making processes.

The Protocol 11 institutional reforms in 1998 led to a dramatic increase in the groups and individuals enabled to participate in litigation as third-party interveners. In the post-1998 period, there were 378 third-party intervention requests, or 81% of the total, which is over four times as many from the pre–Protocol 11 time period.

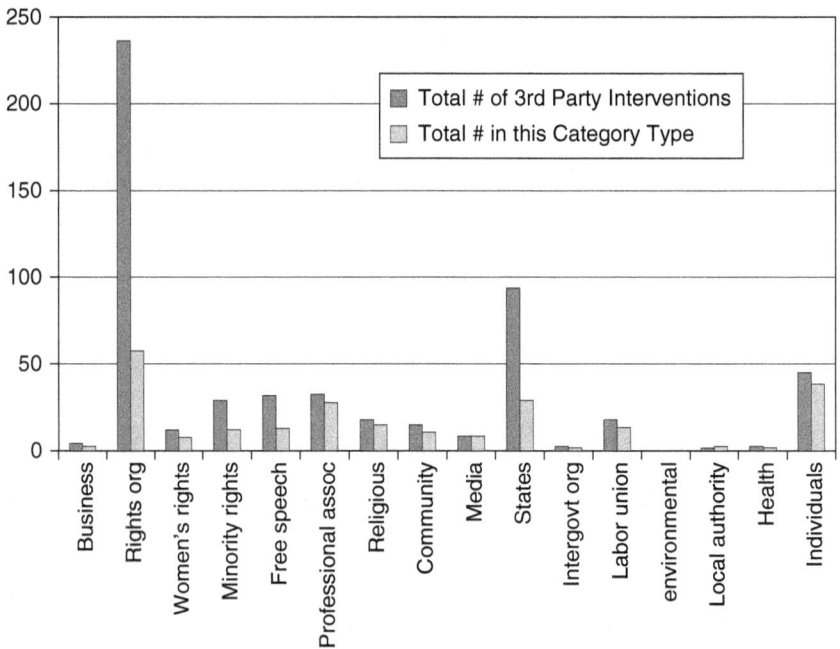

Figure 6.1   Third-party interventions granted by the European Court of Human Rights by total numbers of interventions and intervener type, 1984–2011.

Source: Data compiled by the author from ECtHR HUDOC database. http://www.echr.coe.int/ECHR/EN/Header/Case-Law/Decisions+and+judgments/HUDOC+database/

The data also give us a picture of the types of groups who are utilizing these new opportunities to participate in the litigation process and with what frequency. Figure 6.2 details the types of parties who requested third-party interventions by category and with what frequency from 1984–2011. Not surprisingly, general human rights organizations make up the largest category of interveners, with 58 different rights organizations requesting to intervene. General human rights organizations were granted leave in 237 third-party interventions. Further, there were clearly repeat players among these rights organizations. The London-based international organization Interights submitted third-party interventions in 23 cases. Similarly, the Warsaw-based Helsinki Foundation for Human Rights filed in 18 cases and London-based Liberty was successfully granted leave as a third-party intervener in 17 cases. Member state governments were also proactive in submitting third-party interventions in cases, often in relation to a similar case that may be pending within their own legal system (29 different states were granted leave to submit interventions and they did so for a total of 94 briefs). Individuals are the next highest category of interveners, with 39 different parties submitting third-party interventions a total of 45 times. These individuals are primarily family members, but are also experts[15] and community[16] and political leaders.[17] Professional organizations were granted leave to submit comments 33 times and were more likely to act collectively alongside other professional organizations, with one case including comments from a dozen different professional organizations in the shipping and maritime industry.[18] More

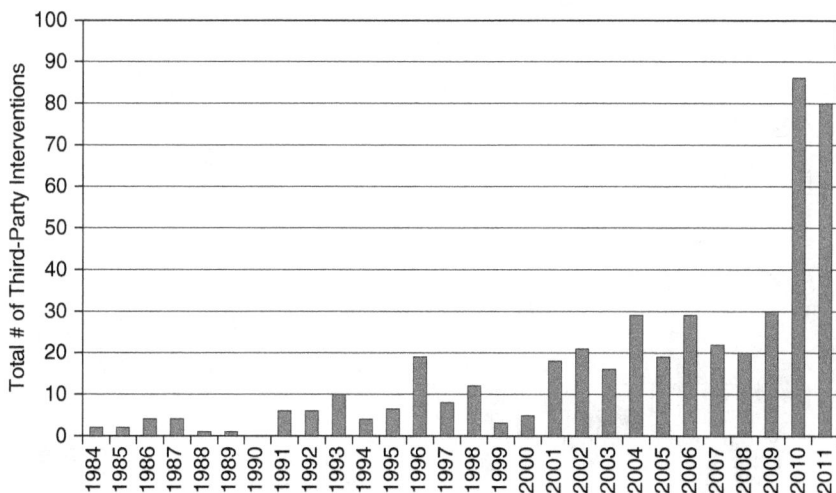

Figure 6.2 Annual number of third-party interventions granted by the European Court of Human Rights, 1984–2011.

Source: Data compiled by the author from ECtHR HUDOC database. http://www.echr.coe.int/ECHR/EN/Header/Case-Law/Decisions+and+judgments/HUDOC+database/

narrowly defined rights organizations were also participating in this process, including minority rights (12 organizations submitting 29 briefs), women's rights (8 organizations submitting 12 briefs), and free speech rights (13 organizations submitting 29 briefs).

Similarly, as the rules of access expanded and as the Court continued to be receptive to this participation, the sheer variety and number of entities requesting to participate as third-party interveners has grown over time. Figure 6.3 includes the annual number of different types of parties acting as interveners in ECtHR litigation from 1984 to 2011. While the number has certainly waxed and waned over this period, what we do see is a steady growth and recent spikes in the sheer number of different types of interveners. In 2010 and 2011 the variation in type of intervener (14 and 13 different types of interveners) was double that of most years up to that time. In the first 10 years that the Court began granting third-party interventions the parties were largely rights organizations, some labor unions, and professional associations. By the end of the 1990s and 2000s we see states, individuals, and an assortment of advocacy groups increasingly active in the litigation process—again not as applicants or defendant states, but as third parties. In sum, the number of cases involving third-party interveners is admittedly a small number compared to the total number of ECtHR cases. But the significance of the case is often high, meaning most of these groups, individuals, and states are very strategic about choosing to participate in cases which they believe have the potential to lead to significant changes in

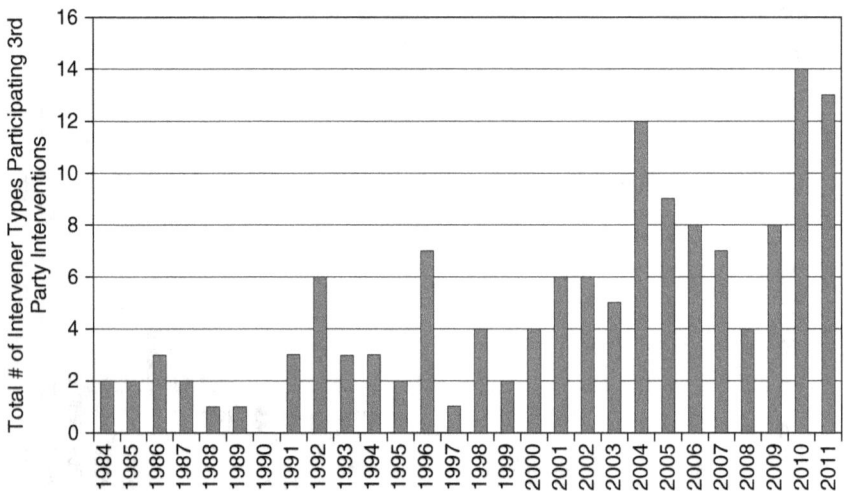

Figure 6.3   Total number of intervener types participating in third-party interventions before the European Court of Human Rights per year, 1984–2011.

Source: Data compiled by the author from ECtHR HUDOC database. http://www.echr.coe.int/ECHR/EN/Header/Case-Law/Decisions+and+judgments/HUDOC+database/

European law and bring maximum reforms to national legal systems. They see it as an opportunity to participate in the development of international human rights law, which subsequently has a direct impact not only at the international level, but on the way international human rights law is upheld by judges and public officials at the domestic level.

Elaborating the data, the following identify the direct effects of these third-party interventions. In the *Soering* case[19] concerning the United Kingdom's involvement in extraditing an individual accused of a capital offense to the United States, Amnesty International was granted leave to submit an amicus brief which ultimately was quoted by the Court in its judgment.[20] The group Article 19 (which focuses on the defense of freedom of expression rights) filed amicus briefs in two cases[21] and played a key role in the Court's decision and dissenting opinions, and was ultimately used to support the Court's finding of a violation.[22] The *Nachova*[23] decision was also particularly important not only for expanding Convention rights to find that Article 14 (prohibition of discrimination) also has a procedural element (obligation of the authorities to investigate possible racist motives), but also that the amicus briefs of three NGOs played prominently in the judgment. The three NGOs, the European Roma Rights Centre (ERRC), Interights, and the Justice Initiative, were all granted leave by the Court to file briefs. By 2005, these groups were directly involved (either as third-party intervention or directly representing a claimant) in more than 80 cases before the ECtHR.

Together, these institutional reforms initiated by the Court and states have led to greater participation by advocacy and interest groups in ECtHR litigation. Clearly, these access points do not create an open flood gate for participation, but instead illustrate the persistence of groups to challenge constraints on the accessibility of the Court and the power of the Court to allow increased participation over time—a decision that often takes place long before states clarified criteria for participation. In sum, while public interest organizations are rarely a litigant before the ECtHR given the constraints by the Article 34 requirement of claiming to be a direct victim of an alleged violation of the Convention, they are able to participate in various ways, and their involvement has directly shaped the ECtHR's decision making—and ultimately the development, reform, and implementation of Convention rights in domestic legal systems.

CONCLUSIONS

This volume highlights the diverse pathways leading to the realization of human rights protection, from treaty adherence (Sandholtz, this volume) to judicial constraint of executive abuses of power (Wright, this volume). Beyond mere compliance, this approach asks us to identify the increasingly dense web that connects up the promise of norms with a fulfillment of rights

(Brysk and Jimenez-Bacardi, this volume). Today, human rights in Europe are not merely a body of laws, but instead are characterized by a dense web of obligation between states, society, and judicial institutions. I argue that the European Court of Human Rights was integral to this transformation.

The ECtHR has a rich history of landmark human rights innovations, and a growing network of advocacy and interest groups participating in this rights development and law enforcement. The findings suggest a set of institutional mechanisms that are critical to this process of change. As Convention rights become more binding and judicially enforceable through ECtHR case law and domestic implementation, individuals and groups are given a growing set of tools leading to increased participation in the rights litigation process. Further, the most dramatic change in the participatory nature of human rights structures came when the ECtHR initiated and states codified reforms in access to justice—opening the door to societal groups as direct individual applicants and third-party interveners. This expanded access created a new repertoire for human rights accountability. Advocacy and interest groups—from rights organizations to professional associations—had a more direct effect on ECtHR decision making—even so far as incorporation of their argumentation into Court judgments. And the subsequent implementation of these rulings led to a host of judicial, legislative, and constitutional reforms within the national legal systems.

Alongside these findings, the analysis also raises a host of unanswered questions that serve as avenues for research in the future. First, do these findings travel across time, region, or area of law? The European Court of Human Rights is exceptional in many ways given its vibrant legacy, large case law, historical network of legal advocacy support, and general compliance among member states. Yet it is also currently facing a massive crisis. Thousands of claims are turned away each year on "admissibility" grounds, with critics pointing to the inability of the institution to handle the real number of violations that exist. And proposed reforms remain in a deadlock, given the power of states to block a system that would ensure greater constraints on national sovereignty.[24] Thus, it remains an important question how the ECtHR's enhancement of participatory governance might evolve in the future to balance the support of member states and citizens.

As evidenced by other chapters in this volume, regional and domestic factors can also greatly constrain this access and protection (e.g., Anaya, this volume). Thus, factors such as domestic rule of law institutions and regional democracy norms may explain variation in the fulfillment of rights across regional human rights legal institutions (e.g., Europe vs. Americas vs. Africa). Others highlight the importance of regional court characteristics such as permeability, rather than mitigating domestic factors, when explaining democracy-enhancing outcomes (Hawkins 2008). These remain important empirical questions. Yet we do know that the globalization of the law today is critically linked to litigation and mobilization—placing courts and societal groups at the center of innovation and change.

NOTES

1. The online database can be accessed at http://www.echr.coe.int/echr/en/hudoc.
2. Decision of 17.5.1983, BverfGE 64, 135 (157); 13.1.1981, VverfGE 74, 102 (128). Essentially, Article 3.1 ("All men shall be equal before the law") is interpreted as a fundamental right protecting against unreasonable (arbitrary) distinctions. The Federal Constitutional Court has brought arbitrary misapplication of law by courts under this provision. See Polakiewicz (1996).
3. See discussion in Loveland (1999).
4. Human Rights Act 1998 S. 3.
5. It would be wrong to suggest that prior to the Human Rights Act, British courts have not engaged Convention rights and ECtHR jurisprudence. In fact, in numerous cases (the Court of Appeals *Derbyshire County Council v. Times Newspaper* [1992] decision is one example), the courts already behave exactly how the Act now requires.
6. In two Austrian cases, December 1987 and March 1988, the Constitutional Court followed the ECtHR interpretation of Article 6 by extending the determination of compensation for hunting damages and for expropriation measures by administrative authorities to civil rights and obligations. A Swiss case that exemplifies this trend was also rendered in 1988 in which the Court went beyond the ECtHR case law to interpret Article 6 in relation to judges.
7. For example, see *Éskomoravsk v. Czech Republic*, no. 33091/96, ECtHR 1999; *ARSEC and Others v. Spain*, no. 42916/98, ECtHR 1999; *Association of Polish Teachers v. Poland*, no. 42049/98, ECtHR 1998; *VgT v. Switzerland*, no. 24699/94, ECtHR 2000; and in two other cases the ECtHR dismissed the claims of the NGO in the case on grounds of not being able to claim direct harm, *Éonka v. Belgium*, no. 51564/99 ECtHR 2001 and *Asselbourg and Others*, no. 29121/95 ECtHR 1999.
8. For example, *Johannische Kirche and Peters v. Germany*, no. 41754/98, ECtHR 2001; *Christian Federation of Jehovah's Witness v. France*, no. 53430/99 ECtHR 2001.
9. For example, *Verdens Gang and Aase v. Norway*, no. 45710/99 ECtHR 2001; *Pasalaris and Foundation de Presse v. Greece*, no. 60916/00 ECtHR 2002; *Independent News and Media plc v. Ireland*, no. 55120/00 ECtHR 2003.
10. For example, *Unison v. UK*, no. 53574/99, ECtHR 2002; *Federation of Offshore Workers' Trade Unions v. Norway*, no. 38190/97 ECtHR 2002.
11. A recent decision is one example. *Women on Waves & Others v. Portugal* (no. 31276/05 ECtHR 2009) involved three NGOs, one Dutch and two Portuguese, who successfully won their claim that the Portuguese government had violated their Article 10 (freedom of expression) rights when it prevented the organizations from disseminating information about reproductive rights and abortion. See country case studies below for further examples.
12. For example, *Comingersoll v. Portugal*, no. 35382/97, ECtHR 2000; *Eielectric Srl v. Italy*, no. 36811/97, ECtHR 2000.
13. For example, the *Aksoy v. Turkey* case was brought by the victim's father along with assistance by a Kurdish human rights group, the KHRP.
14. *Tyrer v. UK*, no. 5856/72 ECtHR 1978; *Winterwerp v. Netherlands*, no. 6301/73 ECtHR 1979; *Young, James & Webster v. UK*, no. 7601/76, no. 7806/77 ECtHR 1981.
15. Professor Geraldine Van Beuren, Director of the Programme on International Rights of the Child, University of London, was granted leave in *T.P. and K.M. v. UK*, no. 28945/95 ECtHR 2001 and also *Z and Others v. UK*, no. 29392/95 ECtHR 2001.

16. Mr. J. Sitruk, Chief Rabbi of France, submitted comments in *Tsedek v. France*, no. 27417/95 ECtHR 2000.
17. Thirty-three Members of the European Parliament were granted leave to file comments in *Lautsi and Others v. Italy*, no. 30814/06 ECtHR 2011. Ms. Kathy Sinnott, Member of the European Parliament, filed a comment in *A, B, C v. Ireland*, no. 25579/05 ECtHR 2010.
18. Over a dozen different professional organizations were granted leave as third-party interveners in *Mangouras v. Spain*, no. 12050/04 ECtHR 2010.
19. *Soering v. UK*, no. 14038/88 ECtHR 1989.
20. The ECtHR stated in para. 102: "This 'virtual consensus in Western European legal systems that the death penalty is, under current circumstances, no longer consistent with regional standards of justice', to use the words of Amnesty International, is reflected in Protocol No 6 to the Convention, which provides for the abolition of the death penalty in time of peace."
21. *Observer & Guardian v. UK*, no. 13585/88 ECtHR 1991; *Sunday Times v. UK*, no. 13166/87 ECtHR 1991.
22. The Court stated in para. 60: "For the avoidance of doubt, and having in mind the written comments that were submitted in this case by 'Article 19' … the Court would only add to the foregoing that Article 10 of the Convention does not in terms prohibit the imposition of prior restraints on publication, as such."
23. *Nachova & Others v. Bulgaria*, no. 43577/98, no. 43579/98 ECtHR 2005.
24. The current debate around reforms to the European Convention system and in particular Russian opposition highlights that for the ECtHR an expanding case law protecting rights may enhance its legitimacy in the eyes of citizens, but at the same time cause a legitimacy crisis in the eyes of national executives. For further discussion of reforms see Mowbray (2009); Caflisch (2006); Greer (2006); Helfer (2008).

REFERENCES

Abbott, Kenneth, and Duncan Snidal. (2000). Hard and Soft Law in International Governance. *International Organization* 54(3): 421–456.
Alter, Karen J. (2011). The Evolving International Judiciary. *Annual Review of Law and Social Sciences* 7: 387–415.
—— (2012). The Global Spread of European Style International Courts. *West European Politics* 35: 135–154.
Anagnostou, Dia. (2010). Does European Human Rights Law Matter? Implementation and Domestic Impact of Strasbourg Court Judgments on Minority-Related Policies. *International Journal of Human Rights* 14(5): 721–743.
Barber, Benjamin. (1984). *Strong Democracy: Participatory Politics for a New Age.* Berkeley: University of California Press.
Barclay, Scott, Lynn Jones, and Anna-Maria Marshall. (2011). Two Spinning Wheels: Studying Law and Social Movements. *Studies in Law, Politics and Society* 54: 1–16.
Bernstein, Mary, Anna-Maria Marshall, and Scott Barclay. (2009). The Challenges of Law: Sexual Orientation, Gender Identity and Social Movements. In S. Barclay, A-M Marshall, and M. Bernstein, eds., *Queer Mobilizations: LGBT Activists Confront the Law*, 1–20. New York: New York University Press.
Bickel, Alexander. (1962). *The Least Dangerous Branch.* New York: Bobbs and Merrill.
Bignami, Francesca. (2005). Creating European Rights: National Values and Supranational Interests. *Columbia Journal of European Law* 11: 242–353.

Black, Charles. (1960). *The People and the Court.* Englewood Cliffs, NJ: Prentice Hall.

Brysk, Alison. (2009). *Global Good Samaritans: Human Rights as Foreign Policy.* Oxford, UK: Oxford University Press.

Caflisch, Lucius. (2006). The Reform of the European Court of Human Rights: Protocol No. 14 and Beyond. *Human Rights Law Review* 6: 403–415.

Cichowski, Rachel A. (2006). Courts, Rights and Democratic Participation. *Comparative Political Studies* 39: 50–75.

—— (2007). *The European Court and Civil Society.* Cambridge, UK: Cambridge University Press.

—— (2011). Civil Society and the European Court of Human Rights. In M. Madsen and J. Christoffersen, eds., *The European Court of Human Rights between Law and Politics,* 77–97.Oxford, UK: Oxford University Press.

Cichowski, Rachel, and Alec Stone Sweet. (2003). Participation, Representative Democracy and the Courts. In B. Cain, R. Dalton, and S. Scarrow, eds., *Democracy Transformed? Expanding Political Opportunities in Advanced Industrial Democracies* (pp. 192–220). Oxford, UK: Oxford University Press.

Conant, Lisa. (2002). *Justice Contained: Law and Politics in the European Union.* Ithaca, NY: Cornell University Press.

Dalton, Russell, Susan Scarrow, and Bruce Cain. (2003). New Forms of Democracy? Reform and Transformation of Democratic Institutions. In B. Cain, R. Dalton, and S. Scarrow, eds., *Democracy Transformed? Expanding Political Opportunities in Advanced Industrial Democracies* (pp. 1–20). Oxford, UK: Oxford University Press.

Epp, Charles. (1998). *The Rights Revolution: Lawyers, Activists and Supreme Courts in Comparative Perspective.* Chicago: University of Chicago Press.

Franck, Thomas M. (1990). *Power and Legitimacy among Nations.* New York: Cambridge University Press.

Fuller, Lon L. (1964). *The Morality of Law.* New Haven, CT: Yale University Press.

Galanter, Marc. (1974). Why the "Haves" Come out Ahead: Speculations on the Limits of Legal Change. *Law & Society Review* 9: 95–160.

Goldsmith, Jack L., and Eric A. Posner. (2006). *The Limits of International Law.* Oxford, UK: Oxford University Press.

Graber, Mark A. (1993). The Non-Majority Difficulty: Legislative Deference to the Judiciary. *Studies in American Political Development* 7: 35–72.

Greer, Steven. (2006). *The European Convention on Human Rights: Achievements, Problems and Prospects.* Cambridge, UK: Cambridge University Press.

Harlow, Carol, and Richard Rawlings. (1992). *Pressure through Law.* London, UK: Routledge.

Hawkins, Darren. (2008). Protecting Democracy in Europe and the Americas. *International Organization* 62: 373–403.

Helfer, Laurence. (2008). Redesigning the European Court of Human Rights: Embeddedness as a Deep Structural Principle of the European Human Rights Regime. *European Journal of International Law* 19: 125–159.

Helfer, Laurence, and Anne-Marie Slaughter. (1997). Toward a Theory of Effective Supranational Adjudication. *Yale Law Journal* 107: 273–391.

Helfer, Laurence, and Erik Voeten. (2012). International Courts as Agents of Legal Change: Evidence from LGBT Rights in Europe. SSRN: http://ssrn.com/abstract=1850526.

Kay, Tamara. (2011). Legal Transnationalism: The Relationship between Transnational Social Movement Building and International Law. *Law & Social Inquiry* 36(2): 419–454.

Keck, Margaret, and Kathryn Sikkink. (1998). *Activists across Borders: Advocacy Networks in International Politics.* Ithaca, NY: Cornell University Press.

Keohane, Robert, Stephan Macedo, and Andrew Moravcsik. (2009). Democracy-Enhancing Multilateralism. *International Organization* 63: 1–31.

Keohane, Robert, Andrew Moravcsik, and Anne-Marie Slaughter. (2000). Legalized Dispute Resolution: Interstate and Transnational. *International Organization* 54(3): 457–488.

Loveland, Ian. (1999). By Due Process of Law?: Racial Discrimination and the Right to Vote in South Africa 1855–1960. Oxford: Hart Publishing.

Lovell, George. (2003). *Legislative Deferrals: Statutory Ambiguity, Judicial Power, and American Democracy.* New York: Cambridge University Press.

Marshall, Anna-Maria. (2006). Social Movement Strategies and the Participatory Potential of Litigation. In A. Sarat and S. Scheingold, eds., *Cause Lawyers and Social Movements,* 164–181. Stanford, CA: Stanford University Press.

McCann, Michael W. (1994). *Rights at Work: Pay Equity Reform and the Politics of Legal Mobilization.* Chicago: University of Chicago Press.

Merry, Sally Engle. (2006). *Human Rights and Gender Violence: Translating International Law into Local Justice.* Chicago: University of Chicago Press.

Morag-Levine, Noga. (2003). Partners No More: Relational Transformation and the Turn to Litigation in Two Conservationist Organizations. *Law & Society Review* 37(2): 457–510.

Mowbray, Alastair. (2009). Crisis Measures of Institutional Reform for the European Court of Human Rights. *Human Rights Law Review* 9(64): 1–10.

Osanloo, Arzoo. (2009). *The Politics of Women's Rights in Iran.* Princeton, NJ: Princeton University Press.

Polakiewicz, Jorg. (1996). The Application of the European Convention on Human Rights in Domestic Law. *Human Rights Law Journal* 17: 405–411.

Scarrow, Susan. (2001). Direct Democracy and Institutional Change. *Comparative Political Studies* 34(6): 651–665.

Shapiro, Martin. (1981). *Courts: A Comparative and Political Analysis.* Chicago: University of Chicago Press.

Sikkink, Kathryn. (2011). *The Justice Cascade: How Human Rights Prosecutions Are Changing World Politics.* New York: W. W. Norton.

Simmons, Beth. (2009). *Mobilizing for Human Rights: International Law in Domestic Politics.* New York: Cambridge University Press.

Stone Sweet, Alec, and Helen Keller. (2008). The Reception of the ECHR in National Legal Orders. In H. Keller and A. Stone Sweet, eds., *A Europe of Rights,* 3–30. Oxford, UK: Oxford University Press.

Tarrow, Sidney. (2005). *The New Transnational Activism.* New York: Cambridge University Press.

Vajic, Nina. (2005). Some Concluding Remarks on NGOs and the European Court of Human Rights. In Tullio Treves, Alessandro Fodella, Attila Tanzi, and Marco Frigessi di Rattalma, eds., *Civil Society, International Courts and Compliance Bodies.* The Hague: TMC Asser Press.

Voeten, Erik. (2008). The Impartiality of International Judges: Evidence from the European Court of Human Rights. *American Political Science Review* 102(4): 417–432.

Zemans, Frances. (1983). Legal Mobilization: The Neglected Role of the Law in Political Systems. *American Political Science Review* 77: 690–670.

Part II

Hard Cases: From Rights to Justice?

7 The Power and Limits of International Law

Challenging the Bush Administration's Extra-Legal Detention and Interrogation System

Arturo Jimenez-Bacardi

In 2008 President Bush stressed that his controversial extra-legal detention and interrogation system (ELD&IS) had "produced critical intelligence that has helped us stop a number of attacks" (Bush 2008). Yet, the Bush administration had already revoked or reformed those same tools that it believed were essential for the national security of the United States. The question that this chapter seeks to answer is: Why did the Bush administration increasingly adhere to the laws governing the treatment of prisoners of war (POWs), even when it believed that doing so would constrain its ability to save American lives? Using a critical constructivist approach this chapter shows how every core aspect of the ELD&IS was either reformed, drawn down, or replaced in a manner more closely aligned with humanitarian and human rights law. These policy shifts were a direct result of the normative challenges pushed by normative and strategic dissenters from within the bureaucracies of the executive branch. Like other chapters in this volume, this is a hard case where the globalization of law improved the fulfillment of human rights by strengthening liberal democratic elements at the domestic level.

There were five major components to the U.S. ELD&IS. First, the United States designated members of al-Qaeda and the Taliban as rights-free "unlawful combatants," unprotected by the Geneva Conventions or any other body of law. Second, the United States created extra-legal zones, at the detention facility in Guantanamo Bay (GTMO), and through a global network of CIA-run detention facilities, known as "black sites," where prisoners were disappeared and routinely tortured (Sikkink 2011). Third, lawyers at the Justice Department's (DOJ) Office of Legal Counsel (OLC) authorized the CIA to use 35 "enhanced interrogation techniques" (EIT) including "waterboarding," a technique classified as torture by the U.S. military since 1898 (Bybee 2002; Solis 2010). Similarly, Secretary of Defense Donald Rumsfeld approved over two dozen EIT to be used by military interrogators that went beyond those permitted by the Army Field Manual (AFM) (Haynes 2002). Fourth, the United States expanded what came to be known as "extraordinary renditions," or the transfer of captured prisoners to third countries for interrogation or trial, even though (or precisely because) the receiving states were known for their use of torture and extra-judicial killings (Mayer

2008). Finally, the Department of Defense (DOD) created military commissions, where suspected terrorists would be prosecuted with minimal legal protections (Forsythe 2011).

By the end of 2002, all of the core elements of the ELD&IS had been established. Yet, by the end of the Bush presidency almost every component had been replaced, reformed, or revoked, in ways more closely aligned with humanitarian and human rights law. The CIA's black sites were closed. EIT were revoked. While still operating, GTMO's prisoner population had decreased more than threefold, and the International Committee of the Red Cross (ICRC) publicly declared that detainee conditions had "improved considerably," though problems remained (Reuters 2006). Similarly, although the military commissions had only seen minimal reforms, and the remaining GTMO detainees were still being held without trial, new suspected international terrorists were increasingly being prosecuted in federal courts (Shane 2011). These reversals in policy are surprising given the power of the United States, the threat perception of policy makers, and the conviction by key members of the administration that international law was at best "obsolete," and at worse, a dangerous and unconstitutional constraint on executive power (Gonzales 2002; Yoo 2006; Cheney 2011; Rumsfeld 2011).

THEORETICAL FRAMEWORK

States observe international law due to a combination of coercion, self-interests, rule legitimacy, communitarian appeals, and socialization (Koh 1998). The latter is the most effective mechanism as it leads to norm-internalization and self-enforcement (Risse, Ropp, Sikkink 1999). Therefore, international law can both constrain state behavior and reconstitute its interests and identity (Jepperson, Wendt, and Katzenstein 1996). However, there is an inherent tension in law as all normative structures contain contradictions within them that generate policy disputes (Sandholtz 2008). Legal disputes arise when laws are ambiguous or incomplete, or when unforeseen scenarios materialize. Most important, in international affairs, actions often evoke overlapping and competing sets of rules that trigger clashes (Sandholtz 2008; Kratochwil 1989). For instance, a state's right to defend itself during wartime frequently clashes with legal protections for enemy combatants. The inherent normative clashes in international relations make it difficult to predict which set of norms will prove to be more salient after any given dispute. As Sandholtz (2008: 103) explains, norm change "occurs in cycles that are linked, forward and backward, in a longer historical dynamic." As this chapter shows, part of the unpredictability of state compliance with international law arises from the fact that norm internalization is an uneven and dynamic process.

Internalization occurs when a state has adopted an international norm and incorporates it, "into its own internal value system," to the point where obedience becomes habitual or instinctive (Koh 1998: 627). But as with most social phenomenon, internalization is a matter of degree. Diverse actors and institutions within a state internalize international law at different levels. *Which* domestic institutions and actors end up internalizing an international rule can make the difference as to whether and how much a state complies with its international obligations. As Scharf and Williams (2010: 12) suggest, in order to understand how international law affects state behavior we need to recognize that the state is not a unitary actor, but "a nexus of competing and contradictory actors that influence its behavior, including bureaucratic subsets within the Executive Branch, political subsets within the Congress, Supreme Court and lower court judges, as well as nongovernmental organizations outside of the government." Thus, we need to disaggregate the state in order to assess which domestic institutions and actors have the most independent influence on state adherence to international agreements.

As the introduction to this volume illustrated, cosmopolitan optimists often emphasize the influence that civil society groups, epistemic communities, nongovernmental organizations (NGOs), lawyers, and courts have on a state's decision to comply with its international obligations. Significantly less attention has been paid to the different executive branch bureaucracies and the individuals that constitute them. The lack of attention is surprising, given the obvious role that the executive has on the decision-making process. This chapter shows that normative contestation within the executive is no less intense and consequential than clashes between the executive and other sectors of society. Understanding the normative clashes between members within the executive bureaucracies is key for uncovering the causal mechanism that can lead to state compliance with humanitarian and human rights law.

THE EXECUTIVE BRANCH BUREAUCRACY AND NORM COMPLIANCE

As the globalization of law intensified over the past few decades, so has the institutionalization of the legal adviser across the various bureaucracies of the executive branch. Today, there are an increasing number of actors with either "a responsibility or an ability to provide counsel to the President on matters of international law" (Scharf and Williams 2010: 199; Goldsmith 2007; Kahl 2007). These include the legal advisers at the Departments of State, Defense, and Commerce, as well as the White House Counsel, the OLC at the DOJ, the CIA's counsel, and the legal adviser at the National Security Council. Equally, important, after the Vietnam War, the DOD further institutionalized the role of the Judge Advocate General (JAGs) in order to increase the military's adherence with the laws of war. Today, the JAGs represent "a dedicated cadre of individuals responsible for training and monitoring compliance during military operations ... legal advisers assist commanders in reviewing operational plans, policies, directives, ROE, and procurements for compliance with the Law of War, and investigate and prosecute potential war crimes" (Kahl 2007: 40–1). Naturally, the influence of any given bureaucracy on the decision-making process varies depending on the issue at hand, as well as the internal politics within the executive.

U.S. compliance with international law is in large part due to the level of internalization of any given norm into the organizational culture of each of these bureaucracies. However, as mentioned earlier, domestic norm internalization is uneven and dynamic. Depending on the degree of bureaucratic internalization of a particular norm, each organization will share a different set of values, interests, and identity. Thus, when the state deviates from its international agreements, this friction will automatically set off a normative clash between the competing executive branch bureaucracies. U.S. adherence to humanitarian and human rights law is in part a synthesis of this process.

In addition to understanding the organizational culture of these competing bureaucracies, it is also essential to look at the individual motivations behind the key personnel in each organization. After all, the organizational culture of any bureaucracy is in part dependent on the identity and interests of the individual personnel that constitute it. As Farrell (2005: 15) explains, "new beliefs and ideas can travel with people into and out of communities ... radical norm change [can occur] when there is a turnover in key people or in a large portion of the community membership." For example, in the Bush administration, the self-proclaimed "War Council"—a cabal of high-ranking like-minded lawyers, including legal counsel to the vice president, David Addington; deputy assistant attorney generals in the OLC, John Yoo and Timothy Flanigan; general counsel of the DOD, William Haynes II; and White House counsel, Alberto Gonzales—decided to unilaterally bypass the interagency process (excluding the State Department and JAGs) and go directly to the president in order to assure that the core elements of the ELD&IS were approved (Mayer 2008). Once Yoo left the administration in mid-2003, not only did the organizational culture at the OLC change, but the influence of the War Council itself suffered an irreversible blow. This personnel change created an opening for other executive bureaucracies and individuals to have more of a say in the decision-making process, which led the United States toward a path of closer adherence to humanitarian and human rights law.

Finally, focusing on the individual motivations of policy makers helps us gain a better understanding of the process of norm internalization, and the ensuing normative clashes that result from uneven levels of internalization. Hawkins (1997) showed that the transnational advocacy campaign against authoritarian Chile was able to succeed partly due to the fact that there were factions inside the Pinochet regime that were responsive to the demands calling for human rights guarantees. Within the Chilean regime there were "hard-liners" that dismissed international demands, as well as "soft-liners," that "emphasized the importance of long-term regime legitimacy, and believed that ongoing extreme repression was counter-productive for long-term political stability" (Hawkins 1997: 415). Similar to Pinochet's Chile, the Bush administration also had its fair share of "hard-liners," mostly concentrated in high-ranking positions throughout the executive bureaucracies. But it also had plenty of "soft-liners," committed to international humanitarian and human rights law. The latter were originally concentrated in the Department of Defense, the military bureaucracies led by the JAGs, and the FBI. But their ranks multiplied as personnel change altered the makeup of competing organizations.

The category of "soft-liners" needs to be further divided into two groups: "strategic" and "normative" dissenters, in order to assess why and how international law shaped their behavior. Normative dissenters stressed the "immorality," "dishonor," or simply the illegality of Bush's ELD&IS. Furthermore, having fully internalized the norms in question, normative dissenters opposed the new policies as soon as they were being proposed and implemented and their opposition was independent of any outside pressure. Following a "logic of appropriateness," these actors had been socialized into accepting the laws governing the treatment of POWs as commonsensical. Humanitarian and human rights law had become part of their internal value system and identity. Consequently, when they perceived that those laws were being violated, they were shocked and forced to react. This allowed them to take further risks than their strategic counterparts. As Finnemore (1996: 29) explains, rather than asking, "How do I get what I want?" normative dissenters ask, "What am I supposed to do now?" Put differently, normative dissenters can be described as "governmental norm entrepreneurs" (Koh 1998). Their stronger sense of conviction and urgency led many to directly challenge their superiors, leak classified information to the press, or simply work against the dominant culture of their bureaucracy, often at the expense of their careers. Normative dissenters were essential in reversing the ELD&IS, not just because they opposed it from the beginning and exerted the most pressure against it, but also because they played a significant role in influencing their strategic counterparts.

Strategic dissenters also opposed elements of the ELD&IS, but their motivation was instrumentalist. They perceived the ELD&IS as counterproductive to U.S. efforts, either due to its overall ineffectiveness, or because the marginal gains from abandoning humanitarian and human rights law were outweighed by the negative consequences of employing such controversial actions. Thus, strategic dissenters were not necessarily opposed to the ELD&IS because they were "illegal" or "immoral" per se—such concerns were epiphenomenal to strategic considerations. Motivated by a "logic of consequence," these actors were also unwilling to oppose the ELD&IS until there was little personal cost in doing so. Thus, strategic dissenters did not oppose the ELD&IS from the beginning, but were instead slowly persuaded or socialized into seeing such policies as counterproductive. Nonetheless, their role was essential in getting the United States to more closely align with international obligations, since their presence increased the degree of internal opposition to the ELD&IS. It should be noted that normative and strategic considerations are not mutually exclusive. As March and Olsen (1998) make clear, any particular action probably involves a combination of normative and strategic concerns.

This chapter shows that internal dissenters had an independent effect on U.S. policy. By 2004, prior to the Abu Ghraib scandal and major news stories that focused the world's attention on U.S. detainee policies; prior to key Supreme Court decisions and Congressional legislation directly challenging the legality of the ELD&IS; and prior to major, focused, and sustained campaigns by human rights organizations coupled with pressure from key U.S. allies against the ELD&IS, dissenters within the administration had already set off normative clashes between the executive bureaucracies that resulted in the reform of core aspects of the ELD&IS. In late 2002, there was a major normative clash at GTMO, led by FBI and senior military personnel, against the EIT that had been approved by the DOD that forced Rumsfeld to suspend the authorized techniques and set up a working group to assess the legality and practicality of the techniques. Consequently, Rumsfeld revoked some of the harshest EIT. Similarly, in December 2003, Jack Goldsmith, assistant attorney general for the OLC, withdrew a key legal opinion written by his predecessor, and had decided to withdraw another (which he would months later), effectively undercutting the legal foundations for the Bush administration's ELD&IS.

This is not meant to suggest that by 2004, the entire ELD&IS was on its way to being completely reversed, far from it. Hard-liners in the administration aggressively fought back attempts to reform the program at every turn. Nonetheless, key victories were achieved prior to the development of a strong and sustained transnational opposition to the ELD&IS, traceable to internal dissent.

THE BUSH ADMINISTRATION'S ELD&IS

Three days after the September 11 attacks, the U.S. Congress authorized the president to "use all necessary and appropriate force against those nations, organizations, or persons he determines planned, authorized, committed, or aided the terrorist attacks." By September 17, the president signed a Memorandum of Notification authorizing the CIA to destroy al-Qaeda and to capture or kill its members and supporters (Woodward 2002). In less than a year, the White House had established an international ELD&IS.

Bush's ELD&IS was based on a series of legal opinions arguing that international law was "quaint" given the "new" nature of the Global War on Terror (Gonzales 2002). Most of the memos followed three main arguments. First, the treaty in question would be interpreted in such a narrow fashion as to make its violation nearly impossible. Second, even if someone managed to violate the law, it would be immaterial since the treaty was deemed non-applicable. Finally, if the treaty did apply, it could be suspended or overruled by the president under his wartime commander in chief powers (Cole 2009).

The savvy legal interpretations concocted by the War Council seemed to provide the perfect antidote to legal restraint. However, the policy makers and their lawyers underestimated two key components of law. First, legal norms are influential not just for their constraining effects, but also in shaping the expectations, interests, and identities of actors. Second, as identities evolve, the normative legal context also changes. As Goldsmith explained, hard-liners in the Bush administration were "naïve" for believing that the Supreme Court would not challenge the wartime powers of the commander in chief given the many Civil War and World War II precedents supporting their case. Legal advisers like Addington were "oblivious to how changes in context and culture might influence the Court's decision to approve presidential action" (Goldsmith 2007: 134). Or as Bradford Berenson, a White House lawyer who agreed with Addington's legal interpretations, would later lament, "[w]hat we underestimated ... was the extent to which the culture had shifted beneath us since World War Two" (Mayer 2008: 88). The normative context had indeed changed, and not only did it affect the judges at the Supreme Court, but also countless members across the various bureaucracies of the executive branch, who fought every element of the ELD&IS until it began to align with international legal standards.

The CIA's role in detaining and interrogating suspected members of al-Qaeda took off after March 2002. That month, Pakistani authorities captured Abu Zubaydah, a high-ranking member of al-Qaeda. Tenet explains that it was with Zubaydah's capture that the CIA "got into holding and interrogating" high-value detainees (HVDs) (Tenet 2007: 231). The CIA followed the situation carefully, as Tenet explains, "[d]espite what Hollywood might have you believe, in situations like this you don't call in the tough guys; you call in the lawyers" (Tenet 2007: 232). The CIA sent a wish list of "stress techniques" it wanted to use on Zubaydeh, but before its operatives could put them into use, they had to make sure that the DOJ gave them an "advanced declination" or a "get-out-of-jail-free card" (Sifton 2010; Goldsmith 2007: 97). It took the OLC several months to approve the techniques, but when it finally did, it did not disappoint.

Although it would take several months for the OLC to approve the EIT for the CIA, the deliberation process was mostly limited to those in the War Council as the regular interagency process was intentionally bypassed, keeping likely dissenters out of the loop (Scharf and Williams 2010). On August 1, two key memos mostly written by Yoo and Bybee legalized 35 EIT for the CIA, including "(1) attention grasp, (2) walling, (3) facial hold, (4) facial slap (insult slap), (5) cramped confinement, (6) wall standing, (7) stress positions, (8) sleep deprivation, (9) insects placed in a confinement box, and (10) the waterboard" (Bybee 2002: 2).

The OLC's August 1 memo quickly made its way to the DOD. In September, Haynes, Gonzales, and Addington, along with CIA General Counsel John Rizzo and Assistant Attorney General of the Criminal Division Michael Chertoff, visited Guantanamo to asses "intelligence successes, failures, and problems" (U.S. Congress 2008). Upon their return, Haynes authored a legal memo clearing the way for EIT to be used by the military (Haynes 2002). Once again, none of the top JAGs were consulted, nor was the State Department. Moreover, interrogators at GTMO began to be routinely pressured to get "tougher" on detainees in order to obtain actionable intelligence (U.S. Congress 2008).

On October 11, 2002, Major General Michael Dunlavey, Commander of GTMO Joint Task Force 170, took the lead by sending a request to SOUTHCOM seeking authorization for a number of EIT (Dunlavey 2002). The timing of the request was in part due to the desire to use EIT on Mohammed al-Qahtani, the so-called 20th highjacker, who had been identified by the FBI through legal means (Mayer 2008). However, when the request reached General James T. Hill at SOUTHCOM, he dissented. Hill sent Dunlavey's request to the Pentagon, but he warned that some of the proposed techniques might run counter to the law (Hill 2002). Haynes disagreed, advising Rumsfeld that all of the techniques were legal, but also argued that the harshest techniques, including waterboarding, "as a matter of policy, a blanket approval … is not warranted at this time" (Haynes 2002: 1). Rumsfeld followed Haynes's advice and overrode the limits outlined in the AFM. Some of the new techniques approved included 20-hour interrogations, sensory deprivation, removal of clothing, the use of personalized phobias including dogs, and stress positions for up to four hours (U.S. Congress 2008).

On November 23, Major General Geoffrey Miller authorized an interrogation plan for al-Qahtani that included many of the Rumsfeld-approved EIT (U.S. Congress 2008: 81–90). Several years later, the U.S. government was forced to drop all charges against al-Qahtani because, as Susan Crawford, the lead authority of the military commissions, explained, "his treatment met the legal definition of torture" (Woodward 2009). Al-Qahtani was interrogated from November 23, 2002, through January 16, 2003. His interrogation ended abruptly due to the dissent of a number of professional military lawyers and FBI agents.

INTERNAL DISSENT AND THE SLOW PROGRESSION TOWARD COMPLIANCE WITH HUMANITARIAN LAW

Both Dunlavey's request for EIT and Miller's specialized interrogation plan for al-Qahtani circulated widely among personnel at GTMO. As soon as the documents reached the desk of FBI agent Jim Clemente, and the senior military lawyers for the Army, Navy, Air Force, and Marines, a normative clash ensued. Major General and U.S. Army JAG, Thomas Romig, led the charge, arguing that several of the proposed interrogations, "cross[ed] the line of 'humane' treatment, [and] would likely be considered maltreatment under Article 93 of the [Uniform Code of Military Justice], and may violate the federal torture statute" (U.S. Congress 2008: 68–9). Clemente concurred, and sent a scathing warning to his superiors at the FBI stating that at least 10 of the 18 techniques violated the Constitution (Mayer 2008: 204).

The JAGs and FBI agents were both normative as well as strategic dissenters. In strategic terms, they feared that military interrogators' might be held legally accountable. Normatively, Major General Romig argued that, "if we mistreat detainees, we will quickly lose the moral high ground" (U.S. Congress 2008: 68–9). The military's image and honor was also a great concern for Major General Jack Rives, who argued that regardless of the legal grounds, EIT should not be introduced because of the negative effects they would have on the organizational culture of the military. The cultural and self-image of the U.S. Armed Forces suffered during the Vietnam conflict and at other times due to perceived law of armed conflict violations. DOD policy, indoctrinated in the Law of War Program in 1979 and subsequent service regulations, greatly *restored the culture and self-image of U.S. Armed Forces. "U.S. Armed Forces are continuously trained to take the legal and moral "high ground" in the conduct of our military operations regardless of how others may operate"* (emphasis added; Reeves 2003: 1).

It is not clear whether the FBI's concerns reached the DOD (Clemente claims they did), but according to Rumsfeld, he was not informed of any criticisms—either from the FBI or the JAGs—until January 2003 (Rumsfeld 2011). As soon as he was, Rumsfeld claims that he suspended the EIT he had approved and ordered Haynes to assemble the "Detainee Interrogation Working Group" in order to "to assess the legal, policy, and operational issues relating to the interrogations of detainees held by the United States Armed Forces in the war on terrorism" (Rumsfeld 2011: 581; U.S. Congress 2008).

Haynes had a tight hold on the Working Group, and the State Department, as well as some of the key JAGs that had dissented, were once again kept out of the loop (Mayer 2008; Scharf and Williams 2010). Nonetheless, dissent within the Working Group intensified, but Haynes maintained that the OLC memos should be treated as authoritative and "supplant the legal analysis being prepared by the Working Group action officers" (U.S. Congress 2008: 119). To strengthen Haynes's hand, Yoo authored another memo in mid-March presenting an even more forceful defense of presidential power than the August 1 memo (Yoo 2003). The new memo was presented to the Working Group as the final say, as far as the law was concerned (U.S. Congress 2008).

Notwithstanding the major limitations, the dissenting JAGs clearly had an impact on Rumsfeld's final decision. The Working Group would end up recommending 35 interrogation techniques to the secretary of defense. Of those, Rumsfeld approved 24, and only 5 were not listed in the AFM; these included, "dietary manipulation, environmental manipulation, sleep adjust-ment, and false flag" (US Congress 2008: 132). However, Rumsfeld included the caveat that, "If, in your view, you require additional interrogation tech-niques for a particular detainee, you should provide me, via the Chairman of the Joint Chiefs of Staff, a written request describing the proposed tech-nique, recommended safeguards, and the rationale for applying it with an identified detainee" (U.S. Congress 2008: 132). Although it is not clear if the exception was ever used, the challenge by the JAGs and the FBI clearly constrained a key component of the ELD&IS, as most of the previously ap-proved techniques for GTMO were no longer available for all situations. This key episode set in motion a reversal of the permissive culture that had engulfed Guantanamo. The partial victory at the DOD was to be followed by a more significant challenge at the OLC, which resulted in the with-drawal of several of the key memos authorizing the ELD&IS.

In mid-March 2003, there were major personnel changes at the OLC that paved the way for internal dissent at this key executive bureaucracy. Bybee would leave the OLC to become a federal judge. Yoo, who wanted to replace Bybee, was not offered the position and decided to resign. These de-partures also affected the influence of the War Council and slowly reinstated the traditional interagency process.

Jack Goldsmith was nominated to replace Bybee, but even before he re-ceived his confirmation, he was approached by Patrick Philbin, a deputy at OLC, warning him of a legal opinion "that may contain serious errors, and that he had been working to correct" (Goldsmith 2007: 142). Goldsmith asked Philbin to send him any additional memos that he felt might be flawed. Philbin responded by sending him the Bybee August 1, 2002, memo, and Yoo's March 14, 2003, memo, the two opinions that provided the legal ra-tionale for the EIT.

As soon as Goldsmith began to read the memos he was shocked, but he did not want to act recklessly and immediately withdraw them, since the ELD&IS was largely dependent on them (Goldsmith 2007). After several months of research, Goldsmith decided that the "opinions written nine [March 13, 2003] and sixteen [August 1, 2002] months earlier by my Bush administra-tion predecessors must be withdrawn, corrected, and replaced" (Goldsmith 2007: 146). By December, he withdrew the Yoo memo, but decided not to withdraw the Bybee memo until he wrote an alternative opinion specifying exactly what was and was not legal with regard to interrogations (Goldsmith 2007). Until he completed the new memo, he told Haynes that the 24 interro-gation techniques that Rumsfeld had authorized could still be used, but the legal reasoning behind them could no longer be relied upon (Mayer 2008). Goldsmith also wrote an opinion concluding that the Geneva Conventions applied to the war in Iraq (although non-Iraqi fighters could be transferred to CIA black sites), forcing Lieutenant General Ricardo S. Sanchez to begin the process of revising U.S. interrogation policy in accordance with the laws of war (Mayer 2008).

As his views spread across the White House, Goldsmith began to be "intimidated" and "pressured" by the hard-liners inside the administration, "to stand by and reaffirm the August 2002 opinion" (Goldsmith 2007: 159). By that point, the interrogation techniques approved by Rumsfeld for GTMO had migrated to Iraq and Afghanistan (U.S. Congress 2008). In late April, the Abu Ghraib scandal broke out. As soon as the pictures began to be shown on television, Gonzales muttered, "this is going to kill us" (Goldsmith 2007: 141).

Gonzalez's intuition was quite prescient: The Abu Ghraib scandal would act as an "outside shock" challenging the legitimacy of the ELD&IS. The pictures of U.S. prisoner abuse would become an undeniable symbol of the excesses of the Bush administration's GWOT. After Abu Ghraib, news reports of American detainee abuse could no longer be ignored. The Abu Ghraib scandal produced immediate international condemnation and opened a discourse that further legitimized the claims of those arguing for adherence to the laws governing the treatment of POWs. Furthermore, a convergence of interests between dissenters inside the administration and actors outside of it emerged. Only three weeks after the publication of the Abu Ghraib photos, a number of the controversial legal memos began to be leaked to the press (Isikoff 2004). Suddenly, the pressure on the administration increased not only by dissenters inside the administration, but also by international allies (and rivals), as well as the press, human rights organizations, members of Congress, and the courts. Opponents could now frame and shame the administration more clearly, as the debates were now taking place in the public sphere, with a clear understanding of what EIT looked like.

In the midst of the international outcry, Goldsmith decided to finally withdraw Bybee's August 1, 2002, memo (Goldsmith 2007). Goldsmith would resign from his post shortly thereafter, without writing a replacement opinion for the withdrawn memo. Yoo would later criticize Goldsmith's decision of withdrawing the memos as a show of weakness and capitulation to political pressure (Yoo 2006: 169). Goldsmith admits that, "Obviously, the public release of the opinions and the resulting outcry precipitated my decision [to withdraw Bybee's memo]" (Goldsmith 2007: 159). However, he maintains that he had made his decision to withdraw the memo six months earlier, well before any major public protest. More important was the support he received from fellow dissenters at the DOJ, including Philbin and Deputy Attorney General Jim Comey, who had also internalized the POW norms (Goldsmith 2007).

Goldsmith's departure from the OLC allowed the hard-liners in the White House to once again exert their influence over the legal bureaucracy. In late December 2004, the temporary head at the OLC, Daniel Levin, issued an unclassified memo to replace the August 2002 opinion (Levin 2004). The memorandum ostensibly argued that the United States no longer needed the broader Commander in Chief Powers accorded in past opinions, nor was the narrow definition of torture still tolerable. On closer inspection, the memo reveals that it was intended for public consumption, as opposed to an actual change in legal interpretation. Hidden in one of the footnotes, the memo made clear that, "[w]hile we have identified various disagreements with the August 2002 Memorandum, we have reviewed this Office's prior opinions addressing issues involving treatment of detainees and do not believe that any of their conclusions would be different under the standards set forth in this memorandum" (Levin 2004: 2). As Yoo explained in his memoir, "in the real world of interrogation policy nothing had changed" (Yoo 2006: 170). Yet, when it came to practice, things continued to change. In mid-2004, the OLC had reauthorized the CIA to use waterboarding; however, the agency chose to stop using the technique regardless of its legal foundation (U.S. Congress 2009). There were reports that interrogation agents had refused to continue to carry out the controversial techniques for fear of prosecution (Mayer 2008). Strategic dissenters were forcing the CIA to internalize POW norms.

Similarly, in 2005, after an internal review of all the EIT was completed, the OLC, now headed by Steven Bradbury, once again concluded that all of the techniques were indeed legal (U.S. Congress 2009; Bradbury 2005). Bradbury went one step further, arguing that the techniques could be used simultaneously without violating the law (Bradbury 2005; Cole 2009). However, in practice, most of the techniques were not reintroduced and other key aspects of the ELD&IS continued to be challenged as the levels of dissent across the executive branch bureaucracies increased.

By 2005, strategic dissenters began to join their normative counterparts in opposing the ELD&IS. None was more important than Condoleezza Rice, who was greatly influenced by her main legal adviser John Bellinger III (Scharf and Williams 2010). For the most part, Rice had stood on the sidelines as the ELD&IS was being created (Mayer 2008; Rice 2011). Abu Ghraib began to change her perception of things. In May 2004, after an internal CIA investigation found many instances of cruel and inhuman treatment of its detainees, Rice began to question the effectiveness and legality of the ELD&IS (Helgerson 2004; Mayer 2008). Once at the State Department, she began to realize that the ELD&IS was counterproductive as, "those policies were creating their own security challenges. Diplomatic relations with our allies, particularly the Europeans, were increasingly strained by the mistaken perception that the United States' detention and interrogation policies operated outside the bounds of international law" (Rice 2011: 497). Rice understood that given the transnational character of al-Qaeda, strong cooperation with other states was essential for both gathering intelligence and carrying out operations against the terrorist organization. Yet the ELD&IS was making such cooperation more difficult. Pushed by Bellinger and others at State, she began to play a more active role opposing the ELD&IS.

Near the end of 2005, the *Washington Post* published a story in its front page disclosing the existence of several CIA secret facilities where high-value detainees were being tortured (Priest 2005). In Europe, a major controversy arose, given that several EU member states had colluded with the ELD&IS.

That same month, the Parliamentary Assembly of the Council of Europe launched its own investigation, which would lead to the censure of several of its member states (Marty 2006). For Washington, the investigation meant that those states that had cooperated with the ELD&IS would seek to sever ties with the program, and possibly try and pressure the United States to close it altogether (Rice 2011; Mayer 2008). For Rice, this diplomatic crisis highlighted the counterproductive aspects of the ELD&IS.

Within the United States, the military had also had enough. In mid-2006, Army Lieutenant General David Petraeus and Marine Lieutenant General James N. Mattis released the military's Counterinsurgency Field Manual. The new document reasserted past military doctrine by only permitting its interrogators to use the techniques outlined in the Uniform Code of Military Justice. In a further blow to the hard-liners, the document also stressed the applicability of the Geneva Conventions and the illegality of any form of abuse. The interrogation policies approved by the DOD had severely damaged the organizational culture of the military. Petraeus and Mattis believed that normative and strategic considerations could not be separated with regard to interrogation, or warfare as a whole. As Petraeus would later explain, "[o]ur values and the laws governing warfare teach us to respect human dignity, maintain our integrity, and do what is right. Adherence to our values distinguishes us from our enemy. This fight depends on securing the population, which must understand that we—not our enemies—occupy the moral high ground" (U.S. Congress 2008: xxv).

For the rest of 2006, the White House would be at war—with itself—over the fate of the ELD&IS. The hard-liners in the administration were losing their influence with the president, as the war in Iraq was quickly deteriorating, and critiques of the ELD&IS continued to strengthen from every corner imaginable. Finally, on June 29, the Supreme Court ruled against the administration in the seminal case of *Hamdan v. Rumsfeld*. In a 5–3 decision, the court decided that the military commissions were unconstitutional because they "violate both the Uniform Code of Military Justice and the four Geneva Conventions of 1949" (Scharf and Williams 2010: 196). The majority decision also made clear that GTMO prisoners were protected under Common Article 3 of the Geneva Conventions. The judicial internalization of the Geneva Conventions was strong, and it provided dissenters within the executive branch with further legitimacy to reform the ELD&IS. As Rice explained, "The Hamdan ruling ... allowed us to go even further in pursuing the goal of establishing an improved legal framework for the war on terror" (Rice 2011: 500). Rice wanted to close the "black sites," make clear that Common Article 3 was applicable to all U.S. detainees, and get Congressional approval for a new military tribunal system. However, the hard-liners, led by Cheney, wanted to push Congress to completely overturn the Supreme Court's ruling on Hamdan, and demand that Congress recognize the president's authority in such matters (Rice 2011). This time, Bush sided with the dissenters.

On September 6, 2006, Bush admitted that the CIA had been interrogating and holding several high-value detainees in secret detention facilities around the world. He also declared that the CIA's prisoners would be transferred to GTMO and be tried in military commissions (Rice 2011). This marked a significant shift in policy as the CIA's "black sites" began to be drawn down. Their closure turned out to be permanent. On several occasions, CIA director Michael Hayden requested to have his agency's detention and interrogation program reinstated, but Rice refused to condone it because it violated Geneva's Common Article 3 (Rice 2011: 503; Cheney 2011). As more executive branch bureaucracies internalized the laws of war, U.S. policy reflected that shift.

The final two components of the ELD&IS—GTMO and the military commissions—remained in use until the last days of the Bush presidency, and remain in place today. In October 2006, Congress passed the Military Commissions Act (MCA), which gave the Bush administration almost everything it had requested. Here, the dissenters within the administration agreed that the military tribunals should not be closed—instead, they sought a legislative foundation for the commissions (Scharf and Williams 2010; Rice 2011). The MCA legalized the military tribunal system, without providing significant reforms to it. Habeas rights were once again denied, and Congress concluded that "humiliating treatment" would no longer be deemed a war crime (Forsythe 2011). In other words, the MCA allowed the Bush administration to maintain its system of administrative detention and military tribunals relatively unchallenged for the remainder of its presidency. On closer inspection, however, once again it was apparent that in practice the administration was changing its policy.

Although GTMO was still open, its prisoner population had decreased sharply since its peak in 2003. From almost 800 detainees, GTMO had a prisoner population of less than 250 by the end of 2008 (Shane 2011). As President Bush lamented, "[w]hile I believe opening Guantanamo after 9/11 was necessary, the detention facility had become a propaganda tool for our enemies and a distraction for our allies. I worked to find a way to close the prison without compromising security" (Bush 2010: 179). The facility could not be closed because several prisoners could not be prosecuted since they had been tortured, nor could they be transferred to other countries since no one would accept them (Mayer 2008). More important, as GTMO dwindled, the U.S. government increasingly depended on federal prosecutions and prisons to deal with international terrorist suspects (Shane 2011). The trend was the mirror opposite of GTMO. Before 9/11 approximately 50 inmates linked to international terrorism were in federal prisons—by the end of 2008, the number exceeded 200 (Shane 2011).

There were clear advantages in using the federal legal system over the military commissions. The federal courts were not controversial, were well tested, less costly, provided more options to get suspects to cooperate, were less vulnerable to appeal—and most important, allies were willing to cooperate with the United States if they knew that a transferred suspect would receive the legal guarantees found in federal courts that the military commissions lacked (Savage and Shane 2010). The change in policy was mostly strategic. For instance, the DOJ and the FBI preferred federal prosecutions, since it allowed them to play a more active role in the GWOT. Thus, even as GTMO and the military commissions lingered, they were a shadow of what the hard-liners had envisioned. Furthermore, the transnational legal process would continue to challenge their legality. In mid-2008 the Supreme Court would once again rule against the administration in *Boumediene v. Bush*. The majority opinion ruled some sections of the MCA unconstitutional and reasserted the right of GTMO detainees to challenge their detention in U.S. courts (Forsythe 2011). However, no further reforms to the military commissions would take place under the Bush presidency.

CONCLUSION

Notwithstanding the fact that certain elements of the Bush administration's ELD&IS remain in effect more than a decade after their inception, today the program is a mere shadow of what it once was. By the end of Bush's second term, EIT were no longer in use, and the global network of CIA black sites had been shut down. Less impressive is the fact that both GTMO and the military commissions survived—however, the government began to use alternative channels to deal with new international terrorism suspects in a way that more closely aligned U.S. policy with its legal obligations. All the core aspects of the ELD&IS were revoked, reformed, drawn down, or replaced. The shift was a direct result of the challenges pushed by strategic and normative dissenters from the different bureaucracies of the executive branch. The globalization of law and the socialization of norms matter, even in the hardest of hard cases.

WORKS CITED

Bradbury, Steven. 2005. "Re: Application of United States Obligations Under Article16 of the Convention Against Torture to Certain Techniques That May Be Used in the Interrogation of High Value al Qaeda Detainees, May 30, 2005." Washington, D.C.: U.S. Department of Justice Office of Legal Counsel.

Bush, George W. 2008. "President's Radio Address to the Nation, March 8, 2008." Washington, D.C.

Bush, George W. 2010. *Decision Points*. New York: Crown.

Bybee, Jay S. 2002. "Interrogation of al Qaeda Operative, August 1, 2002." Washington, D.C.: U.S. Department of Justice Office of Legal Counsel.

Cheney, Richard B. 2011. *In My Time: A Personal and Political Memoir*. New York: Threshold Editions.

Cole, David, ed. 2009. *Torture Memos: Rationalizing the Unthinkable*. New York: New Press.

Dunlavey, Michael E. 2002. "Counter Resistance Strategies, October 11, 2002." Guantanamo Bay, Cuba APO-AE: U.S. Department of Defense Joint Task Force 170.

Farrell, Theo. 2005. *The Norms of War: Cultural Beliefs and Modern Conflict.* Boulder, CO: Lynne Rienner.

Finnemore, Martha. 1996. *National Interests in International Society.* Ithaca, NY: Cornell University Press.

Forsythe, David P. 2011. *The Politics of Prisoner Abuse: The United States and Enemy Prisoners After 9/11.* New York: Cambridge University Press.

Goldsmith, Jack L. 2007. *The Terror Presidency: Law and Judgment Inside the Bush Administration.* New York: W. W. Norton.

Gonzales, Alberto R. 2002. "Re Application of the Geneva Convention on Prisoners of War to the Conflict with al Qaeda and the Taliban, January 5, 2002." Washington, D.C.: White House General Counsel, http://www.torturingdemocracy.org /documents/20020125.pdf (retrieved December 2012).

Hawkins, Darren G. 1997. "State Responses to International Pressures: Human Rights in Authoritarian Chile." *European Journal of International Relations* 3(4): 403–434.

Haynes, William J. 2002. "Counter-Resistance Strategies, October 25, 2002." Washington, D.C.: U.S. Department of Defense General Counsel.

Helgerson, John. 2004. "Special Review [Redacted] Counterterrorism Detention and Interrogation Activities (September 2001–October 2003)." Washington, D.C.: Central Intelligence Agency.

Hill, James T. 2002. "Counter-Resistance Techniques, 25 October, 2002." Miami, FL: Department of Defense United States Southern Command.

Isikoff, Michael. 2004. "Memos Reveal War Crimes Warnings." *Newsweek,* May 16, http://www.thedailybeast.com/newsweek/2004/05/16/memos-reveal-war-crimes-warnings.html (retrieved December 2012).

Jepperson, Ronald L., Alexander Wendt, and Peter J. Katzenstein. 1996. "Norms, Identity, and Culture in National Security." In *The Culture of National Security: Norms and Identity in World Politics,* ed. P. J. Katzenstein, 33–75. New York: Columbia University Press.

Kahl, Colin H. 2007. "In the Crossfire or the Crosshairs? Norms, Civilian Casualties, and U.S. Conduct in Iraq." *International Security* 32(1): 7–46.

Koh, Harold. 1998. "Frankel Lecture: Bringing International Law Home." *Houston Law Review* 35: 623–77.

Kratochwil, Friedrich V. 1989. *Rules, Norms, and Decisions: On the Conditions of Practical and Legal Reasoning in International Relations and Domestic Affairs.* New York: Cambridge University Press.

Levin, Daniel B. 2004. "Re: Legal Standards Applicable Under 18 U.S.C. § 2340–2340A, December 30, 2004." Washington, D.C.: U.S. Department of Justice Office of Legal Counsel.

March, James G., and Johan P. Olsen. 1998. "The Institutional Dynamics of International Political Orders." *International Organization* 52(4): 943–969.

Marty, Dick. 2006. "Alleged Secret Detentions and Unlawful Inter-State Transfers Involving Council of Europe Member States." Strasbourg, France: Parliament Assembly of the Council of Europe, Committee on Legal Affairs and Human Rights.

Mayer, Jane. 2008. *The Dark Side: The Inside Story of How the War on Terror Turned into the War on American Ideals.* New York: Doubleday.

Priest, Dana. 2005. "CIA Holds Terror Suspects in Secret Prisons." *Washington Post,* November 2. http://www.washingtonpost.com/wp-dyn/content/article/2005/11/01/ AR2005110101644.html (retrieved December 2012).

Reeves, Jack L. 2003. "Comments on Draft Report and Recommendations of the Working Group to Assess the Legal, Policy and Operational Issues Relating to Interrogations of Detainees Held by the U.S. Armed Forces in the War on Terrorism,

February 6, 2003." Washington, D.C.: U.S. Department of the Air Force Office of the Judge Advocate General.

Reuters. 2006. "Guantanamo Bay Conditions Have Improved: Red Cross." *Reuters News*, April 25.

Rice, Condoleezza. 2011. *No Higher Honor: A Memoir of My Years in Washington*. New York: Crown.

Risse, Thomas, Stephen C. Ropp, and Kathryn Sikkink, eds. 1999. *The Power of Human Rights: International Norms and Domestic Change*. New York: Cambridge University Press.

Rumsfeld, Donald. 2011. *Known and Unknown: A Memoir*. New York: Sentinel.

Sandholtz, Wayne. 2008. "Dynamics of International Norm Change: Rules Against Wartime Plunder." *European Journal of International Relations* 14(1): 101–131.

Savage, Charlie, and Scott Shane. 2010. "Experts Urge Keeping Two Options for Terror Trials." *New York Times*, March 8, http://www.nytimes.com/2010/03/09/us/politics/09terror.html?_r=0 (retrieved December 2012).

Scharf, Michael P., and Paul R. Williams. 2010. *Shaping Foreign Policy in Times of Crisis: The Role of International Law and the State Department Legal Adviser*. New York: Cambridge University Press.

Shane, Scott. 2011. "Beyond Guantánamo, a Web of Prisons for Terrorism Inmates." *New York Times*, December 10. http://www.nytimes.com/2011/12/11/us/beyond-guantanamo-bay-a-web-of-federal-prisons.html?pagewanted=all (retrieved December 2012).

Sifton, John. 2010. "The Get Out of Jail Free Card for Torture: It's Called a Declination; Just Ask the CIA." *Slate*, March 29. http://www.slate.com/articles/news_and_politics/jurisprudence/2010/03/the_get_out_of_jail_free_card_for_torture.html (retrieved December 2012).

Sikkink, Kathryn. 2011. *The Justice Cascade: How Human Rights Prosecutions Are Changing World Politics*. New York: W.W. Norton.

Solis, Gary D. 2010. *The Law of Armed Conflict: International Humanitarian Law in War*. New York: Cambridge University Press.

Tenet, George. 2007. *At the Center of the Storm: My Years at the CIA*. New York: HarperCollins.

U.S. Congress, Senate. 2008. "Inquiry into the Treatment of Detainees in U.S. Custody; Report of the Committee on Armed Services, United States Senate." Washington, D.C.: Library of Congress, 110th Congress, 2nd Session, November 20.

U.S. Congress, Senate. 2009. "OLC Opinions on the CIA Detention and Interrogation Program, Report of the Select Committee on Intelligence, United States Senate." Washington, D.C.: Library of Congress, 111th Congress, 1st Session, April 22.

Woodward, Bob. 2002. *Bush at War*. New York: Simon & Schuster.

Woodward, Bob. 2009. "Guantanamo Detainee Was Tortured, Says Official Overseeing Military Trials." *Washington Post*, January 14. http://www.washingtonpost.com/wp-dyn/content/article/2009/01/13/AR2009011303372.html (retrieved December 2012).

Yoo, John. 2003. "Re: Military Interrogation of Alien Unlawful Combatants Held Outside the United States, March 14, 2003." Washington, D.C.: U.S. Department of Justice Office of Legal Counsel.

Yoo, John. 2006. *War by Other Means: An Insider's Account of the War on Terror*. New York: Atlantic Monthly Press.

8   States of Emergency, Courts, and Global Norms in Latin America

Claire Wright

Regimes of exception[1] are an old foe of human rights in Latin America. These constitutional clauses have become infamous for facilitating military intervention and restricting the enjoyment of civil and political rights in "emergency" situations to deal with social unrest, ever since the 19th century (Loveman, 1993). In fact, the "regime of exception" mechanism itself is an example of how the globalization of law has the potential to be a double-edged sword; the mechanism was imported from European constitutional models by Latin American legislators during the 19th century (Aguilar Rivera, 1996; Fix-Zamudio, 2004). The specific question we pose in this chapter is: How have constitutional courts been able to protect human rights during regimes of exception in Bolivia, Ecuador, and Peru? And how have global treaty norms been used by national judiciaries to shift globalized repressive legal practices?

Regimes of exception became the favorite tool for repression on the part of military governments that seized power in various parts of the region during the 20th century. By declaring a regime of exception, the military was able to seize power over civilians for several years.[2] Although often linked with the countries of the Southern Cone—where the greatest abuses of civil rights undoubtedly occurred—at the end of 1970s two thirds of Latin American states were under states of emergency (Despouy, 1997). Given this situation, it would be logical to assume that the series of democratic governments that came to power towards the end of the same decade would remove these clauses from their normative frameworks. However, this was not the case; in fact, all new constitutions adopted between 1978 and 1993 reaffirmed and broadened emergency powers available to Latin American presidents, with the only exception being Paraguay (Loveman and Davies, 1997: 376).

The continuing and increasing presence of these mechanisms in the constitutions of the region is a key legacy of authoritarian regimes that has survived the so-called third wave of democracy and which continues to offer the military a key area of influence in the region (Hagopian 2005; Karl 1996). In another study (Wright 2012), we found that as of 2012, 13 constitutions in Latin America establish formal regimes of exception and a further three establish a clause that allows the limitation of the enjoyment of certain rights in emergency situations. Loveman (1993) offers an excellent analysis of the use of regimes of exception in various Latin American countries from independence until the third wave of democracy. In recent years, there are case studies that point to a continuing use of these mechanisms, in several countries, including Colombia (Iturralde, 2003), Bolivia (Alenda, 2003), and Ecuador (Dávalos Muirragui, 2008). Likewise, data from the United Nations suggest that between 1985 and 2005, "states of emergency" were declared in Argentina, Bolivia, Colombia, Ecuador, Guatemala, Honduras, Nicaragua, Paraguay, Peru, and Venezuela (Wright, 2012: 311). Regimes of exception are a feature of Latin American politics that did not come to a sudden halt with the return of the military to the barracks.

Undoubtedly, regimes of exception pose a threat to fulfillment of civil rights specifically, due to the suspension of human rights and the use of military force that they may entail.[3] In this chapter, we concentrate on three Latin American countries where declarations of regimes of exception have been common throughout recent history: Bolivia, Ecuador, and Peru. In the study cited above (Wright, 2012), a total of 290 presidential declarations of regimes of exception were found in the three countries between 2000 and 2010. According to the analysis carried out, 85 of these decrees employed the use of military force or the suspension of human rights, with just over half of them being in response to social unrest, corresponding to the traditional use of these mechanisms in the region. Clearly old practices die hard, but what has been done to protect human rights under these circumstances?

The aim of this chapter is to focus on the role of national judiciaries in the protection of human rights during declarations of regimes of exception. We consider that constitutional courts in democratic regimes could offer much needed protection in these circumstances, given the prevalence of international and regional norms on the protection of human rights during declarations of regimes of exception, and the language of rights which this type of court manages. We aim to ascertain whether constitutional courts have been able to offer protection for human rights in recent years and what political or institutional factors can help or hinder this process. This chapter is divided into four main sections: first, we offer a revision of international norms and recommendations on the protection of human rights during "regimes of exception"; second, we offer evidence from the Bolivian Constitutional Tribunal; third, we consider the case of Ecuador's Constitutional Court; and fourth, we evaluate the role of Peru's Constitutional Tribunal. Finally, we offer a reply to the research question and take into account what light this chapter can shed on the issue of the globalization of human rights as it is presented in this volume.

THE GLOBALIZATION OF LAW AND PROTECTION OF HUMAN RIGHTS UNDER REGIMES OF EXCEPTION

The issue of human rights protection during regimes of exception has been analyzed in depth by several Latin American scholars (García-Sayán, 1989;

Zovatto, 1990; Delfino, 2000; and Fix-Zamudio, 2004). In the following section we summarize the key precepts and instruments defined at both the international and regional levels, in order to offer an outline of the existing normative framework regarding the use of regimes of exception both globally and regionally. It is worth noting that we consider that the rights framework when dealing with regimes of exception to deal with internal affairs falls under international human rights law rather than international humanitarian law, given that in the region in question they have been used to deal with "states of internal tension and disturbance" (see Despouy, 1997).

At the International Level

The primary reference point for the protection of human rights during regimes of exception at the international level is the International Covenant on Civil and Political Rights (ICCPR), in its Article 4. According to this article, when there is an emergency that "threatens the life of the nation," states parties to the Covenant may derogate certain obligations, provided that the derogation is declared publicly, communicated to the United Nations, is not discriminatory, and respects other obligations under international law. Furthermore, the article establishes obligations which are not subject to derogation: the right to life (Article 6); freedom from torture or cruel, inhuman, or degrading treatment or punishment (Article 7); freedom from slavery or servitude (Article 8); freedom from imprisonment on the grounds of inability to fulfill a contractual obligation (Article 11); freedom from being found guilty of an offense which did not constitute a criminal offense at the time it was committed (Article 15); right to recognition as a person before the law (Article 16); and right to freedom of thought, conscience, and religion (Article 18). Finally, it is worth mentioning that in 2001, the General Comment No. 29 on States of Emergency (Article 4)[4] stipulated further exigencies for states beyond Article 4 of the Covenant: All persons deprived of their liberty should be treated with humanity and respect for the dignity of the human person; prohibitions against taking hostages, abductions, or unlawful detention should remain in place; the protection of the rights of minorities cannot be derogated; and forced displacement can never be permitted.

The United Nations became interested in the issue of situations known as states of siege or states of emergency in 1977, via the Sub-Commission on Prevention of Discrimination and Protection of Minorities, which requested that the Economic and Social Council carry out a detailed analysis of the issue. After the report by Questiaux,[5] several guidelines on the use of regimes of exception have been developed at the international level: the Siracusa Principles, the Paris Minimum Standards, and Despouy's principles. Below we shall outline the contributions of all of them.

In 1984, an international conference took place on the limitation and derogation of provisions of the International Covenant on Civil and Political

Rights, at Siracusa in Italy, resulting in the adoption of a series of principles entitled "The Siracusa principles on the limitation and derogation provisions in the International Covenant on Civil and Political Rights."[6] The principles offer interpretations of key terms such as *national security, public safety,* and the *exigencies of the situation* and also highlight the importance of notifying the Secretary General of the United Nations. In terms of the derogation of certain rights, it stipulates that "All limitation clauses shall be interpreted strictly and in favour of the rights at issue" (A.3) and goes on to stress protection for nonderogable rights and include limits on those that may be derogated according to the Covenant. In order to protect rights, the principles establish that ordinary courts should maintain their jurisdiction, to determine whether a nonderogable right has been violated (D.60).

For its part, in 1984 the International Law Association established the "Paris Minimum Standards of Human Rights Norms in a State of Emergency." In terms of human rights protection, it offers more detail on the nonderogable rights established in Article 4 of the Covenant. Furthermore, it makes explicit the need to respect guarantees such as *habeas corpus,* in order to determine the need to suspend certain rights as well as protect due process. It also highlights the role of the Legislative Branch in offering a check on executive power during emergency situations and the importance of a time limit and restoration of all rights once the emergency period is over. It also stresses the possibility of judicial oversight, the need for the judicial branch to be independent, and prohibits the use of states of emergency to remove judges or restructure the justice system.

The next important development at the international level for the protection of human rights under regimes of exception was the extensive work carried out on regimes of exception by the UN Special Rapporteur, Leandro Despouy.[7] He was appointed as Special Rapporteur on the question of States of Emergency in 1985 and published a series of reports on states that had proclaimed, extended, or terminated a state of emergency since he took on the role.[8] As a result of his work on the issue, Despouy (1997) drew up a set of principles that have become a key reference point for the protection of human rights and which summarize the other developments in international law and jurisprudence to date, including cases from Europe and Latin America. The principles are as follows: legality (a legal basis for the declaration); proclamation (to the population affected); notification (to the international community); a time limit, an exceptional threat (to the life of a nation); proportionality (of the measures to the situation); nondiscrimination; and compatibility, concordance, and complementarity of the various norms of international law (with the precedence of norms most favorable to human rights). In the same report, Despouy highlights the need for an independent judiciary and legislature which can oversee the constitutionality and compatibility of the declaration and the measures involved.

At the Regional Level

The main reference point for the protection of human rights under regimes of exception at the regional level is the American Convention on Human Rights (ACHR) adopted in San José, Costa Rica, on 22 November 1969. In its Chapter 4, entitled "Suspension of Guarantees, Interpretation and Application," the ACHR establishes the possibility of a state derogating from its obligations under the Convention, provided that there is a time limit according to the "exigencies of the situation," the measures are compatible with international law, and that there is no discrimination of certain groups as a result (Article 27.1). Furthermore, it requires that these derogations are declared to the Secretary General of the Organization of American States (Article 27.3) and that the interpretation of the restrictions should be limited to what is permitted in international law (Article 29). Undoubtedly, Articles 27–30 are entirely in keeping with Despouy's principles. In terms of the protection of human rights specifically, Article 27 establishes various rights that can never be derogated: Article 3 (Right to a Juridical Personality), Article 4 (Right to Life), Article 5 (Right to Humane Treatment), Article 6 (Freedom from Slavery), Article 9 (Freedom from Ex Post Facto Laws), Article 12 (Freedom of Conscience and Religion), Article 17 (Rights of the Family), Article 18 (Right to a Name), Article 19 (Rights of the Child), Article 20 (Right to a Nationality), and Article 23 (Right to Participate in Government), or of the judicial guarantees essential for the protection of such rights. Consequently, the American Convention offers greater protection for human rights in emergency situations than does the ICCPR.

In 1975, the First Latin American Congress on Constitutional Law—which was held in Mexico—analyzed the situation of regimes of exception, at a time when various countries were living under military dictatorships and concluded that for national courts to carry out their role in overseeing the constitutionality of these measures, these measures should be truly *exceptional* (Fix-Zamudio, 2004). Then, during the 1980s, at the start of the third wave of democratization, there was considerable concern regarding the use of regimes of exception in Latin America. For example, in 1985 the Instituto Interamericano de Derechos Humanos organized a conference on "states of emergency" in the Southern Cone (Despouy, 1997) and in 1986 the Comisión Andina de Juristas organized a conference on "states of emergency" in the Andean Region (García-Sayán, 1987).

The conference on the Andean Region gave rise to a series of observations directed to the Secretary General of the United Nations, including the following: the fact that there are no clear and effective mechanisms for the judicial and legislative powers to offer effective oversight; that the use of states of exception respond to temporary political concerns rather than specific threats to the life of the nation; the problem of military intervention via these mechanisms; the use of military tribunals to judge civilians;

and the systematic lack of proclamations of emergency situations by states to the United Nations (García-Sayán, 1989: 117–121). Consequently, the recommendations revolve around a need for increasing control of these mechanisms, including a greater role for the judicial branch, a limited interpretation of situations that can give rise to declarations of regimes of exception, limits on the duration of the declarations, and monitoring on the part of the UN's Human Rights Commission, the Inter-American Commission of Human Rights, and the Inter-American Court of Human Rights (García-Sayán, 1989: 121–124).

In this sense, it is worth highlighting the significance of two consultative opinions of the Inter-American Court of Human Rights in the 1980s, which have also served as a reference point at both the national and international levels. The first, of January 1987, is in relation to *habeas corpus*[9] under regimes of exception, in answer to a petition from the Inter-American Commission of Human Rights, given a widespread practice in suspending this guarantee on the part of states party to the ACHR (OC-8/87). Considering experiences of massive illegal detentions in the Americas in the decades prior to the decision, the Court determines that this guarantee cannot be suspended and that any national legislation that permits the executive to do this in emergency situations is implicitly incompatible with the Convention.

The second recommendation, of October 1987, is in relation to judicial guarantees in general and answers a query from the government of Uruguay on exactly which judicial guarantees cannot be suspended (OC-9/87). The Court finds that any guarantee which can guarantee the respect for the rights and liberties whose suspension is not authorized by the Convention cannot be suspended, including—but not limited to—*habeas corpus* and *amparo*. Once again, the Court refers to massive human rights abuses in the past in many countries in Latin America as a reason for offering further protection in emergency situations.

While the Inter-American Commission has addressed several instances of potential human rights violations during states of emergency, in various reports[10] and the Inter-American Court has dictated several sentences related to the implementation of states of emergency,[11] there is currently no systematic monitoring of declarations of regimes of exception at the regional level, as is the case at the international level. Nevertheless, the fact that the regional norms not only incorporate international law but build on them reflects a profound awareness of how toxic these measures can be, based on first-hand experiences in the region's recent past.

Now that the international and regional framework on human rights protection in emergency situations has been outlined, we shall consider how the Constitutional Tribunals in three Latin American countries—Bolivia, Ecuador, and Peru—have served to protect civil rights during regimes of exception, in the context of the globalization of law.

BOLIVIA

The use of regimes of exception in recent history in Bolivia is extensive and well documented, both under military regimes in the 1960s and 1970s (Loveman, 1993) and during the transition to democracy (Alenda, 2003). There are two regimes of exception that have been in place in Bolivia since its transition to democracy (that took place with several interruptions between 1978 and 1982): the "state of siege" in the Constitution of 1967 and the "state of exception" in the Constitution of 2009. Below we offer a very brief analysis of these two mechanisms, focusing on their implications for human rights and the possibility of oversight by the judicial or legislative branches.[12]

The "state of siege" contemplated in the Constitution of 1967 established the possibility of increasing the reserves of members of the Armed Forces (112.1) and the suspension of human rights and guarantees (112.3). Nevertheless, it safeguards the guarantee of *habeas corpus* and establishes that anyone carrying out orders that violate guarantees may be tried at any time (112.5). While there is no specific role assigned to the Constitutional Tribunal, the Congress has a key role in overseeing the action of the executive (113) and even has the power to put a stop to a "state of siege" that has already started (111.2). Finally, a clear time limit of 90 days is also stipulated. Despite the fact that the key judicial guarantee of *habeas corpus* is maintained, civil servants can be tried, and a time limit is included, since the "state of siege" does not stipulate which rights obligations *cannot* be derogated, it is not in keeping with an important element of the international and regional legal framework.

The "state of exception" established in Articles 137–140 of the Constitution of 2009 brings regimes of exception in Bolivia further in line with the international and legal framework. In the very first article, it establishes that guarantees cannot be restricted and that certain rights can never be derogated, including all fundamental rights, the right to due process, the right to information, and the rights of people deprived of their freedom. Nevertheless, there is no mention of a potential time limit of a "state of exception," something which is at odds with international and regional principles on regimes of exception. As was the case with the "state of siege," the power to oversee the declaration rests firmly with the legislative branch and whoever violates rights enshrined in the Constitution can be tried at any time (Article 139)—hence there is no move towards a greater role for the judicial branch in this most recent regime of exception.

Between 2000 and 2010, two "states of siege" were declared in Bolivia, both of which attracted considerable media attention and public debate. Although—as we have seen—the role of the judicial branch in overseeing the use of regimes of exception is not clear in the normative framework, in 2000 an important case was presented before the Superior Court of La Paz. Below we describe the act, the sentence, and the implications of this case for human rights protection during declarations of regimes of exception in Bolivia.

Habeas Corpus and the Constitutional Tribunal, 2000

On 8 April 2000, President Gonzalo Sánchez de Lozada declared a "state of siege" throughout Bolivia via the DS25730. The declaration was a response to the climax of the so-called Guerra del Agua, an intense social conflict which began in Cochabamba and quickly spread throughout Bolivia, including La Paz (see Romero 2005; Assies and Salman 2003). The episode was debated extensively by human rights defenders, the press, and even in Congress.[13] One particular incident that was highly controversial was the detention of several protest leaders the *night before* the official declaration of the state of siege, which led to the Human Rights Ombudsman giving notice of a *habeas corpus* appeal to the Superior Court of Justice of La Paz.[14]

The notice was given just two days after the declaration of the state of siege, on 10 April. The Defensora del Pueblo Ana María Romero de Campero acted on behalf of 4 citizens detained in La Paz, 18 citizens detained in Cochabamba, and 23 citizens detained in Patacamaya. Given that no official warrant for arrest had been ordered and the detained had not been brought before a judge with 48 hours of their detention, the notice claims that the arrests were illegal and unconstitutional. In order to back up the claim, there is a reference to Article 7 of the ACHR, the consultative opinion of 30 January 1987 of the Inter-American Court of Human Rights, as well as Article 9 of the ICCPR, highlighting the importance of the international and regional framework in this case.

The Superior Court of La Paz resolved in favor of the Defensora del Pueblo and the detained were duly brought before a judge in order to determine the legality of their arrest. A month later, the Constitutional Tribunal confirmed the constitutionality of the decision,[15] again referring to the ACHR as well as national legislation in order to support the need to protect the judicial guarantee of *habeas corpus* during the declaration of a "state of siege."

This case represented a major step forward for the protection of human rights under "states of siege," a mechanism that is synonymous with the worst type of state repression in Bolivia (see Romero 2005). Three elements are particularly striking: the degree of public concern over the use of this mechanism to repress a protest with widespread popular support; the organized, well-referenced, and swift defense by the national human rights ombudsman; and the use of international and regional norms for support in the notice itself. While the victory in this case was specific to those detained in the name of this measure, it set an important precedent at the symbolic and normative levels in Bolivia.

ECUADOR

The use of regimes of exception in recent history in Ecuador has also been extensive and well documented (Loveman, 1993; Dávalos Muirragui, 2008).

Between 2000 and 2010, two regimes of exception that offered the possibility for military intervention and the suspension of rights were contemplated in Ecuadorian constitutionalism: the "state of emergency" of 1998 and the "state of exception" of 2008. Below we offer a very brief analysis of these two mechanisms, focusing on their implications for human rights and the possibility of oversight by the judicial or legislative branches.

The "state of emergency" established in Articles 180–182 of the Constitution of 1998 in many respects is in keeping with international and regional norms on human rights protection during regimes of exception. It is important to note that none of the rights it establishes as subject to derogations are at odds with the standards set at the international and regional levels[16] (Article 181.5), a clear time limit of 60 days is established (182), and the Congress can revoke the declaration at any time (Article 182). However, there are several causes for concern: first, it does not explicitly confirm respect for guarantees under a "state of emergency"; second, it does not refer to any type of judicial review or responsibilities on the part of civil servants; and finally, via Article 181.4 it offers the military extensive powers, even establishing the possibility of military jurisdiction over civilians during "states of emergency" (referring to the National Security Act of 1979, Article 147).

In 2007 and 2008, a Constituent Assembly drew up a new constitution, amidst a degree of debate on regimes of exception, in the context of a publicly criticized "state of emergency" declared in the town of Dayuma, in the province of Orellana.[17] The result of these debates was the "state of exception" mechanism, included in Articles 164–166. This regime of exception appears to be much more in keeping with the tenets of international and regional human rights norms: as in the Constitution of 1998, the rights it establishes as subject to derogation are permitted at both the international and regional levels[18] (Article 165). It also refers to several of Despouy's principles, including legality, a time limit, proportionality, and concordance with international treaties and introduces other principles including necessity, territoriality, and reasonability.[19] Along with the Congress, the Constitutional Tribunal is given an explicit role to check the constitutionality of the decrees (Article 166), and the national security law referenced no longer establishes military jurisdiction over civilians (Article 165). Consequently, the "state of exception" established by the Constitution of 2008 appears to fulfill many of the requirements of regimes of exception established at the international and regional level.

Between 2000 and 2010, a total of 110 decrees emitted by Ecuadorian presidents declaring a "state of emergency" or "state of exception" have been identified.[20] Despite the fact that most of these decrees were used to offer an administrative solution to different types of crises, a total of 18 declarations during this period employed the use of force to quell episodes of social unrest, and therefore correspond to the classic use of regimes of exception (data taken from Wright 2012). In the case of Ecuador, the emblematic case of the

Constitutional Tribunal's role in protecting human rights during regimes of exception was a resolution on military jurisdiction in 2008 which is analyzed in depth below.

Military Jurisdiction and the Constitutional Tribunal, 2008

As with the state of siege in Bolivia in 2000, it was a specific declaration of a state of emergency that propelled several human rights defenders to make an appeal to the Constitutional Tribunal.[21] In the face of protests over social and environmental rights in the region of Sucumbíos and Orellana, the president dictated DS1204 to declare a state of emergency, which he altered by DS1214 in order to apply different elements of the Law of National Security of 1979. In this context, an observer was detained, the resolution to grant *habeas corpus* was never fulfilled, and the observer was tried by a military authority. The plea notes that this is not an isolated case but rather symptomatic of the kind of abuses that occur under states of emergency.

The human rights defenders sought to declare several articles of the Law of National Security (145 and 147) that permitted military authorities to judge infractions unconstitutional, rather than simply redressing the specific wrongs that had occurred—as was the case in Bolivia. In order to support their arguments, the human rights defenders refer to due process, established in Article 8.1 of the Inter-American Convention on Human Rights as well as the national Constitution.

The sentence of the Constitutional Tribunal of 10 June 2008 accepted the demand for unconstitutionality, given Article 187 of the Constitution that establishes that only members of the Armed Forces who commit an infraction related to their responsibilities as military personnel may be judged by military authorities. Furthermore, the sentence refers to the recommendation made by the Inter-American Commission on Human Rights in its Annual Reports of 1996, 1997, and 1998 on the limitations of military jurisdiction, which state that military personnel who commit an infraction in ordinary circumstances and civilians who commit infractions should always be subject to normal jurisdiction. Furthermore, the Annual Reports of 1999 and 2005 single out the use of military tribunals to judge civilians in Ecuador specifically, something that sentence also highlights. Summing up, the Tribunal rules in favor of the unconstitutionality of the articles of the law and bases its decisions on its duties under the national Constitution as well as under the ACHR.

Without a doubt, the ruling of the Constitutional Tribunal constituted an important change in the normative framework surrounding states of emergency in Ecuador. Again, there was a confluence of three factors that were present in the case from Bolivia analyzed above: specific wrongs in the context of a publicly debated declaration of a regime of exception; a well-prepared defense by human rights defenders; and extensive references to international law by the plaintiffs and the Constitutional Tribunal. The key difference is the effect of the Court's decision: in this instance it changed a key aspect of the normative framework rather than establishing responsibilities in a specific case.

PERU

Regimes of exception have been used widely in Peru by both military and democratic regimes (Loveman, 1993; Power Manchego-Muñoz, 1989). The relevant normative framework in the period between 2000 and 2010 is the Constitution of 1993, which establishes in its Article 137: two regimes of exception the "state of emergency" and the "state of siege," which will be outlined briefly below.

The "state of emergency"—for situations of internal disorder—permits the suspension of several rights, including personal liberty and security, the inviolability of the home, freedom of assembly, and freedom of movement. Nothing is said of respect for guarantees,[22] but forced exile is forbidden. Likewise, it establishes a fixed time limit of 60 days, in keeping with international and regional guidelines. However, no role is established either for the Congress or the Judicial Power in overseeing the measures used, and the Armed Forces are given *carte blanche* to control internal order, if the president so chooses. Given these shortcomings, the "state of emergency" clause is extremely vague[23] and ill at ease with international and regional norms.

The "state of siege" mechanism—for international or civil conflict—on the other hand is even less specific. It establishes a time limit of 45 days and some sort of oversight by the legislative branch, mainly for approving a time extension. In terms of rights, the clause states that the decree will establish which rights can be restricted, without stating what rights can or cannot be limited. The state of siege mechanism is even more vague than the "state of emergency" and could lead to a wide range of human rights abuses, in the wrong hands.

Fortunately, a "state of siege" has never been declared in Peru, but ample use has been made of the "state of emergency" mechanism. Throughout the 1980s and 1990s, large parts of the territory were under military command in the context of the fight against the *Sendero Luminoso* guerrilla.[24] The tendency to use a "Classic Repressive" type of regime of exception has clearly continued into the 21st century; of 115 declarations of "states of emergency" between 2000 and 2010, 32 suspended human rights or employed military force in the face of internal disorder, in many cases in areas still linked to the activity of the *Sendero Luminoso* group (Wright, 2012). In the case of Peru, the role of the courts over the question of military jurisdiction over civilians during "states of emergency" shifted between 2000 and 2010.

Military Jurisdiction and the Constitutional Tribunal, 2004

As with the cases in Bolivia and Ecuador outlined above, it was a particularly scandalous declaration of a regime of exception that led to a group of human rights defenders—from the Defensoría del Pueblo or national human rights ombudsman—to resort to the Constitutional Tribunal in an attempt to protect human rights in the context of regimes of exception. In this case, in the face of mass protests against a proposed Free Trade Agreement with the United States, President Alejandro Toledo emitted the DS-55–2003-PCM declaring a "state of emergency" throughout the nation. As a result of this case, the Defensoría del Pueblo established a set of guidelines for its intervention during "states of emergency" and outlined how it could oversee human rights violations and potential abuses of power.

In point 4 of these guidelines, the Defensoría del Pueblo declares that ordinary justice still operates in areas declared in emergency and therefore homicides, kidnapping, torture, or forced disappearances fall under the competence of the ordinary justice system. In order to support this statement, the guidelines refer to the recommendations of the Inter-American Court of Human Rights. Consequently, the Defensoría prepared an act of unconstitutionality against various clauses of the Law No. 24150, which regulated the role of the military in emergency zones. Interestingly, both the act itself and the sentence of the Constitutional Tribunal refer to the Peruvian Constitution rather than regional or international norms, reflecting a prominence of national norms in this case. Furthermore, the reasoning in both cases revolves around the role of the military in domestic affairs rather than the protection of human rights as such, particularly Article 10 of the aforementioned law on the question of military jurisdiction.

In any case, the Tribunal found in favor of the Defensoría del Pueblo and declared Article 10 unconstitutional, on the grounds that it applies military jurisdiction on the basis of being in active service in an emergency zone rather than on the nature of the infraction committed. The ruling constituted an important step forward for the protection of the right to due process in the context of states of emergency, particularly bearing in mind the catalogue of abuses carried out via this mechanism in the fight against *Sendero Luminoso* in the 1980s and 1990s (Comisión de la Verdad y Reconciliación (CVR) 2003). Nevertheless, it is worth highlighting that the victory was short-lived; the Law No. 29166 of 2007 reintroduced an ample understanding of military jurisdiction under states of emergency, completely ignoring the ruling of the Constitutional Tribunal in 2004 (Jaskoski, 2011: 13).

CONCLUSIONS

The aim of this chapter has been to determine whether constitutional courts have been able to use international and regional norms to offer a degree of protection for human rights under regimes of exception, mechanisms that are synonymous with the restriction of civil liberties and military intervention in Latin America. Having outlined the relevant international, regional, and domestic normative framework on the issue, we analyzed exemplary cases from three countries where regimes of exception have been declared repeatedly: Bolivia, Ecuador, and Peru.

All three cases have several features in common: a highly contentious and controversial declaration of a regime of exception immediately preceding the case; concern over the lack of due process for those detained in the context of a regime of exception; the presentation of a lawsuit by highly organized human rights defenders; references to *regional* human rights norms; a favorable sentence by the Constitutional Tribunal; and a highly symbolic victory for the protection of civil rights under regimes of exception. These cases demonstrate that Constitutional Courts can have an important role in the safeguarding of human rights, given the continuing use of a measure that continues to jeopardize them at regular intervals in the region.

In this context, could the highest level of the judicial branch constitute an important counterweight for the executive branch when designing and enacting emergency norms in Latin America? Despite the positive evidence offered here, it is wise to be cautious regarding the long-term implications. First, the victories won may prove short-lived, given executive and military persistence, as was the case with the law on military jurisdiction in Peru. Second, at the normative level the role of the judicial branch in overseeing the use of regimes of exception is generally undefined, with the legislative branch—in the best cases—taking on this role. While the Ecuadorian Constitution of 2008 stipulates that the Constitutional Tribunal must be notified of every declaration of a "state of exception," as of 2010 no declarations had been sentenced as unconstitutional.[25] Rather, the Constitutional Tribunal's repeated declarations of the "constitutionality" of the declarations suggest that the Court is more interested in justifying rather than challenging the regimes of exception declared by the president.

Thus, in keeping with the framework outlined in the introduction, this chapter shows that the globalization of law is a multifaceted process, and that institutions do make a difference in determining its impact on human rights. In Latin America, some positive challenges to regimes of exception signal the potential for strengthening the rule of law, but the other positive elements of the political process have not yet caught up to this promise. Shifts in the self-determination of the Latin American state and the empowerment of citizens will be needed to fully tame the legalization of repression through states of emergency.

NOTES

1. We use the term *regime of exception* as an inclusive term of those legal mechanisms that offer previously contemplated, special powers in emergency situations—given the use of different terms at the national legal level—including "state of siege," "state of emergency," "state of exception," "state of alarm," and so on.

2. For example, in Chile a regime of exception was in place for over 12 years (García-Sayán, 1989).
3. As Despouy (1997) explains, regimes of exception may also pose a secondary threat to social and economic rights. However, in the first instance it is civil and political rights that suffer from the use of this type of mechanism.
4. CCPR/C/21/Rev.1/Add.11.
5. E/CN.4/Sub.2/1982/15.
6. E/CN.4/1984/4.
7. Nonetheless, it is worth mentioning the Johannesburg Principles of 1995, which regulate the restriction of freedom of information under states of emergency.
8. E/CN.4/Sub.2/1993/23, E/CN.4/Sub.2/1994/23, E/CN.4/Sub.2/1995/20, E/CN.4/Sub.2/1996/19, E/CN.4/1998/41/Add.1, E/CN.4/Sub.2/1999/31, E/CN.4/Sub.2/2001/6, E/CN.4/Sub.2/2001/6/Corr.1, E/CN.4/Sub.2/2003/39, E/CN.4/Sub.2/2005/6.
9. *Habeas corpus* offers protection for personal or physical liberty against arbitrary detention, by taking the detained before a judge so that he or she can decide upon the legality of the detention.
10. For instance Report 48/00 Case 11.166 Walter Humberto Vásquez Vejarano, Peru; Informe de País—Nicaragua 1978; Informe Anual 1980–1981; Informe de País—Chile 1985; and Capítulo 4—Ecuador. Reports available at www.cidh.oas.org.
11. See Sentence of 4 July 2007 Caso *Zambrano Vélez y otros v Ecuador*.
12. It is worth noting that a very different framework for regimes of exception was established under Law No. 2140, with the figures of "emergency" and "disaster." Nevertheless, as the two figures do not contemplate explicitly the use of military force or the suspension of human rights, they are not of relevance for this study. For an in-depth legal and political analysis of these mechanisms see Wright (2012).
13. This was confirmed in personal interviews with Ana María Romero in La Paz and Kathia Saucedo in Sucre, April 2007.
14. For an in-depth account of this episode and its importance for the protection of human rights in Bolivia, see Romero (2005).
15. Constitutional Sentence No. 439/2000.
16. Freedom of opinion (Article 23.9); inviolability of the home (Article 23.12); inviolability of correspondence (Article 23.13); freedom of movement (Article 23.14); freedom of association (Article 23.19).
17. Personal interview with David Cordero, Quito, Ecuador, July 2010.
18. The right to the inviolability of the home, the inviolability of personal correspondence, freedom of movement, freedom of association and reunion, and freedom of information.
19. For several Ecuadorian analysts, the predominance of "principles" creates a degree of ambiguity in the new constitutional framework. Personal interview with Fabián Corral, Quito, Ecuador, July 2010.
20. According to Wright (2012) the total may be more, given the problems in accessing the decrees in the Official Registers.
21. Acción de Inconstitucionalidad Presentada por Luis Ángel Saavedra et al., caso 42–2007-TC.
22. There was an intense debate on the issue of the suspension of *habeas corpus* and international legal norms in the 1980s; see García-Sayán (1989).
23. Personal interview with Carlos Rivera Paz, Lima, Peru, April 2007.
24. See Comisión de la Verdad y Reconciliación (CVR) (2003).
25. Personal interview with David Cordero, Quito, Ecuador, July 2010.

REFERENCES

Aguilar Rivera, José Antonio. (1996). "El manto liberal: emergencias y constitutciones." *Política y Gobierno* 3(2): 327–362.

Alenda, Stéphanie. (2003). "Bolivia: la erosión del pacto democrático." *Revista Fuerzas Armadas y Sociedad* 18(1–2): 3–22.

Assies, Willem, and Salman, Ton. (2003). *Crisis in Bolivia: The Elections of 2002 and Their Aftermath.* London: Institute of Latin American Studies.

Comisión de la Verdad y Reconciliación (CVR). (2003). "Cronología 1978–2000." *Informe Final de la Comisión de la Verdad y Reconciliación.* www.cverdad.org.pe

Dávalos Muirragui, María Daniela. (2008). "Estados de excepción: ¿Mal necesario o herramienta mal utilizada? Una mirada desde el constitucionalismo contemporáneo." In Ramiro Ávila Santamaría (Ed.), *Neoconstitucionalismo y Sociedad,* 123–162. Quito, Ecuador: Flacso.

Delfino, María de los Ángeles. (2000). "El desarrollo de los estados de excepción en las Constituciones en América Latina." In Eduardo García de Enterría Martínez-Carande (Eds.), *Constitutción y constitucionalismo hoy. Cincuentenario del Derecho constitucional comparado de Manuel García Pelayo,* 507–532. Caracas, Venezuela: Fundación Manuel García Pelayo.

Despouy, Leandro. (1997). *Report by the UN Special Rapporteur, Mr Leandro Despouy, on the Question of Human Rights and States of Emergency.* United Nations Document No. E/CN.4/Sub.2/1997/19.

Fix-Zamudio, Héctor. (2004). "Los estados de excepción y la defensa de la constitución." *Boletín Mexicano de Derecho Comparado* 37(111): 801–860.

García-Sayán, Diego (Ed.). (1987). *Estados de emergencia en la región andina.* Lima, Peru: Comisión Andina de Juristas.

García-Sayán, Diego. (1989). *Hábeas Corpus y Estados de Emergencia.* Lima, Peru: Comisión Andina de Juristas/Fundación Friedrich Naumann.

Hagopian, Frances. (2005). "Conclusions: Government Performance, Political Representation and Public Perceptions of Contemporary Democracy in Latin America." In Frances Hagopian and Scott P. Mainwaring (Eds.), *The Third Wave of Democratization in Latin America: Advances and Setbacks,* 319–362. New York: Cambridge University Press.

Iturralde, Manuel. (2003). "Guerra y Derecho en Colombia: el decisionismo político y los estados de excepción como respuesta a la crisis de la democracia." *Revista de Estudios Sociales no. 15*: 29–46.

Jaskoski, Maiah. (2011). "Civilian Control of the Armed Forces in Democratic Latin America: Military Prerogatives, Contestation and Mission Performance in Peru." *Armed Forces and Society* 38(1): 70–91.

Karl, Terry Lynn. (1996). "Dilemmas of Democratizaton in Latin America." In Roderic Ai Camp (Ed.), *Democracy in Latin America: Patterns and Cycles.* Wilmington, DE: Scholarly Resources.

Loveman, Brian. (1993). *The Constitution of Tyranny: Regimes of Exception in Spanish America.* Pittsburgh: University of Pittsburgh.

Loveman, Brian, and Davies, Thomas M. (1997). *The Politics of Antipolitics: The Military in Latin America.* Pittsburgh: University of Pittsburgh.

Power Manchego-Muñoz, Jorge. (1989). "La constitución peruana de 1970: los estados de excepción." PhD diss., University of Valencia, Spain.

Romero, Ana María. (2005). "El Defensor del Pueblo como puente entre la sociedad y el Estado." In Domingo de Pilar (Ed.), *Bolivia: Fin de un ciclo y nuevas perspectivas políticas (1993–2003),* 119–130. Barcelona: Edicions Bellaterra.

Wright, Claire. (2012). "¿De la seguridad nacional a la gestión de riesgos? El uso político de los regímenes de excepción en Bolivia, Ecuador y Perú." PhD diss., University of Salamanca, Spain.

Zovatto, Daniel. (1990). *Los Estados de Excepción y los Derechos Humanos en América Latina*. Caracas/San José: Instituto Interamericano de Derechos Humanos/Editorial Jurídica Venezolana.

9   Barriers to Rights in the Israeli-Palestinian Conflict

Gershon Shafir

How much has the globalization of legal norms contributed to the fulfillment of human rights in the "hard case" of Israel-Palestine? From the legal
perspective, a complicating circumstance that makes the relevance and application of human rights to the conflict problematic is that the Palestinians
of the Gaza Strip and the West Bank are not Israeli citizens but live under military occupation. As a consequence, the controlling international legal framework is that of international humanitarian law (IHL), sometimes referred to
as the law of international armed conflict. The nature of the difficulty is not
the somewhat inchoate nature of humanitarian responsibilities; in fact the
law of belligerent occupation has a long history and is the most codified part
of humanitarianism. From the legal perspective, the case is hard precisely
because of the co-existence of—and, indeed, inherent conflict between—two
frameworks of international law: human rights and humanitarian law. This
legal duality is due to the unsolved political question of sovereignty in the
Occupied Palestinian Territories (OPT). From the practical perspective, the
co-existence of humanitarian law and human rights leaves a great deal of
wiggle room to the Israeli authorities, and serves as an obstacle to the spread
of human rights norms—and international jurisprudence in general.

A further complication is Israel's mixed, in fact contradictory, attitude to
its obligations to the occupied Palestinian residents under IHL. Under the
Hague Regulation of 1907 and the 1949 Fourth Geneva Convention relative to the Protection of Civilian Persons in Times of War, international organizations, such as the UN, the International Committee of the Red Cross
(ICRC), and the International Court of Justice to name a few, all view Israel
as a belligerent occupier of the part of Palestine it conquered in the June
1967 War. The Israeli legal system recognizes the state's obligations under
IHL, but the legal and executive branches of the state sometimes accept
them and at other times ignore them or altogether reject their applicability.

The Supreme Court, as a court of first instance, that is, a High Court of
Justice (HCJ), decided in 1972 that it will review petitions from the OPT,
and over the years has come to adjudicate them on the basis of Israeli administrative law, IHL, and on occasion international human rights law. The
High Court holds that the Fourth Geneva Convention is the controlling legal

authority in the OPT and has relied extensively on its provisions in adjudicating relevant cases. It holds that the Palestinian residents of the OPT are protected persons under the Convention, while the Israeli settlers are not. In fact, as Orna Ben-Naftali points out, the HCJ's continuous involvement makes this "the most legalized occupation in world history" (Ben-Naftali, 2011: 130).

At the same time, the Israeli government asserts that the Fourth Geneva Convention is inapplicable to the OPT because they are not occupied. Occupation, in this view, means the displacement of a previous sovereign whereas both Egypt and Jordan were themselves occupiers and cannot be construed as High Contracting Parties to the Convention in regard to Gaza and the West Bank, respectively. A fundamental premise of this approach was that Palestinians, a stateless people, cannot be a party to the Geneva Conventions. Further, the government holds—in contradiction to international legal convention—that the Convention is not binding on Israel, since it is conventional rather than a customary international law (at least in part) and since the Knesset has not domesticated it, it cannot supersede domestic law. At the same time, the government agreed to abide by what it views as the Convention's "humanitarian provisions," notwithstanding the ICRC's view that all of the provisions are humanitarian, and without specifying which provisions it considers to fall under the humanitarian category (Hajjar, 2005: 53–56; Hajjar, 2006: 25–27).

Similarly, there is a considerable gap between the government and the High Court's views on the applicability of international human rights conventions to the Occupied Territories. Israel is a signatory to major human rights conventions; in 1991, in one energetic bout when Dan Meridor (from the liberal wing of Likud) served as its Minister of Justice, it ratified the Covenant on Economic, Social and Cultural Rights; the Covenant on Civil and Political Rights; the Convention on the Elimination of All Forms of Discrimination Against Women; the Convention on the Rights of Children; the Convention Against Torture, and Other Forms of Cruel, Inhuman or Degrading Treatment or Punishment. However, in the absence of their domestication by the Knesset, Israel has not acceded to any of them (http://www1.umn.edu/humanrts/research/ratification-israel.html). As a signatory to such treaties, Israel is obligated to submit periodic reports to the international committees established under these conventions and, in fact, has done so. Israel submits such reports, for example, on its enforcement of the provisions of the Convention on the Rights of Children and the Convention on Torture. At the same time,

> Israel denies that the International Covenant on Civil and Political Rights and the International Covenant on Economic, Social and Cultural Rights, both of which it has signed, are applicable to the occupied Palestinian territory. It asserts that humanitarian law is the protection granted in a conflict situation such as the one in the West Bank and Gaza Strip, whereas human rights treaties were intended for the protection of citizens

from their own Government in times of peace. (Summary Legal Position of the Government of Israel, par. 4. http://www.icj-cij.org/docket/files/131/1497.pdf)

Eyal Benvenisti, a prominent Israeli scholar of international humanitarian law, takes the opposite view. He concluded that, even if international human rights conventions must be incorporated through domestic legislation to take effect within Israel, the mere ratification of such treaties by the government requires them to be implemented in the Occupied Territories (Benvenisti: 35).

The High Court, in contrast to the government, recognizes the applicability of the international human rights conventions in the OPT and has repeatedly sought to balance human rights conventions with humanitarian law, as well as the provisions of the IHL with one another. Even so, in cases of divergence between IHL and human rights norms and treaties, the HCJ held that "the extent of permitted restrictions on human rights is determined ... by humanitarian law contained in the law concerning armed conflict" (HCJ 7015/02, *Adjuri v the Commander of the IDF Forces in the West Bank*, in *Judgments*, Vol. 1, par. 16, p. 157). Human rights are limited in yet another way: Even when part of common and not conventional law, according to the HCJ, conflicts with provisions of a Knesset law, the latter prevails (HCJ 1661/05, Regional Council, *Coast of Gaza v. Knesset of Israel*).

While the Israeli government has rejected the applicability of either IHL or human rights conventions to the OPT, so far it has not tried to overturn or bypass HCJ rulings that rely on them. It seems that over the years, Israeli governments have been willing to live with the High Court's judicial interpretation in regard to the OPT, since the HCJ has never ruled on the legality of the most crucial Israeli policies such as settlement in the OPT (although after many court rulings there are attempts on the part of some members of the Knesset to propose laws that would bypass the HCJ). The military, on its part, has dawdled and taken its time to implement court resolutions, but has ultimately complied with them.

In this chapter I compare two human rights campaigns waged through the Israeli High Court of Justice by Israeli and Palestinian advocacy groups: against the use of torture in the 1990s and the building of a separation wall or barrier in the 2000s, respectively. The outcomes of the two cases were significantly different. The HCJ's decision from September 1999 forbade the General Security Services (*Shin Beth* or *Shabak*) from using several methods of physical pressure against terror suspects, even though it did not close all the loopholes (Israel, Supreme Court, 1999, cited as SC). The HCJ received dozens of appeals against the separation barrier, and heard several concerning both the legality of the separation barrier as a whole and against its path in particular locations. While rejecting the former comprehensive challenges, the Court required the government to amend the fence's course in several instances. This and the court's other decisions provided only very limited relief to the Palestinians affected by the barrier directly, and also stands in stark contrast with the 2004 advisory decision of the International Court of Justice—which found the barrier illegal and demanded its dismantling. The contrasting decisions of the Israeli HCJ allow us to inquire into the relative weight of the multiplicity of factors that shape the outcomes of legal human rights campaigns.

TORTURING DEMOCRACY

The Israeli experience with torture is Janus-faced: It alone among democracies has sanctioned the use of torture, euphemistically called "moderate physical pressure," on terror suspects—yet 22 years later reversed itself. What circumstances changed between these dates, and just how closely are they related to the globalization of human rights?

When the *London Sunday Times* broke the topic wide open in 1977 (June 19, July 3, 10, 1977), concluding after a five-month-long investigation that "Israeli interrogators routinely ill treat and often torture Arab prisoners" and had done so "throughout the ten years of Israeli occupation," the Israeli government denied the charge. The exposure of foreign media, even as respectable as the British *Times*, carried little weight in Israeli governmental calculations. A decade later, grave suspicions arose, this time in the Israeli media, but their impact remained minimal. In April 1984, Israeli troops stormed the number 300 bus hijacked by four Palestinian terrorists, killed two of the terrorists, and freed their Jewish hostages. Though two of the terrorists survived, they were later pronounced dead. An Israeli tabloid, *Yediot Achronot*, defying the military censor, published a photo in which the two were seen taken alive at the conclusion of the military action. The Attorney General (AG) (in Israel roughly combining the tasks of the Solicitor General and the Government's Legal Counsel) uncovered that the terrorists were beaten to death, apparently under the orders of Avraham Shalom, the head of the General Security Services (GSS—*Shin Bet*). The AG was pressured to halt his investigation—and when he refused, he was fired. Shalom and his underlings, who lied to cover up the beating but later cooperated with the investigation, were pardoned by the Israeli president.

The mistreatment of suspects became public knowledge only in 1987, when the Supreme Court agreed to hear the case of a former Israel Defense Force lieutenant, Izat Nafsu, who was convicted of espionage on behalf of Syria. Nafsu's appeal was based on the fact that one of the security agents involved with Bus 300, who was exposed lying, also served as his interrogator (Shelef, 1990: 186, fn 3.) The Court ruled that Nafsu's conviction was based on a confession extracted under duress by GSS interrogators who falsely testified in court to cover up their illegal actions. As an Israeli citizen (of the Circassian minority), Nafsu's mistreatment generated the kind of legal alarm that the killing of Palestinian Arab terrorists by the GSS three years earlier did not.

The Israeli government officially appointed a "Commission of Inquiry into the Methods of Investigation of the General Security Service Regarding Hostile Terrorist Activity [HTA]," known by its Chair—retired Supreme Court Justice Moshe Landau, in the wake of the Nafsu Affair. The Landau Commission determined that GSS personnel had been using physical pressure on terror suspects and lying to cover it up in court for the past 16 years (LC, 1987: 2.27–2.28, p. 23; Kremnitzer, 1989: 218). The Landau Commission, however, accepted *prima facie* the GSS's view that physical pressure was necessary to conduct effective interrogation of terror suspects. But the commission members expressed fear of moral corruption resulting from infringement of the rule of law. The Landau Commission's preferred option was to confront the dilemma openly and, by justifying the exceptional use of force under the "necessity" defense, make the use of "moderate physical pressure" permissible only under some circumstances (LC, 1987, 4.7, p. 80; Gross, 2004: 372; Kremnitzer, 1989: 217). Such pressure, the Commission, asserted, should "never reach the level of physical torture or maltreatment or grievous harm to his honor which deprives [the suspect] of his human dignity" (LC, 1987: 3.16, p. 61).

The commission established a regulatory mechanism to oversee the use of physical pressure. Though the part of its report which specified what constituted allowable physical pressure remains secret to this day, the particular practices employed have come to light in legal appeals and demands for compensation, some of which were uncontested by the GSS. Five of them have been listed by the Supreme Court in 1999 as no longer legal. The latter are forceful shaking, the "Frog Crouch," excessive tightening of hand or leg cuffs, sleep deprivation, and the infamous "Sabach Position," in which the suspect "is seated on a small and low chair, whose seat is tilted forward, towards the ground. One hand is tied behind the suspect and placed inside the gap between the chair's seat and back support. His second hand is tied behind the chair, against its back support. The suspect's head is covered by an opaque sack, falling down to his shoulders and powerfully loud music is played in the room" (SC, 1999: 3; Bowden, 2003: 64).

In 1987, the influence of the court and the legal apparatus on the use of torture was limited and mixed. Acting as a court of appeal, the Supreme Court was willing to expose and reject the gaining of confession through torture in the case of a single individual—an Israeli minority citizen. But a commission of inquiry, even one headed by one of the most respected members of the Supreme Court—Justice Landau chaired the court in the trial of Adolf Eichmann—and one which recognized the mendacity of the GSS, chose to defend the practice, even as it sought to limit its intensity and restrict it to cases dictated by "necessity." The main legal significance of the Landau Commission's recommendation to permit the use of "moderate physical pressure" on the basis of an a-priori "necessity" defense is in the legitimation of this defense, and allowing governmental authority to inflict such "pressure."

Subsequent to the adoption of the Landau Commission's recommendations, the government set up a special ministerial committee to monitor and
routinely renew the GSS's interrogation guidelines. The new official policy
was fortuitously adopted on the eve of the First *Intifada*, a mostly nonviolent Palestinian uprising which saw mass demonstrations, tire burning, stone
throwing, tax strikes, and similar expressions of protest. Even so, it gave
license to interrogators to use "humiliating and brutal coercive techniques"
against thousands of Palestinian arrested during the *intifada* (Lelyveld 2005:
60). In the second year of the mostly nonviolent *intifada*, when the GSS expressed its need for better information, the monitoring committee authorized the GSS to upgrade its methods and use "enhanced physical pressure"
(B'Tselem, 1991: 34; Pacheco, 1999: 6).

By replacing the absolute prohibition on torture with one based on distinction between degrees of physical pressure, the Landau Commission, in
effect, contributed to the erosion of the law's restraining influence. Though
the Landau Commission approved "only" the use of moderate physical pressure, during the first *intifada*, about "16 Palestinians are reported to have
died after punitive beatings at the time or shortly after arrest by Israeli forces.
At least eight others died in detention centers … " (Amnesty International,
1994: 21). One of them, Abdel Samad Harizat, died as a consequence of
having been administered violent shaking, a fact not denied by the GSS
(Pacheco: 7). Two GSS interrogators were sentenced to six months in jail
for causing Khaled Shaik Ali's death by negligence (Amnesty International,
1994: 21). Justice Landau himself admitted to feeling betrayed by the GSS's
practice of regularly exceeding the constraints his commission sought to
impose (Felner, 2005: 39).

According to an 1998 estimate of B'Tselem, the Israeli Information Center for Human Rights in the Occupied Territories, the GSS annually interrogated between 1,000–1,5000 Palestinian suspects and "some eighty-five
percent of them—at least 850 prisoners a year—are tortured during investigation" (B'Tselem, 1998: 8). On the higher end, Israeli attorney Allegra
Pacheco, who defended many Palestinian terror suspects, puts the number
of Palestinians tortured by Israel at 50,000 (Pacheco, 2001).

Examining the chronology of Israeli legal and legislative actions in regard
to torture, we come across a most surprising and counterintuitive finding.
Israel signed the United Nations Convention Against Torture on 22 October
1986, ratified it on 4 August and deposited its instrument of ratification on
3 October 1991. In other words, the Israeli government committed itself
to legally ban torture and cruel, inhuman, and degrading treatment and
punishment at the very time when it authorized its own security services to
engage in just these kinds of actions. This inconsistency can be profitably
interrogated to assess the relative weight of the factors that enable effective
legal globalization.

There appear to be two alternative explanations—one which focuses on
international, the other on domestic legal factors—as to what enabled the

Israeli government to so blatantly bifurcate its words and deeds. Though ratifying CAT, Israel also made a number of significant reservations to its implementation. Among them, it did not recognize the Committee Against Torture's competence to carry out special investigations, including on-site visits, when there are indications that torture is being systematically practiced. It also does not recognize the Committee's competence to receive interstate complaints against it, or permit the Committee to receive individual complaints. Finally, Israel stated that it will not be bound by the provision allowing disputes concerning the interpretation or application of the Convention to be submitted to arbitration or referred to the International Court of Justice (Implementation: 5). Israel has submitted periodic reports, as required by CAT, but these are met with the Committee's firm rejection of Israel's judicial justification for acts prohibited under the Convention. Several alternative reports have been published, sometimes jointly by the Public Committee Against Torture in Israel (PCATI); *Al-Haq* (The Law), the Palestinian Society for the Protection of Human Rights and the Environment; and the World Organization Against Torture (OMCT), but these do not appear to have had any discernible effect on Israeli practices. In sum, one explanation suggests that while accepting the principles and requirements, Israel reserved for itself the monitoring and implementation of the Convention.

At the same time, Israel entered neither reservations that pertain to what constitutes torture or other ill treatment, nor any granting immunity to torturers. It would seem that the government concluded that Israel's own methods of interrogation, under the Landau Commission's framework, were too mild to fall under the international prohibition of torture and other ill treatment. Israeli governments view themselves as enjoying immunity in part due to the reservations sovereign countries can place on the implementation of international human rights conventions, and in the Israeli case, the lack of CAT's domestication by the Knesset precludes courts from applying it to the behavior of Israeli state institutions. In addition, as Lisa Hajjar has pointed out, Israel is an effective practitioner of "lawfare," a legal strategy used by both states and their challengers. States use law to abet serious violations of the laws of war, while opponents use law to challenge the legitimacy of the state's war-making policies and practices. Israel has created its own alternative domestic legality (Hajjar, 2006: 27; Hajjar, 2012). The second explanation highlights the immunity Israel has because it has an active domestic legal system which has been sufficiently autonomous to assume jurisdiction over government and military polices in the OPT, even if it has recused itself from passing on the legality of important issues, such as the establishment of settlements, on the grounds that they are "acts of state" and as such nonjusticiable (Kretzmer: 19–24).

Six years after the signing of the Oslo Declaration of Principles and Israeli withdrawal from Gaza and the West Bank towns, the threat posed by the PLO and Palestinian terror could no longer be defined as one against the "survival of Israel" (Gross, 2001: 31). The Supreme Court abruptly chose to take up the issue of torture. After ignoring the steady stream of petitions from Palestinians in regard to physical mistreatment, in 1999 it joined several of them with two public petitions, one of which was brought in 1994 by the Public Committee Against Torture in Israel, and the other in 1995 by the Association for Citizen's Rights in Israel (ACRI). These organizations repeatedly petitioned the Supreme Court to review the Landau Commission guidelines and revoke them, and to have its secret annex made public. ACRI was established in 1972; it is Israel's oldest and largest human rights organization and addresses the entire spectrum of human rights and civil liberties issues in Israel and the Occupied Territories. PCATI was founded in 1990, in direct response to the ongoing policy of ill treatment and torture of Palestinian terror suspects.

On September 9, 1999, the Israeli Supreme Court sitting as the High Court of Justice, in an opinion written by Chief Justice Aharon Barak, boldly asserted that:

> although a democracy must fight with one hand tied behind its back, it nonetheless has the upper hand. Preserving the rule of law and recognition of an individual's liberty constitutes an important component in its understanding of security. At the end of the day, they strengthen its spirit and its strength and allow it to overcome its difficulties. (SC, 1999: 15)

In its ruling, the HCJ forbade the GSS from using several methods of physical pressure against terror suspects, though it did not close all loopholes (SC, 1999). In short, Israel stands out not only for having legalized certain forms of physical pressure which fall under the "torture, cruel, inhuman, and degrading treatment" as described in the 1987 international Convention on Torture, but also in having, in a meaningful way though not fully, reversed that decision.

Pursuant to this decision, the Israeli Attorney General, Elyakim Rubinstein, carefully circumscribed the GSS's interrogation practices in an internal memo in which he explained that in the future "means of interrogation immediately necessary to yield vital information" cannot be used as a routine matter or be part of ongoing investigations to gather information about terrorist organizations. When such means were used, he stated his intention to weigh the threat's immediacy, concreteness, and gravity, alternatives available, and the interrogator's state of mind, and the involvement and deliberations of upper echelons in each case separately. In no case were the methods used to amount to "torture" as defined in the Convention Against Torture (AGD, par. 7).

About a year after the HCJ's decision, a second *intifada* broke out—with the extensive use of horrific suicide bombings in restaurants, discotheques, bus stations, shopping malls, festivities, and other locations by Hamas, Islamic Jihad, Fatah's Al-Aksa Brigades, and the Popular Front for the Liberation of Palestine. Whereas the first *intifada* was by and large nonviolent, Human

Rights Watch's report on the second *intifada* concluded that "the scale and systematic nature of these attacks ... meet the definition of a crime against humanity. When these suicide bombings take place in the context of violence that amounts to armed conflict, they are also war crimes" even when perpetrated on civilian settlers (http://www.hrw.org/reports/2002/isrl-pa/). Even against the backdrop of such repeated and ongoing purposeful and indiscriminate attacks on Israeli civilians, the HCJ's decision and the attorney general's legal opinion had a clear restraining impact. The GSS trained new interrogators, disciplines and monitors them, requires them to work in pairs, and videotapes interrogations. The low, tilted chairs used in the "Sabach" position were replaced with regular chairs, suffocating hoods with blackened goggles, the violent shaking methods with repeated shoving. No detained terror suspects died in custody. All the same, while legal constrains always matter a great deal, physical pressure had only been reduced by the Court decision, not eliminated.

Lisa Hajjar, one of the most astute participants in the torture debates in Israel and the United States, aptly captures the meaning of the Supreme Court decision:

> A qualified victory in this struggle was achieved in September 1999, when the Israeli High Court finally rendered a decision against the commonplace use of state-sanctioned "pressure" tactics, although this decision does not go so far as to close the widow of opportunity for continuing torture. (Hajjar, 2000: 105)

The decision, in fact covers neither ill treatment during the predetention period when the suspects are in the hands of the military or the police, nor forms of "moderate physical pressure" not on the Landau Commission's list. The court also acceded to the infliction of "sleep deprivation," when it was not an end in itself but a side effect of the interrogation (SC, 1999: 12). The Supreme Court, significantly, retained the "necessity" defense for the use of physical pressure in the case of "ticking bombs," though only as an ex post-facto defense and, as the Landau Commission before it, allowed for its expansive use by defining the "imminence" of the threat to mean that "the danger is certain to materialize," "even if the bomb is set to explode in a few days or even in a few weeks" (SC, 1999: 13). Similarly, the attorney general's guidelines, following this ruling, also allowed for the "necessity" defense (AGD, par. 7).

The Court also chose a narrow legal basis for concluding that the prior authorization of specific practices was unlawful. It held that the executive branch alone could not adopt such a policy and that it had to be done, if it was to be done, by the legislature. At the same time, though the Court did not invoke the "Basic Law: Human Dignity and Liberty" as the grounds for its decision, it pointed out that legislation will have to, thus raising a high barrier to the passing of such a law (SC, 1999: 15). Parliamentary and governmental attempts to adopt such a law, significantly, came to naught (B'Tselem, 2000).

Even in the wake of the Supreme Court decision, as documented in the April 2003 Report of the Public Committee Against Torture in Israel, there exists ongoing ill treatment of terror suspects and in some cases torture. Many of these took place during arrest and on the way to the GSS detention facility, such as tight shackling for many hours with hard-plastic disposable shackles that can be tightened but not loosened, detention in open air without food and provisions, beatings with rifle butts and slapping, and threats against relatives (PCATI, 2003: 9). Though the number of terror suspects subjected to "special methods" declined from hundreds, during the first *intifada*, to dozens a year during the second, the use of such methods persisted (Lelyveld, 2005: 66). A major adverse outcome in the aftermath of the Court's decision has been its unwillingness to hear subsequent petitions of terror suspects concerning incidents of torture. PCATI had submitted 124 petitions requesting permission for detainees to meet with their lawyers during the course of their interrogation, but the court accepted none (PCATI, 2003: 8). In 2002, the GSS acknowledged that since the Supreme Court ruling 90 Palestinian terror suspects were defined as "ticking bombs" and subjected to "physical pressure, though PCATI believes that the actual number might be higher" (Harel; PCATI, 2003: 17). The state prosecutor referred complaints to the GSS itself for investigation, and the latter had found none in which physical pressure was deemed unnecessary. Finally, though the attorney general, as we have seen, defined the applicability of the "necessity" defense very narrowly in his guidelines (AGD, par. 7), he granted his approval *ex post facto* for every single case in which physical pressure was used (PCATI, 2003: 12). In August 2012, the HCJ rejected petitions of ACRI, PCATI, and Adalah to require that every complaint against the GSS over torture or abuse of detainees during investigation automatically lead to a criminal investigation. The Court left standing the current policy of investigating such complaints by the state's attorney general's office to determine whether the evidence warrants the launching of such an investigation. In the past, the attorney general's office has not brought criminal charges against GSS interrogators (*Ha'aretz*, August 7, 2012).

A BARRIER TO RIGHTS

For a long time, Israel has been repeatedly held in violation of the human rights of Palestinians in the OPT by UN bodies, Israeli and other NGOs, and many scholars of human rights (B'Tselem, 2011; Peleg). The construction of the separation wall, barrier, or fence has added its own and unique set of violations. Whereas many aspects of the subject of torture remained shrouded in secrecy and protest was confined to a small group of concerned

NGOs, the pros and cons of the separation barrier were debated in the court of public opinion as well as in the halls of justice.

The decision to construct the wall was made at the height of the Second *Intifada* in June 2002, by a reluctant Sharon government in response to public clamor to prevent the infiltration of Palestinian suicide bombers from the West Bank into Israeli population centers. Since the barrier's construction began, the number of suicide bombings and attempted bombings within Israel has fallen dramatically. For most of its length, the barrier consists of a sensor-equipped intrusion detection fence, with a dual set of paths equipped to detect footprints, a patrol road, and a ditch containing a pyramid-shaped stack of six coils of barbed wire on the eastern side of the structure and barbed wire on the western side, extending to an average width of 65 yards. In built-up and narrow places an actual concrete wall of 6.5 to 8.5 yards was put in place. The decision to construct the barrier for all practical purposes meant the end of the dream of Greater Israel, but did not signal the end of territorial expansion. The barrier was not built on the 1948 ceasefire line, the so-called Green Line, but was planned to place as many of the Israeli settlements as possible with as few Palestinians as practical on the western, Israeli side of the fence. About 85% of the barrier's route is within the West Bank proper. Its goal was to serve as the permanent future border of Israel, according to pronouncements by many Israel leaders at the time and since (Arieli: 325–326).

As a consequence of its routing inside the West Bank, the separation barrier has created a new subgroup of the Palestinian population: those from the West Bank whose villages, residences, or agricultural lands are found on the western, that is, "Israeli," side of the separation barrier; those living in what Israel calls "the seam zone" (*merchav hatefer*). The seam zone, which is spread over a few hundred miles east of the Green Line, is separated both physically and legally from the rest of the West Bank—it is a closed military area—and the entry and exit of its Palestinian residents is regulated and limited (Arieli: 357). All told, the barrier affects close to 12% of the West Bank's land mass.

The residents of the Palestinian villages in the seam zone require a permit to live in their own homes and villages, which they can leave only through a specified gate in the barrier—for which they also need a permit. Those Palestinians who live east of the wall, and wish to enter the seam zone to cultivate their land or for other purposes, also need permits. As of July 2008, there were 39 open gates to serve Palestinians that are divided into daily crossing gates, agricultural gates—which are open several times a day to allow the tending of crops that require daily care—and seasonal gates, for crops that require only intermittent care (B'Tselem, 2010). There also are several areas east of the Green Line that have been enclosed to separate them from adjacent Jewish settlements. Due to the barrier's meandering course, some Palestinian communities are surrounded on three sides by the barrier—and some on all four sides, to be connected to the rest of the West Bank with a tunnel or road (UN, 2008).

It is difficult to provide an accurate number of individuals whose lives and rights are affected by the separation barrier, since its course has changed several times and only about 40% of it is completed. A further difficulty in coming up with a consensus estimate is that while some of those Palestinians are "locked in" the seam zone, others are "locked out"; for example, villagers from communities neighboring East Jerusalem will not be able to visit the city, and while some sources count only the former, others count both groups. The largest estimate, from an unnamed UN source, suggests that "if the series of walls, fences, barbed wire and ditches is completed along its planned route, about a third of West Bank Palestinians will be affected. About 274,000 will be trapped in enclaves and about 400,000 blocked from their fields, jobs, schools and hospitals" (CBC News, 2006). Another UN agency, the United Nations Relief and Works Agency for Palestinian Refugees (UNWRA) estimates that 14 communities would be completely isolated between the barrier and the Green Line, numbering 13,636 Palestinians, as well as 15 communities on its eastern side affecting "approximately 138,593 Palestinians." Finally, at least 33 communities will be affected, to some degree, numbering 69,019 Palestinians. Altogether UNWRA's number is 207,612 (UNWRA, 2003). B'Tselem's estimate numerates 27,520 Palestinians from 17 villages west of the barrier plus 247,800 on the east side whose 54 communities are completely or partially surrounded, and all of East Jerusalem's 222,500 residents; all told 497,820 (B'Tselem, 2010). A 2008 UN Report concludes that approximately 35,000 West Bank Palestinians will be in the seam zone, in addition to the majority of the approximately 250,000 residents of East Jerusalem, and another 125,000 Palestinians in 28 communities will be surrounded on three sides, while 26,000 Palestinians in 8 communities will be surrounded on four sides by the barrier. This estimate has the advantage of coinciding with the High Court's calculation of at least one number—the number of Palestinians west of the barrier (UN, 2008).

The barrier violates many of the human rights decreed in the International Covenant on Economic, Social and Cultural Rights, such as the right to work (Articles 6 and 7); protection and assistance accorded to the family and to children and young persons (Article 10); the right to an adequate standard of living, including adequate food, clothing, and housing, and the right "to be free from hunger" (Article 11); the right to health (Article 12); the right to education (Articles 13 and 14), as well as similar provisions in other Covenants, such as the Convention on the Rights of the Child. It affects Palestinian farming particularly adversely, since the land lying west of the barrier is among the most fertile regions of Palestine (UN, 2008). Eighty percent of the Palestinians who do not reside in the seam zone but own land there did not receive permits that would allow them to continue cultivating their land (UN (ESCWA), 2008: 5). The construction of the barrier led to the loss of land by Palestinian farmers. "For example, the barrier surrounds the town of Qalqiliya, with the only exit and entry point controlled by an Israeli military checkpoint. This has isolated the town from almost all its agricultural land, while surrounding villages are separated from its markets and services. The barrier has a particularly damaging effect on Palestinian health. A United Nations hospital in the town has experienced a 40 per cent decrease in caseloads" (UN, 2003).

The barrier has been at the center of both international and domestic litigation. The International Court of Justice issued an advisory opinion in response to a referral by a special emergency session of the United Nations General Assembly. The opinion was advisory, rather than binding, because Israel had refused to accept jurisdiction over the issue by the Court. The ICJ based its decision on the two central documents of international humanitarian law (IHL), the Hague Regulation of 1907 and the Fourth Geneva Convention relative to the Protection of Civilian Persons in Times of War of 1949, as well as on provisions of the International Covenant on Economic, Social and Cultural Rights. The ICJ concluded that by constructing the wall Israel violated its obligations as belligerent occupier under IHL. The ICJ also listed multiple human rights violations that result from the construction of the barrier, among them land confiscations, house demolitions, the creation of enclaves, and restrictions on movement and access to water, food, education, health care, work, and an adequate standard of living. The ICJ advised Israel that it was obligated to cease the construction of the barrier in the OPT, including East Jerusalem, dismantle the structure already completed, repeal all related legislative and regulatory acts and make reparation for all damage caused by the construction of the wall (ICJ, 2004).

As the Israeli High Court views the OPT as being under Israeli jurisdiction, it has accepted petitions from its Palestinian residents from the very beginning of the territories' occupation by Israel. Dozens of Palestinians petitioned for court redress in regard to the separation barrier, frequently with help from an Israeli human rights NGO, such as B'Tselem, the Association for Civil Rights, and Rabbis for Human Rights—or a Palestinian human rights NGO, among them Adalah Legal Centre for Arab Minority Rights in Israel and *Al-Haq*—the Palestinian Society for the Protection of Human Rights and the Environment. The Israeli High Court agreed to review and sometimes group several of these petitions, and has handed down significant decisions. I will examine two such decisions: the Beit Sourik and the Alfe Menashe cases.

The residents of Beit Sourik raised two legal objections; on the principled level, they argued that since the barrier de facto annexes parts of the West Bank to Israel, and does so in the service of the occupying power, it runs afoul of IHL obligations of belligerent occupation to ensure the protection of the occupied population. On a more practical level, they suggested that in determining the barrier's route the security benefits have outweighed the severe harm caused to large numbers of Palestinians, and consequently, demanded its rerouting. The HCJ concurred with the petitioners' insistence that Israel is obligated to uphold the requirements of a belligerent occupier, since that is the legal basis of its presence in the West Bank. At the same time, it rejected the opposition to the barrier, on the basis that under the self-same IHL that prevents Israel from building the barrier for political reasons, the occupier is entitled to carry out temporary measures to ensure security. The Court accepted an affidavit provided by the military commander of the Central Command which includes the West Bank area to the effect that the barrier is a temporary fence erected for security needs. The High Court concluded, notwithstanding the construction of the barrier east of main settlement blocs rather than on the Green Line, that "we have no reason to assume that the objective is political rather than security-based" (HCJ 2056/04, *Judgments*, Vol. 1; Lynk: 11).

At the same time, the application of the proportionality test, balancing the humanitarian harm caused by the barrier against the security benefits, led the Court to conclude that segments of the 40 km under construction would harm Palestinians disproportionately. Examining issues such as Palestinian access to lands and orchards, unemployment rate, and the like, it concluded that a 25-km segment of the barrier injures "the fabric of life of the entire population" and instructed the Israeli military to reroute the relevant section (HCJ 2056/04, *Judgments*, Vol. 1; Lynk: 13–14).

The dual rulings ignited an internal Israeli debate over Israel's legal responsibilities in the OPT. The minister of justice, Yosef Lapid, and Mechanem Mazuz, the attorney general who serves as the government's legal counsel, suggested, respectively, that nonadherence to human rights or the unwillingness to fully apply the Fourth Geneva Convention puts Israel in danger of an international campaign of boycotts akin to the one that was directed at South Africa. Though Israeli elites were dismayed by the ICJ's advisory opinion, which the government proceeded to ignore, they embraced the Supreme Court's much more modest subsequent decision (Lynk: 16).

The HCJ's Alfe Menashe decision, from September 2005, was practically identical to its previous ruling. It accepted the legality of building the barrier within the OPT, but concluded that since the wall around the Alfe Menasha settlement, itself located in the seam zone in the central West Bank, formed a "chokehold" on its neighboring five Palestinian villages, it failed the proportionality test and needed to be moved (HCJ 7957/04, *Judgments*, Vol. 2; Lynk: 18). This time, however, the Court explicitly accepted that the security of Israeli settlers in the OPT is a legitimate security concern, equivalent to the security of the occupying state. Though the settlers are not protected persons under IHL, the construction of the barrier to protect them was viewed as lawful by the HCJ and is not affected by the legality of the settlements themselves (HCJ 8414/05, *Yassin v Government of Israel*, par. 28, p. 213 in *Judgments*, Vol. 3; Dinstein: 257). This ruling, which resembles past ones, extends the concept of security in a way that ignores the Fourth Geneva Convention's prohibition of belligerent occupiers to move their population to the conquered territory.

The cumulative result of the Supreme Court decisions, combined with international pressure, is surprisingly far-reaching. The routing of the separation barrier, as conceived in 2003, would have placed 20% of the West Bank on its Israeli side. By 2009, the barrier included only 4.5% of West Bank territory, in effect reducing the land mass east of the Green Line by 60%. Running up against legal and political obstacles, 40% of the barrier remains unbuilt, without evident damage to Israeli security. In fact, since November 2007, the barrier's construction has practically ceased (Arieli: 351).

The construction of the barrier has generated considerable and persistent Israeli and foreign opposition. The best-known flashpoint is the village of Bil'in. With a population of 1,800, Bil'in is a village of farmers and a bedroom suburb of nearby Ramallah, and is located about 4 km east of the Green Line. In September 2005, the head of the village council petitioned the Court against the separation barrier's route. The petition pointed out that the barrier was designed to follow a route that would have placed on its east side the yet unplanned and built neighborhood, Matetyahu East. In 2006 the Supreme Court concluded that the proposed route in fact offers inferior security to patrolling Israeli troops and ruled that the route is to be changed. In fact, the Court intimated that the military was willing to sacrifice security in order to advance the political goal of expanding a settlement. Further, the Court ruled that the barrier is to be built on available state-owned rather than private Palestinian land (Arieli: 355; *Jerusalem Post*, February 11, 2010). The military's proposed new route was also rejected by the Court, since it only included marginal and cosmetic changes. Though the Court ordered the military to dismantle the existing barrier without further delay, it took four years after the Supreme Court ruling for the military to dismantle the wall and for the villagers of Bil'in to regain access to part, but not all, of their land.

Parallel with the legal petitions, the villagers of Bil'in and their Bil'in Popular Committee conduct weekly demonstrations against the separation barrier. The protests start after Friday prayers at the village's mosque, and when the protesters head towards the separation barrier they are joined by Israeli supporters, some of whom are affiliated with Israeli Anarchists Against the Wall, and by members of the International Solidarity Movement, mostly European and American opponents of the occupation. The protests are meant to be nonviolent but as young Palestinians hurl stones and the Israeli security forces fire tear gas, stun grenades, and rubber bullets, they frequently end in clashes. Several demonstrators have been injured in the past six years and one Palestinian villager was killed when a canister hit his chest.

The barrier, unlike the torture issue, generated considerable public debate in Israel. Israeli Jews felt immune to physical mistreatment by the security forces, whereas the barrier affected their public security and the country's future agreements with the Palestinian Authority. While only a handful of NGOs petitioned the Court to review torture applications, and they were the dedicated human rights organizations, the Court received amicus briefs from the Council for Peace and Security, an organization of retired military officers. The Council did not object to the location of the largest parts of the barrier in the OPT, but argued that its proposed route was injurious not to Palestinians but to Israeli security and, consequently, suggested alternative routes. Routing the fence too close to Palestinian homes and villages, in its professional opinion, made it harder to protect Israel and its settlements (Arieli: 331). Its submission removed the monopoly of the military and provided the Court with competing military options. In fact, the Court preferred the evidence provided by the Council that alternative routes, further removed from Palestinian homes and communities, would provide equivalent or better security for Israel (Lynk: 9, 14).

CONCLUSION

The Israeli-Palestinian conflict is a "hard case" for human rights advocates who would like to see a more thorough application of human rights and resort to international legal institutions to address violations. The main obstacle to effective appeal to and implementation of human rights norms in the case of the Israeli-Palestinian conflict is the fact that Palestinians live under Israeli military occupation, and the resulting use of an alternative legal framework, international humanitarian law. When two controlling legal frameworks exist, there is ample wiggle room to disregard or diminish the enforcement of human rights.

The Israeli perspective, described by Dinstein as a general principle, is that "the special law of belligerent occupation trumps the general law of human rights on the ground of *lex specialis derogat lex generali*" (Dinstein: 85). This view has been rejected in the advisory opinion of the ICJ, which holds that human rights and humanitarian law should be in concord. The current situation, however, is one in which even the Israeli High Court—which in contrast to the government's position holds that humanitarian law is applicable in the OPT and regularly invokes it in its decisions—has accepted the primacy of IHL over human rights. Furthermore, the HCJ, as we have seen, applies IHL selectively. The consequence of the occupation and the application of IHL is that human rights norms and international enforcement institutions have only the most limited impact.

At the same time, a comparison of the two legal campaigns surveyed in this chapter—against torture and physical mistreatment and against the separation barrier—shows that even within these limits human rights conventions and norms do matter. The potential usefulness of human rights in addressing the rights of Palestinians under occupation is due in large part to the availability of international legal *fora* as well as NGOs which have come into existence as part of the growing reach of human rights, through norms, conventions, domestic legislation, universal jurisdiction, and the formation of a transnational network of advocacy. The international and regional climate of human rights compliance, even more than the actual ascension to international conventions by a state or the recognition of its obligations under such conventions, serves as an enabling condition for respecting human rights: the institutional depth and autonomy of civil society, the sense of security within the regional order, and the relative weight and influence of human rights in the international and regional arenas.

A comparison of the relative success of legal restrictions by Israeli courts following international standards on the use of torture with the failure of international legal appeals to deter Israel's construction of demarcations that impede Palestinians' access to social and economic rights such as health care allows us to assess the relative weight of these factors. I argue that the difference in human rights protection in these cases results from differences in the nature of the norms claimed, the relationship between international and domestic law in these cases and, in particular, the level of the domestic empowerment of the claimants. Norms against torture are more developed and transcend sovereignty, while state sovereignty over security trumps social rights and the weaker mechanisms of international humanitarian law. Most significantly, Israeli civil society was empowered to contest torture as part of an advocacy coalition, while international venues granted Palestinians standing to object to construction of the barrier wall that were not matched at a domestic level. Thus, this case follows the pattern of this project, in which the impact of the globalization of law is conditioned by institutional autonomy and civil society empowerment.

The autonomy and vibrancy of Israel's civil society, as exemplified in the activism of its NGOs and their alliance with and mobilization on behalf of Palestinian human rights, however, is jeopardized by Israel's growing turn away from democratic principles in the past decade. Already in 1999, 43 legislators proposed a law permitting "physical pressure," but it was never passed (Gross, 2004: 375–377). More recently, Israel has shown growing signs of retreating from its qualified cooperation with international judicial bodies connected with the UN; and its Knesset has passed a flurry of laws which have a chilling effect on the operations of human rights NGOs and even the Supreme Court. In February 2011, the Knesset passed the "Law on Disclosure Requirements for Recipients of Support from a Foreign State Entity," requiring certain NGOs to list foreign state contributions in quarterly financial reports and state that such funds were used in specific campaigns. The law's goal allegedly was to increase transparency in NGO funding, but as is clear from the parliamentary debates, its goal is to delegitimize certain kinds of NGOs. Though appearing to target all NGOs, this law singles out civil and human rights organizations (http://www.acri.org.il/en/2012/02/05/update-anti-democratic-legislation-initiatives/). Bills restricting NGO activities even further have been submitted to the Knesset, bringing the chief justice of the Supreme Court, Dorit Beinish, to declare that she fears greatly for Israel's constitutional enterprise. Former chief justice Aharon Barak stated that the Knesset is considering proposed bills that appear unconstitutional, and that the courts are witnessing attacks that border on incitement. The attorney general warned that attempts to restrict foreign governments' donations to Israeli NGOs are unconstitutional, and declared his unwillingness to defend them in court (*Ha'aretz*, December 11, 2011).

The Knesset has also reduced the autonomy of the appointment process for Supreme Court justices, by passing a law that alters the composition of the Judicial Appointments Committee, making it more political. As part of this process, in early 2012 the Knesset passed a law that changed the retirement age limits, in order to allow the appointment of Asher Grunis as chief justice—a conservative justice "who made a name for himself as a supporter of judicial restraint" and opponent of petitions from parties that have no legal standing since they are not directly affected by official actions [such as some advocates] (*Ha'aretz*, January 1, 2012; http://www.jewishpress.com/news/israel/will-israels-supreme-court-tilt-right-under-new-chief/2012/02/29/). In early 2012, Grunis wrote, in the decision upholding a law that prevents Palestinians who marry Israelis from living with their spouses, that "human rights are not a prescription for national suicide" (http://mondoweiss.net/2012/02/asher-grunis-discriminates-his-way-to-the-top-of-the-supreme-court.html). The Court now also has its first member, Justice Noam Sohlberg, who is the resident of a settlement in the West Bank. These changes are likely to signal a turn away from the liberal approach of the Court under chief justices Barak and Beinish—though even the previous interventionist approach habitually gave preference to broadly defined security concerns over human rights and excluded a host of issues as "state acts" from judicial review.

The legal constraints on Israeli NGOs and the attempts to reign in the Supreme Court potentially threaten Israel's civil society and even the narrow application of human rights conventions and norms that its Supreme Court has ensured in the OPT. Like the physical barriers between Israel and Palestine, the barriers to rights and to the globalization of law are growing in this hard case.

NOTE

I would like to thank Yuval Ginbar, Louis Frankenthaler, Menachem Hofnung, and Ilan Saban for their advice and insight.

BIBLIOGRAPHY

Amnesty International, *Israel and the Occupied Territories: Torture and Ill-Treatment of Political Detainees*, New York, April 1994.

Arieli, Shaul, *Zchut hachasiva: Osef maamarim al hasichsuch hayisreli palestinai* (The Right of Reflection: A Collection of Articles on the Israeli-Palestinian Conflict), Tel Aviv, 2010. (For English translations of some of the articles, see http://www.shaularieli.com/?lat=en)

Attorney General, "GSS Interrogations and the Necessity Defense—Framework for Attorney General's Deliberation (Following the HCJ Ruling)," Jerusalem, Memo, October 28, 1999 (cited as AGD)

Ben-Naftali, Orna, "Pathological Occupation: Normalizing the Exceptional Case of the Occupied Palestinian Territory and Other Legal Pathologies," in Orna Ben-Naftali, ed., *International Humanitarian Law and International Human Rights Law: Pas de Deux*, Oxford, Oxford University Press, 2011, pp. 129–200.

Benvenisti, Eyal, "The Applicability of Human Rights Conventions to Israel and to the Occupied Territories," *Israel Law Review*, Vol. 26, No. 1, Winter 1992, pp. 24–35.

Bowden, Mark, "The Dark Art of Interrogation," *Atlantic Monthly*, Vol. 292, No. 3, October 2003, pp. 51–76.

B'Tselem, *The Interrogation of Palestinians During the Intifada: Ill-Treatment, Moderate Physical Pressure or Torture?* Jerusalem, March 1991.

B'Tselem, *Routine Torture: Interrogation Methods of the General Security Service*, Jerusalem, February 1998.

B'Tselem, *Legislation Allowing the Use of Physical Force and Mental Coercion in Interrogations by the General Security Service*, Jerusalem, January 2000.

B'Tselem, *The Separation Barrier—Statistics*, May 2010, http://www.btselem.org/separation_barrier/statistics

B'Tselem, *Human Rights in the Occupied Territories: 2011 Annual Report*, Jerusalem, 2011.

CBC News Online, Indepth: Middle East, *Israel's Barrier*, January 6, 2006, http://www.cbc.ca/news/background/middleeast/israel_barrier.html

Dinstein, Yoram, *The International Law of Belligerent Occupation*, Cambridge, Cambridge University Press, 2009.

Felner, Eitan, "Torture and Terrorism: Painful Lessons from Israel," in Kenneth Roth and Minky Worden, eds., *Torture: Does It Make Us Safer? Is It Ever OK?: A Human Rights Perspective*, New York, New Press, 2005, pp. 28–43.

Gross, Michael L., "Just and Jewish Warfare," *Tikkun*, Vol. 16, No. 5, 2001, pp. 31–36.

Gross, Michael L., "Regulating Torture in a Democracy: Death and Indignity in Israel," *Polity*, Vol. 34, No. 3, April 2004, pp. 367–388.

Hajjar, Lisa, "Sovereign Bodies, Sovereign States and the Problem of Torture," *Studies in Law, Politics, and Society*, Vol. 21, 2000, pp. 101–134.

Hajjar, Lisa, *Courting Conflict: The Israeli Military Court System in the West Bank and Gaza*, Berkeley, University of California Press, 2005.

Hajjar, Lisa, "International Humanitarian Law and 'Wars on Terror': A Comparative Analysis of Israeli and American Doctrines and Policies," *Journal of Palestine Studies*, Vol. 36, No. 1, Autumn 2006, pp. 21–42.

Hajjar, Lisa, "Lawfare and Targeted Killing: Developments in the Israeli and US Contexts," *Jadaliyya*, January 15, 2012, http://www.jadaliyya.com/pages/index/4049/lawfare-and-targeted-killing_developments-in-the-i

Harel, Amos, "GSS Used 'Exceptional Interrogation Means' 90 Times Since HCJ Ruling," *Ha'aretz*, July 25, 2002.

"Implementation of the Convention Against Torture by Israel," November 2001, http://www.omct.org/files/2003/05/2345/isr_cat_impl.pdf (cited as Implementation)

International Court of Justice, "Legal Consequences of the Construction of a Wall in the Occupied Palestinian Territory," July 9, 2004, http://www.icj-cij.org/docket/index.php?pr=71&p1=3&p2=1&case=131&p3=6 (cited as ICJ)

Judgments of the Israeli Supreme Court: Fighting Terrorism Within the Law, Vol. 1 (1999–2004) & Vol. 2 (2004–2005) & Vol. 3 (2006–2009), Jerusalem, Supreme Court of Israel, http://www.mfa.gov.il/MFA/Government/Law/Legal+Issues+and+Rulings/Judgments_Israel_Supreme_Court-Fighting_Terrorism_within_Law-Vol_3 (cited as Judgments)

Kremnitzer, Mordechai, "The Landau Commission Report—Was the Security Service Subordinated to the Law or the Law to the 'Needs' of the Security Service?" *Israel Law Review*, Vol. 23, Nos. 2–3, Spring/Summer 1989, pp. 216–279.

Kretzmer, David, *The Occupation of Justice: The Supreme Court of Israel and the Occupied Territories*, Albany, State University of New York Press, 2002.

Lelyveld, Joseph, "Interrogating Ourselves," *New York Times Magazine*, June 12, 2005, pp. 36–43, 60, 66–69.

Lynk, Michael, "The High Court of Israel, International Law, and the Separation Wall," *Journal of Palestine Studies*, Vol. 35, No. 1, Autumn 2005, pp. 6–24.

Pacheco, Allegra, ed., "The Case Against Torture in Israel: A Compilation of Petitions, Briefs and Other Documents Submitted to the Israeli High Court of Justice," Public Committee Against Torture in Israel, Jerusalem, May 1999.

Pacheco, Allegra, "UN and International Law: Possibilities and Limitations in Palestine," *Guild Practitioner*, Vol. 58, No. 1, 2001, pp. 20–26.

Peleg, Ilan, *Human Rights in the West Bank and Gaza: Legacy and Politics*, Syracuse, Syracuse University Press, 1995.

Public Committee Against Torture in Israel (PCATI), *Back to a Routine of Torture: Torture and Ill-Treatment of Palestinian Detainees During Arrest Detention and Interrogation, Jerusalem, September 2001–April 2003*, 2003.

Shelef, Leon, "The Lesser Evil and the Greater Good—On the Landau Commission Report, Terror and Torture," *Plilim: Israel Journal of Criminal Justice*, Vol. 1., 1990, pp. 185–219 (in Hebrew).

State of Israel, *Commission of Inquiry into the Methods of Investigation of the General Security Service Regarding Hostile Terrorist Activity* (a.k.a. Landau Commission Report), Jerusalem, October 1987. (Translation of selections from the report can be found in *Israel Law Review*, Vol. 23, Nos. 2–3, Spring/Summer 1989, pp. 146–188.) (cited as LC)

"Text of Israeli Supreme Court Decision on GSS Practices," September 6, 1999, http://www.totse.com/en/politics/foreign_military_intelligence_agencies/ua92170.html (cited as SC)

United Nations, "Report of the Secretary-General Prepared Pursuant to General Assembly Resolution ES-10/13," November 23, 2003, http://www.icj-cij.org/docket/files/131/1497.pdf

United Nations, "Four Years After the Advisory Opinion of the International Court of Justice on the Barrier, The Humanitarian Impact of the Barrier," July 2008, http://unispal.un.org/pdfs/BR_Update8July2008.pdf

(United Nations) Economic and Social Commission for Western Asia (ESCWA), "Economic and Social Repercussions of the Israeli Occupation Facts and Figures," October 2008, http://unpan1.un.org/intradoc/groups/public/documents/unescwa/unpan035390.pdf

United Nations, Office for the Coordination of Humanitarian Affairs: Occupied Palestinian Territory, "The Humanitarian Impact of the Barrier," July 2012, http://www.ochaopt.org/documents/ocha_opt_barrier_factsheet_july_2012_english.pdf

United Nations Relief and Works Agency for Palestinian Refugees (UNWRA), "The Impact of the First Phase of Security Barrier on UNRWA-registered Refugees," 1 October, 2003, http://unispal.un.org/UNISPAL.NSF/0/8D642E64DC68377685256DB4004C3869

10   Non-state Actors as Violators in Mexico

A Hard Case for Global Human Rights Norms

Alejandro Anaya Muñoz

Mexico is going through a severe human rights crisis—perhaps the worst in its recent history—whose sources and potential solution are both highly globalized. Thousands of people are being denied their physical integrity rights as a result of the rampant wave of drug-related violence that has savaged the country during the past few years. Although the involvement of the armed forces in the government's struggle against drug cartels has been the source of numerous violations of human rights, the bulk of the executions, torture and disappearances have been perpetrated by members of transnational drug cartels. Furthermore, a majority of the victims of violence are male adults presumably involved in drug-related activities. In this sense, the current human rights crisis in Mexico implies a double challenge for global human rights norms and the actors that advocate them—the main victims are not readily perceived as vulnerable and/or innocent, and the direct perpetrators are not agents of the state. This chapter explores whether transnational advocates of human rights can frame the situation in a way that they can convince larger audiences to join them in the exertion of pressure over the Mexican government. In this sense, the chapter ultimately explores up to what point extent global human rights norms can be relevant for the fulfillment of rights in the current crisis in Mexico.

As the introduction suggests, political processes govern the extent to which the globalization of law can contribute to strengthening human rights. In this case, despite increasing rule of law and autonomy of institutions, the Mexican state lacks critical elements of sovereignty, and Mexico's civil society lacks leverage and traction over nonstate perpetrators. However, this chapter argues that transnational activists could exert pressure over the Mexican government and advocate in favor of a human rights–based approach to the struggle against organized crime in the country. The chapter is, in this way, cautiously optimistic about the possible relevance of global norms for those most in need of protection in Mexico.

INTRODUCTION

Mexico has faced important human rights problems in the past—the repression of the students' movement in the late 1960s and early 1970s, the "dirty war" against radical dissidents that ensued, the violations in the framework of the indigenous uprising in Chiapas in the mid-1990s, and the disappearances and killings of women towards the early 2000s (see Anaya Muñoz 2009a and 2011). However, the atrocities currently taking place in the country have no precedent in recent history. According to official figures, over 47,000 people were killed in drug-related violence between December 2006 and September 2011 (Muedano 2012; also see Booth 2011; Ballinas 2011).[1] About 5,000 people are said to have disappeared in the same period (OUNHCHR 2011a; Becerril and Ballinas 2011). Similarly, the National Commission on Human Rights has reported that tens of thousands of migrants have been abducted by organized crime and brutally abused in order to force their families to pay for their release (Comisión Nacional de los Derechos Humanos 2009 and 2011). Thousands of people are being denied their rights to life, physical integrity and liberty in contemporary Mexico; and the main source of this massive infringement on human rights is a brutal turf war between drug cartels, and in general the criminal activity conducted by non-state actors.

It has been strongly argued in the literature that the actions of non-state actors can be considered as entailing human rights responsibilities for states or even constitute violations of human rights by themselves (Brysk 2005; Hessbruegge 2005; Jochnick 1999; Clapham 2006; Paust 1992). And it has also been argued that given the decreasing power of many states vis à vis other actors (such as multinational corporations, international financial institutions, terrorist groups, and insurrection movements), the negative effects on human rights of the actions of nonstate actors is "one of the most critical human rights matters of our time" (Hessbruegge 2005, 23; also see Jochnick 1999). But, going back to the situation in Mexico, the perpetrators of this massive abuse of physical integrity rights are members of a particular kind of nonstate actor that has not been associated in the literature with the violation of human rights—organized crime, and more specifically, drug cartels. Can we then consider the current situation in Mexico as *a human rights problem*?

Navi Pillay, United Nations High Commissioner for Human Rights, stressed during a recent visit to the country:

> I am deeply concerned by the very high and still escalating levels of violent crime in some parts the country. Organized crime, with its brutal actions and methods, threatens the very core of the state *and attacks the basic human rights* we are struggling so hard to protect. Let us not forget that ensuring citizen security means upholding the right of the

whole population to live free of threat to their basic rights—such as life, physical integrity and liberty, and justice—and for the state to respond and provide redress when those rights are violated. (OUNHCHR 2011b, my emphasis)

Of course, the military and other security forces have been directly involved in the violation of human rights within the framework of the "war against drugs" deployed by the government of President Felipe Calderon (2006–2012). But these "ordinary" or "traditional" violations of human rights have been described and scrutinized elsewhere (Human Rights Watch 2011; Anaya Muñoz 2012). The main focus of this chapter, then, is the executions, acts of torture and disappearances perpetrated by organized crime in the country.

Mexico has figured within the international human rights agenda for at least twenty years now. Particularly since the mid-1990s, after the *Zapatista* uprising in Chiapas, international nongovernmental organizations (NGOs), organs and bodies of the United Nations (UN) and the Organization of American States (OAS) specialized in human rights and (to a lesser degree) governments of developed democracies have monitored the situation in the country and exerted normative pressure over its government.[2] This process of transnational pressure on the bases of global norms has empowered local civil society and has contributed to transformation of the country's human rights laws and institutions.[3] In other words, in the recent past, through the activism of transnational advocates, global human rights norms have been an important force in shaping the domestic politics of human rights in Mexico (Keck and Sikkink 1998, 110–116; Anaya Muñoz 2009b and 2011). Can global human rights norms and the transnational activism around them make a significant contribution in the current crisis in Mexico? Can they influence domestic politics to facilitate the fulfillment of human rights in practice? Can they be relevant to the thousands of victims of drug-related violence in the country?

A growing literature shows that global human rights norms gain salience and influence within domestic political processes when transnational advocates exert significant levels of norms-based pressure over rights-violating governments (see Brysk and Jimenez-Bacardi, this volume). In this sense, global human rights norms can be relevant in the current situation in Mexico if a broad and persistent network of transnational advocates exerts pressure over the government, on account of its failure to meet its international normative obligations. But in order for such a process of broad and consistent transnational pressure to emerge, the situation has to be framed in a way that different international actors are drawn into adopting it, and thus contributing to pressure the Mexican government. Indeed, not all grievances or situations of human suffering are amenable to such an effective framing exercise (see Carpenter 2007; Anaya Muñoz 2011). In this sense, the central question addressed in this chapter is whether the situation of massive infringement of physical integrity rights perpetrated by organized crime is amenable to an effective human rights framing exercise. If the situation can be effectively framed so as to animate the emergence of a broad network of advocates of human rights, then global human rights norms might become relevant in this situation and thus might be able to make a contribution to the fulfillment of rights in the country.

The chapter proceeds as follows. In the first section, it proposes a framework to identify the situations that are more amenable to an effective framing exercise. It argues that cases that involve the violation of physical integrity rights of vulnerable or innocent individuals, and those in which state responsibility is easy to determine, will be more likely to be framed in a way that generates a forceful reaction by international advocates of human rights. The second section describes the situation in Mexico, showing the severity of the infringements on physical integrity rights and the blatant impunity in which violence takes place. In the third section, the chapter explores up to what point the situation is likely to be effectively framed, focusing on the types of violations, victims and perpetrators involved, and on the issue of impunity. The chapter argues that even if the current crisis of physical integrity rights in Mexico is a "hard case" for the globalization of human rights norms, national and international activists could try to frame the situation in a way that they can generate a broader process of transnational pressure over Mexico, and thus contribute to empowering the local actors that are trying to defend the victims of violence in the country.

FRAMING SITUATIONS: VICTIMS, NORMS AND STATE RESPONSIBILITY

As reviewed by Brysk and Jimenez-Bacardi in the introductory chapter to this volume, a sizable international relations literature has studied whether global human rights norms have an influence on state behavior. Indeed, some of this literature shows that, under certain circumstances, global norms have been relevant in the redefinition of state-society relations in a way that favors the human rights agenda (see Brysk and Jimenez-Bacardi, this volume). The literature on international human rights has focused on the role played by the normative pressure exerted "from above" by transnational advocacy networks; it has shown that in a good number of cases (many of them from Latin America), under some circumstances and to different degrees, transnational advocates have influenced domestic political processes in such a way that they contributed to the redefinition of government interests and preferences. In this way, this literature suggests that global human rights norms acquire significance in practice when transnational activists get involved and make them matter, exerting pressure over rights-violating governments (see Brysk 1993 and 1994; Sikkink 1993; Keck and Sikkink 1998; Risse, Ropp and Sikkink 1999; Foot 2000; Burgerman 2001; Thomas 2002; Hawkins 2002; Khagram, Riker and Sikkink 2002; Anaya Muñoz 2009b; cf Neumayer 2005; Franklin 2008; Hafner-Burton 2008; Cardenas 2007; Shor 2008).[4]

But not all situations of violation of human rights result in a similar response from transnational activists—some generate broader and deeper processes of transnational pressure than others, and more easily so (Keck and Sikkink 1998, 26–27; Anaya Muñoz 2011; cf Carpenter 2007). In order to give rise to broad processes of transnational activism and pressure, human rights situations must be credible and shocking; or be presented or framed as such. The occurrence of violations of human rights must be convincingly demonstrated—allegations have to be well documented and must be based on sufficient and reliable evidence. Facts, moreover, must be strategically framed in order to generate a greater impact on international audiences. Broad transnational pressure campaigns need to be based, in the words of Keck and Sikkink, on "credibility and drama"; "cold facts" need to be turned into shocking "human stories" (Keck and Sikkink 1998, 18–22). So a key element for undertaking effective framing exercises is the occurrence of severe human suffering by people that are likely to generate empathy and solidarity from others. Situations that imply bodily harm (i.e., the violation of physical integrity rights) of people considered vulnerable or innocent are more amenable to being presented in a highly shocking manner and therefore to be effectively framed (Keck and Sikkink 1998, 26–28; Sikkink 1993; Burgerman 2001, 31–47; Brysk 1993, 270–271; Hawkins 2004).[5]

Ideas, arguments or demands are likely to be more influential if they are internationally legitimate (Brysk 1994 and 1995). In other words, they will have a greater impact if they "resonate" with existing international understandings about appropriate behavior; that is, with international norms (Brysk 1994 and 1995; Khagram, Riker and Sikkink 2002; Hawkins 2002 and 2004; Price 1998; Thomas 2002). What this means for this chapter's discussion is that issues or situations of human suffering that are proscribed, condemned or delegitimized by global norms are more likely to generate processes of transnational pressure against the governments involved. In this sense, the convergence of the situation with the global normative context is also of central importance for framing exercises.

An important point for the discussion addressed in this chapter is that international human rights norms are traditionally understood as limits on state action; as tools to curtail abuses by government agents. Indeed, as advanced by Alison Brysk, "[t]he human rights tradition [is] a necessary and continuing struggle to limit *state* repression" (2005, 1, my emphasis). In other words, "the human rights regime is based on the enduring principle of state responsibility" (Jochnick 1999, 58). Acts by private citizens or groups that affect the rights of others are generally perceived as crimes, not as violations of human rights. There is, however, as mentioned in the Introduction, a growing concern about "private wrongs" and the fact that abuse "does not always wear a uniform" (Brysk 2005, 1; Jochnick 1999; Hessbruegge 2005).

States, furthermore, not only have a responsibility to respect human rights, but also to ensure or secure their enjoyment by those under their jurisdiction. The International Covenant on Civil and Political Rights, for example, establishes in this respect that each State Party "undertakes to *respect* and to *ensure* to all individuals within its territory and subject to its jurisdiction the rights recognized in the present Covenant."[6] The American Convention on Human Rights includes a very similar clause, while the European Convention on Human Rights establishes that State Parties "shall *secure* to everyone within their jurisdiction the rights and freedoms" established therein.[7] This is what Hessbruegge has called "diagonal obligations": the obligation of the state to protect individuals and groups from the acts of nonstate actors "with due diligence, by preventing or at least reacting to certain non-state conduct" (2005, 24 and 25).[8] States can be responsible not only for directly abusing human rights, but also for failing to protect individuals from abuse by third parties.

EXECUTIONS, TORTURE AND DISAPPEARANCES PERPETRATED BY ORGANIZED CRIME IN MEXICO

Contrary to common perceptions, the murder rate in Mexico declined consistently from 1992 to 2007—from nineteen murders per 100,000 habitants in 1992 to eight in 2007. In this period, Mexico was far less violent than countries such as Colombia, Venezuela, Guatemala or El Salvador. Colombia, for example, had a rate of nearly eighty murders per 100,000 habitants in 1992 and of around thirty-five in 2007 (Escalante Gonzalbo 2007, 25–33). Since 2008, however, the situation has deteriorated, escalating to the levels of the early 1990s—twelve murders per 100,000 habitants in 2008 and eighteen in 2009 and 2010. This growing violence, furthermore, has been clearly concentrated in a few states and cities—those in which the military has been deployed to fight drug-traffickers (Escalante Gonzalbo 2011).[9] Still, overall, Mexico continues to have a murder rate lower than other Latin American countries—that is, Brazil, Guatemala, El Salvador, Venezuela, Colombia and Honduras. However, states like Chihuahua have a rate (120 murders per 100,000 habitants in 2009) much higher than that of Honduras, which has the highest country-rate in Latin America (80 murders per 100,000 in 2010) (Escalante Gonzalbo 2011; United Nations Office on Drugs and Crime 2011).

The recent peak in murder rates in Mexico coincides with an increase in drug-related violence and the so-called war against drugs launched by President Calderon. As mentioned in the Introduction, official figures report that nearly 50,000 people were killed in drug-related violence during the first five years of the Calderon government; while at least 31,000 were "executed" between December 2006 and the end of 2010.[10] A recent journalistic account describes a common execution scene: "one after the other, fifty-eight men and fourteen women, amongst them children, were placed against the wall inside a warehouse (...) Then, they were forced to keep their heads down and were shot by a fire-squad with assault rifles. At the end, the killers shot each of their victims on the head" (*El Universal* 2010). Indeed, independently of the causes of the dramatic increase in violence and murder in Mexico, the fact remains that thousands of people are being denied their right to life as a direct result of drug-related violence and in general the activities of organized crime (such as the kidnapping of migrants).

It is estimated that 90% of the victims of homicide in Mexico are young male adults.[11] The aforementioned increase in the homicide rate in the country has particularly affected men between 20 to 39 years of age. However, "the upsurge in homicide even affected the 15–19 age group, either as members of drug trafficking groups or simply because they were in the wrong place at the wrong time. And there is evidence that some organized criminal groups employ even younger boys within their ranks, which exposes them to a higher risk of being killed" (United Nations Office on Drugs and Crime 2011, 65). So even if young male adults constitute the group most affected by drug violence, children are also victims. According to the Network for the Rights of Children in Mexico (*Red por los Derechos de la Infancia en Mexico*), 900 children (17 years old and younger) have died in violent incidents related to drug trafficking in recent years (Barra and Joloy 2011, 7–8); according to other sources, however, the number of victims reaches more than 1,300 minors (Ballinas 2011).[12] The Network for the Rights of Children in Mexico has also reported that the rate of homicides of children has tripled in some states—for instance, in Baja California, this rate increased from 8.3 per 100,000 people in 2007 to 24.3 in 2008, while in Chihuahua the rate grew from 12.6 to 45.9 in the same period. The rate of homicides of children in Chihuahua in this period is actually twice as high as that for all age groups in Mexico and higher than that of countries like Colombia. In this sense, the killing of children in the context of drug-related violence has recently gained salience in public opinion; particularly after news reports about different massacres of people between 15 and 19 years of age, which have taken place in Chihuahua, Durango, Baja California and Coahuila (Barra and Joloy 2011, 7–8).

Though there are no systematic data on the use of torture in the context of drug-related violence, journalistic accounts suggest that executions are sometimes preceded by torture. A common news report containing information about executions would read, for example: "Thirty-five dead bodies, *with signs of torture*, were abandoned inside two trucks on a heavily transited street in the tourist area of Veracruz-Boca del Río" (*El Universal* 2011b, emphasis added). A search of news reports in leading Mexican newspapers (*El Universal* and *Reforma*) that contain the terms *cadáver* (corpse) and *tortura* (torture), published in a period of five years (from November 2006 to October 2011), produces a list of 274 news stories.[13] So even if we lack a more detailed and systematic account on the occurrence of torture and its relation to executions within the framework of drug-related violence, there is enough evidence to determine that it is also an important part of the picture.

This scenario is further complicated by the occurrence of disappearances, also perpetrated by organized crime within the framework of drug-related violence. According to local human rights nongovernmental organizations (NGOs), about 3,000 people disappeared in the country between 2007 and 2011 (OUNHCHR 2011a). The National Commission on Human Rights, however, reported that the number reached nearly 5,500; while other sources claim that up to 10,000 people have gone missing during the government of Felipe Calderon (Becerril and Ballinas 2011; Ballinas 2011).[14] Again, even if we lack systematic data, it is clear that disappearances further aggravate the situation of massive and systematic violation of physical integrity rights in Mexico.

Thousands of those affected by criminal violence are poor migrants from Central America; men, women and children en route to the United States. Before the recent breakout of criminal violence in Mexico, it was thought that the main risks faced by migrants transiting through Mexico were those related to the inherent dangers of traveling on foot through jungles and deserts, or riding on the top of cargo trains. Human rights advocates were particularly concerned about the legality of the detention practices used by Mexican authorities and the deplorable conditions in detention centers, together with abuses of labor rights of those migrants who chose to work in Mexico (see Anaya Muñoz 2011; Comisión Nacional de los Derechos Humanos 2005). However, as drug-related violence increased in the country, activists' concerns started to focus on the massive and systematic kidnapping and extortion of migrants by organized crime. As mentioned in the Introduction, the National Commission on Human Rights has reported that, between 2009 and 2010, over 20,000 migrants were kidnapped and extorted by organized crime; many of them were tortured, sexually abused or even killed in the process (Comisión Nacional de los Derechos Humanos 2009 and 2011). Kidnapped migrants are forced to provide the telephone number of their relatives in the United States or in their countries of origin, in order to demand a ransom. According to numerous testimonies, those who refuse to cooperate are tortured or even brutally executed in front of others. Migrant women, on their part, suffer particularly from sexual abuse—Amnesty International argues that 60% of migrant women are raped while they transit through Mexico towards the United States (Comisión Nacional de los Derechos Humanos 2009 and 2011; Amnesty International 2010).

According to official narratives, most of the victims of drug-related violence are people involved in criminal activities—in April 2010, President Calderon argued that more than 90% of the registered murders and executions were related to direct intercartel fighting (Ramos and Gomez 2010; BBC 2011). Such statements seem to suggest that those deaths "do not matter," at least not from the official perspective. But in any case, in addition to persons allegedly involved in criminal activities, hundreds of members of the security forces have also been killed, while innocent civilians (who happen to be at the wrong place at the wrong time) have been killed, tortured and disappeared by organized crime. The most dramatic attack on civilians took place in Monterrey, Nuevo León, in August 2011, when a group of armed men belonging to one criminal group set fire to a casino that had apparently refused to pay for "security," killing more than 50 people inside (*El Universal* 2011a).

Human rights activists and journalists have speculated about the reproduction in Mexico of the Colombian "false positives" scenario—the presentation of innocent civilians, extra-judicially executed by security forces, as guerilla fighters, paramilitaries or drug-traffickers that supposedly fell in combat. These arguments have emerged around the hundreds of (unidentified) bodies that in 2011 have been found buried in clandestine mass graves in the states of Tamaulipas and Durango. The official account is that the bodies belong to people that refused to join criminal groups, and were thus executed in reprisal. Indeed, this argument leads to suspicion since, as noted by Emilio Álvarez Icaza (a leading human rights activist), the *narcos* do not hide the bodies of their victims (Reveles 2011, 170). In this framework, some speculation about "false positives," "death squads" and "social cleansing" has started to emerge (Reveles 2011; also see Booth 2011; Miroff and Booth 2011).

This situation, in which thousands of Mexicans are being denied the enjoyment of their physical integrity rights, develops and flourishes in the midst of blatant impunity. The direct victims of violence and their families seldom receive any kind of reparation or compensation. Executions that are considered by the authorities as resulting from intercartel fighting are not investigated. The National Commission on Human Rights asserted in October 2011 that nearly 9,000 bodies had not been identified (Becerril and Ballinas 2011). According to some journalistic estimates, only 5% of drug-related murders are investigated (Otero 2010). This coincides with academic research on overall impunity in Mexico, which has estimated that only 4.5% of crimes are fully investigated by prosecutors, while in only 1.6% of all cases somebody is taken to trial (Zepeda Lecuona 2003, 2005; also see Shirk 2010; Magaloni Kerpel 2007). Similarly, the growing reports of missing or disappeared people are routinely ignored by authorities.

President Calderon stated in late 2011 that he is "concerned about the fact that the number of disappeared people in the country is very high" and acknowledged that "we do not know the dimensions of this problem." In this context, he praised the creation of the "Social Attorney's Office for the Support of the Victims of Crime" and the creation of a database of missing people (*La Jornada* 2011; Ramos 2011; Becerril and Ballinas 2011). This Social Attorney's Office (which does not have prosecutorial powers) has been recently established by the Calderon government with the intention of supporting the victims of crime and, in particular, promoting an efficient response from the authorities in cases of disappearances. This new entity, however, has been dismissed by national activists as irrelevant, arguing that it lacks the necessary resources and criticizing that it has been established to support victims of *crime* as opposed to victims of the violation of human rights (Movimiento por la Paz con Justicia y Dignidad 2011; Instituto Mexicano de Derechos Humanos y Democracia 2011). In any case, the point that is important to stress here is that the state is blatantly failing to provide effective access to justice for the massive number of executions, torture and disappearances.

DEVELOPING AN EFFECTIVE FRAMING EXERCISE

As reviewed in the first section of this chapter, according to the literature, the possibilities for developing an effective framing exercise (and thus for generating a broad and persistent process of transnational human rights pressure) are higher in situations that entail the violation of physical integrity rights of individuals or groups that are perceived as vulnerable or innocent. In addition, the responsibility of the state has to be clearly established. As clearly shown in the previous section, the crisis of drug-related violence in Mexico implies the massive denial of physical integrity rights. Thousands of people are being affected in their rights to life and to be free from torture and disappearance. So the situation is related to the human rights that are most amenable to an effective framing exercise—physical integrity rights. However, while many of the victims can be readily considered as vulnerable or innocent—notably children, women and migrants—the bulk of those executed, tortured and disappeared are male adults that appear to be directly involved in criminal activity. They are not, in other words, "good victims," from the perspective of an effective framing exercise. In addition, and perhaps more important, the direct perpetrators of the abuses are not state agents, but members of organized crime.

What are the real chances of effectively framing the current crisis in Mexico as one of the violation of international human rights norms? Can international human rights norms provide an appropriate answer for the thousands of Mexicans that are being killed, tortured or disappeared? Should domestic and international human rights advocates devote a considerable share of their energy to try to present the situation within a human rights framework and in this way try to contribute to the fulfillment of rights in practice? Is it worth the effort?

As stressed above, the first obstacle to develop an effective framing exercise is that most of the victims are young male adults allegedly involved with drug cartels. Thus, most victims are not readily perceived as innocent or vulnerable. It could be argued that these individuals opted to take part in a dangerous illegal activity, and thus they must accept the consequences of their own choices. On a closer examination, however, the situation is more complex than that.

Thousands of migrants have suffered from the wave of brutal violence exerted by organized crime. Migrants are not involved in criminal activity—and thus are clearly innocent. Most of them have been driven out of their home countries in Central America by extreme poverty. A good part of these migrants are women, who are highly exposed to sexual abuse. Overall, migrants transiting through Mexico are highly vulnerable—given their un-documented status, they have to travel through deserted clandestine routes, in which they are easy prey for organized crime. According to human rights groups, Mexican authorities have not really tried to protect migrants; even worse, they are sometimes part of the criminal networks that abuse them (see Amnesty International 2010; Centro de Derechos Humanos Miguel Agustín Pro Juárez 2010; Comisión Nacional de los Derechos Humanos 2009, 2011). So migrants can readily be considered as innocent and highly vulnerable victims.

As also mentioned in Section 2 above, hundreds of children are being killed. Stories of massacres of children are not rare. In Durango, for exam-ple, a group of ten children and young adults (aged 8 to 21) were massacred by an armed group after they had received an award for their performance in school. In Ciudad Juárez, at least three massacres of teenagers took place between September 2009 and February 2010 (Barra and Joloy 2011, 8). In most such cases, the connection between those killed and organized crime was not clear. But even if they were part of a criminal group, following the international consensus on children in armed conflict, it could be argued that more than perpetrators they are victims that need to be protected (see Carpenter 2007). Focusing on children as victims, the possibilities for an effective framing exercise increase.

Finally, an argument could be made to challenge the view that members of organized crime made a free choice to get involved in an illicit and dan-gerous business. It is commonly accepted that the cadres of criminal groups come from marginal and deprived socioeconomic groups. Faced with no other viable option for social mobility, a good proportion of the *ni-nis* gener-ation is almost inexorably drawn into the lower ranks of criminal groups.[15] Can we really consider a decision made under these circumstances a "free choice"? Though controversial, this is highly relevant, particularly because those more likely to be killed in the turf wars between cartels are those in the lower echelons of the criminal hierarchy.

The most significant obstacle to undertake an effective framing exercise, however, is that the direct perpetrators are not state agents. Can state respon-sibility be established in this case? Situations characterized by executions, torture or disappearances perpetrated by nonstate actors have been framed in a human rights framework in the past when the direct perpetrators are sponsored, supported or at least tolerated by the state or its agents. That is, when nonstate actors are *de facto* agents of the state (see Hessbruegge 2005, 53–59). This has been the case, for example, of violations by paramilitary groups (see Human Rights Watch 2010). But this does not initially seem to be the case in Mexico. Members of drug-trafficking organizations are not *de facto* agents of the state.[16]

An increasing amount of evidence, however, shows that police forces and other government agents (particularly at the state and municipal levels) are often co-opted by the different drug cartels and thus play an active and direct role in actions (Miroff and Booth 2011; Amnesty International 2010; Centro de Derechos Humanos Miguel Agustín Pro Juárez 2010). In other words, some members of the security forces often *do* act as *de facto* agents of the drug cartels. Even if the bulk of the executions, torture and disappearances are perpetrated by members of organized crime, there is evidence that shows that state agents are sometimes directly involved. In these kinds of cases, the *direct* responsibility of the state could be easily presented to wider audiences. In other words, it could be convincingly argued that, in a number of cases or situations, the Mexican state is not fulfilling its "vertical" human rights obligations: that is, its direct obligations to respect human rights.

But the main argument could be that of "diagonal obligations": that is, the obligations of the state that emerge from the actions of nonstate actors. Transnational advocates of human rights could stress that the Mexican state is utterly failing to act with due diligence in order to control violence and to prevent the occurrence of executions, torture and disappearances perpetrated by private actors. In other words, they could stress that the state is failing to protect thousands of people, and thus to *ensure* or *secure* the enjoyment of their physical integrity rights. This could be linked to the situation of blatant impunity described in the previous section. Passive or active omission produces an undeniable failure to conduct effective investigations, bring those responsible to justice and provide remedy and compensation to the victims. In this way, there is sufficient evidence to also frame the situation as one of denial of the right to access to justice, which in turn feeds into the vicious cycle in which executions, torture and disappearances take place.

Framing the situation in Mexico in terms of the "diagonal obligations" of the state could be buttressed making reference to extant norms. Indeed, international human rights instruments, such as the International Covenant on Civil and Political Rights and the American Convention on Human Rights, explicitly establish the duty of diligent protection of rights (Hessebruegge 2005, 70–71). Furthermore, the duty to protect physical integrity rights against attacks by private actors has been explicitly stressed (around cases of other Latin American countries) by the jurisprudence of the Human Rights Committee of the United Nations and the Inter-American Court of Human Rights (Hessebruegge 2005, 72–74). Key players in the transnational advocacy of human rights in Mexico have made the argument of "diagonal obligations" before, in relation to other countries. A similar argument could be made again by these actors, this time in respect to Mexico.

Another relevant point of reference could be the "Campaign to Stop the Use of Child Soldiers," which in the 1990s and early 2000s successfully moved the international community into trying to protect human rights against the abuses of nonstate actors. As is widely known, the Campaign resulted in the adoption of the Optional Protocol to the Convention on the Rights of the Child on the involvement of children in armed conflict "as well as a whirlwind of activity around the issue of children and war" (Carpenter 2007, 105–108).[17] This situation, however, is different than the one addressed here in two key respects: the victims and the perpetrators. Indeed, children are more likely to elicit sympathy from international audiences than "drug dealers" and "criminals." On the other hand, rebel or insurgent groups have been regularly included within the group of nonstate actors that can potentially violate human rights; drug cartels, as mentioned before, have not.

CONCLUSIONS

The uncontrolled wave of drug-related violence in Mexico has generated a severe crisis of physical integrity rights in the country, perhaps the worst since the 1910 Mexican Revolution. Nearly 50,000 people have been denied the right to life during the first five years of the Calderon government, while an undetermined number have been tortured or disappeared. This terrible crisis of human rights fulfillment, however, cannot be easily presented to international audiences as one of the violation of human rights norms. In other words, the characteristics of the situation itself make it difficult for activists to frame it as a credible and shocking story of the violation of human rights, and thus to convince different international actors that they should exert pressure over the Mexican government. This is a "hard case" for the globalization of human rights law. The most evident framing difficulties arise from two concrete characteristics of the situation. First, a large proportion of the victims of violence are presumed to be actively involved in criminal activities, and thus can hardly be perceived as innocent or vulnerable individuals, worthy of solidarity and protection from international actors. Second, the direct perpetrators are nonstate actors. This latter point is particularly problematic for framing efforts because advocates would need to argue convincingly that the brutal abuses by organized crime have to be understood as entailing human rights obligations for the state.

This chapter, however, argues (speculatively) that these two obstacles for an effective framing exercise, however important, are not insurmountable. Advocates could stress, first of all, that in fact a massive number of children, women and migrants are being affected in the enjoyment of their human rights. Thousands of innocent and vulnerable victims are being killed, tortured and disappeared. The case could also be made that many of the young male adults that take part in criminal activities and that have been killed, tortured or disappeared are the victims of poverty and marginalization and thus worthy of international solidarity and protection. On the other hand, it could be argued that even if most of the times the direct perpetrators of the abuses are nonstate actors, security forces sometimes directly participate in the abuses. The responsibility of the state (or the breach of its "vertical obligations") in this type of case is straightforward. Furthermore, advocates could stress that the Mexican state is not fulfilling its "diagonal" human rights obligations. They could underline that the Mexican state is blatantly failing to implement a security policy that protects the persons under its jurisdiction and thus ensures or secures the enjoyment of physical integrity rights in the country. This could further be linked to the issue of impunity, which feeds into the vicious cycle of murder, torture and disappearances by failing to impose credible costs for those taking part in violent criminal activity. Furthermore, through blatant impunity, the Mexican state is itself directly denying the right to access to justice. The lack of reparation, in the broad sense of the term, further violates the human rights of the thousands of victims and their relatives.

In sum, the current crisis of physical integrity rights in Mexico can be understood within a human rights framework. It can be framed as a situation of massive *violation of human rights* that deserves international attention. As recognized above, however, this is a speculative argument. Unfortunately, it seems that there are no cases of successful advocacy in similar circumstances from which we could derive more solid (empirically founded) expectations. The optimistic cosmopolitan literature would lead us to expect that if international advocates were to succeed in effectively framing the situation and thus in drawing the support of broader international audiences, then they would in turn contribute to empower local human rights organizations and those groups who are struggling to uphold the rights of the victims of violence in Mexico. This optimism for bringing the globalization of human rights to the hard case of Mexico will be tested by the practice of human rights in Mexico in the months or years to come.

NOTES

1. An official database, with the number of drug-related killings disaggregated by month and municipality, can be consulted at http://www.presidencia.gob.mx/base-de-datos-de-fallecimientos/.
2. For an initial approach on the Zapatista uprising in Chiapas see Harvey 1998 and Womack 1999.
3. For the importance of the empowerment of civil society and the strengthening of local institutions see Brysk and Jimenez-Bacardi, this volume.
4. This is not to argue that transnational human rights pressure necessarily leads to a significant improvement in the actual respect of human rights. Target governments are expected to take the situation more seriously and adopt reforms and new policies, which in principle should improve the prospects for social mobilization and litigation by domestic actors, but do not result, per se, in a dramatic improvement in the fulfillment of human rights in practice (see Cardenas 2007; cf Simmons 2009). As proposed by Brysk and Jimenez-Bacardi (this volume), the ultimate impact of the globalization of law in specific

countries is contingent on local factors: autonomous justice institutions, and empowered civil society and a minimum degree of self-determination.

5. Keck and Sikkink acknowledge that "who is vulnerable or innocent may be highly contested." They conclude, nevertheless, that "campaigns against practices involving bodily harm to populations *perceived as* vulnerable or innocent are most likely to be effective" (Keck and Sikkink 1998, 27, emphasis added).

6. International Covenant on Civil and Political Rights (Article 2.1, emphasis added), adopted December 16, 1966; entered into force March 23, 1976.

7. American Convention on Human Rights (Article 1.1), adopted November 22, 1969, entered into force July 18, 1978; European Convention on Human Rights (Article 1, emphasis added) as amended by Protocols Nos. 11 and 14, which entered into force November 1, 1998, and June 1, 2010, respectively.

8. "Vertical obligations" are those that a state has in respect to human rights: "The state (S) has an obligation to do or not do X in its dealings with a non-state actor (N), because N can invoke a human right against S." On the other hand, "horizontal obligations" are the direct human rights obligations of non-state actors: "N1 must do or not do X to N2, because N2 has a human right corresponding to an obligation of N1" (Hessbruegge 2005, 25).

9. This is not to suggest that military presence has *caused* the increase in the murder rates. More likely, security forces have been sent to where violence has escalated.

10. See the government's database at http://www.presidencia.gob.mx/base-de-datos-de-fallecimientos/. Also see BBC 2011; Ballinas 2011. Though the government's database does not specify what exactly constitutes an "execution," it is likely that it is the murder of a person in a noncombat context.

11. A recent report by the UN Office on Drugs and Crime argues that, in countries heavily affected by growing murder rates related to organized crime, young males are at a higher risk, "due to their more likely participation in violence-prone activities such as street crime, gang membership, drug consumption, possession of weapons, street fighting, etc." (United Nations Office on Drugs and Crime 2011, 12).

12. This figure was given by a group of activists that presented to the Prosecutor of the International Criminal Court a petition to investigate President Felipe Calderon for crimes against humanity. For the original document see http://www.petitiononline.com/CPI/petition.html.

13. The total number of stories containing only the term *cadaver* holding constant the rest of the search parameters is 3,838. All searches were made using the "Power Search" engine in *Lexis Nexis Academic*.

14. Also see http://www.petitiononline.com/CPI/petition.html.

15. The term *ni-nis* colloquially refers to those who "*ni* estudian, *ni* trabajan"; that is, those who neither study nor work. According to the Organization for Economic Cooperation and Development (OECD), over 7 million Mexicans aged between 15 to 29 would fall in this category (Avilés 2011).

16. Some politicians, journalists and parts of the general public have suspected that the Calderon government has been lenient towards the powerful *Sinaloa* cartel, showing a stronger stance towards the rest of the drug-trafficking groups, in particular the ruthless *Zetas* cartel. These accusations have, of course, been strongly denied by the government (Beltrán 2010; Booth 2011; Herrera Beltrán 2010).

17. Article 4 of the Optional Protocol establishes that "States Parties shall take all feasible measures to prevent" that "[a]rmed groups that are distinct from the armed forces of a State" recruit or use children in hostilities.

REFERENCES

Amnesty International (2010) *Invisible Victims: Migrants on the Move in Mexico*, London: Amnesty International (http://www.amnesty.org/en/library/asset/AMR41/014/2010/en/8459f0ac-03ce-4302-8bd2-3305bdae9cde/amr410142010eng.pdf) (last consulted 28 October 2011).

Anaya Muñoz, Alejandro (2009a) "Mexico after the Institutional Revolutionary Party (PRI)," in David Forsythe (ed.), *Encyclopedia of Human Rights*, Oxford, UK: Oxford University Press.

—— (2009b) "Transnational and Domestic Processes in the Definition of Human Rights Policies in Mexico," *Human Rights Quarterly*, Vol. 31, No. 1, pp. 35–58.

—— (2011) "Explaining High Levels of Transnational Pressure over Mexico: The Case of Disappearances and Killings of Women in Ciudad Juárez," *International Journal of Human Rights*, Vol. 15, No. 3, pp. 339–358.

—— (2012) "Security versus Human Rights: The Case of Contemporary Mexico," in Paul Kenny and Mónica Serrano (with Arturo Soto Mayor) (eds.), *Mexico Security Failure: Collapse into Criminal Violence*, New York: Routledge, pp. 122–140.

Avilés, Karina (2011) "OCDE: *ninis*, 7 millones 226 mil mexicanos de entre 15 y 29 años," *La Jornada*, Society and Justice Section, 13 September, p. 36.

Ballinas, Victor (2011) "Denunciarán a Calderón en La Haya por crímenes de lesa humanidad," *La Jornada*, Politics Section, 11 October, p. 5.

Barra, Aram, and Joloy, Daniel (2011) *Niños: Las víctimas olvidadas en la guerra contra las drogas en México*, Mexico City: Espolea A.C.

BBC (2011) "Mexico Updates Four Years of Drug War Deaths to 34,612," News Latin America & Caribbean, 13 January (http://translate.google.com.mx/translate?hl=es&sl=en&tl=es&u=http%3A%2F%2Fwww.bbc.co.uk%2Fnews%2Fworld-latin-america-12177875&anno=2) (last consulted 20 October 2011).

Becerril, Andrea, and Ballinas, Victor (2011) "El gobierno retirará reservas a la convención internacional," *La Jornada*, Politics Section, 20 October, p. 10.

Beltrán, José Alfredo (2010) "El Narco en Sinaloa no ha sido tocado," *El Universal*, National Section, 19 February (http://www.eluniversal.com.mx/nacion/175758.html) (last consulted 26 December 2012).

Booth, William (2011) "10 Years On, Mexican Drug Lord Still Dodges Capture," *Washington Post*, 27 October (http://www.washingtonpost.com/todays_paper?dt=2011-10-28&bk=A&pg=1) (last consulted 28 October 2011).

Brysk, Alison (1993) "From Above and Below: Social Movements, the International System and Human Rights in Argentina," *Comparative Political Studies*, Vol. 26, No. 3, pp. 259–285.

—— (1994) *The Politics of Human Rights in Argentina: Protest, Change and Democratization*, Stanford, CA: Stanford University Press.

—— (1995) " 'Hearts and Minds': Bringing Symbolic Politics Back In," *Polity*, Vol. 27, No. 4, pp. 559–585.

—— (2005) *Human Rights and Private Wrongs: Constructing Global Civil Society*, New York: Routledge.

Brysk, Alison, and Arturo Jimenez-Bacardi (2013) "The Politics of the Globalization of Law," in Alison Brysk (ed.), *The Politics of the Globalization of Law: Getting from Rights to Justice*, New York: Routledge.

Burgerman, Susan (2001) *Moral Victories: How Activists Provoke Multilateral Action*, Ithaca, NY: Cornell University Press.

Cardenas, Sonia (2007) *Conflict and Compliance: State Responses to International Human Rights Pressure*, Philadelphia: University of Pennsylvania Press.

Carpenter, Charli (2007) "Studying Issue (Non)-Adoption in Transnational Networks," *International Organization*, Vol. 61, No. 3, pp. 643–667.

Centro de Derechos Humanos Miguel Agustín Pro Juárez (2010) *Secuestros a Personas Migrantes Centroamericanas en Tránsito por México*, Mexico City: Centro de Derechos Humanos Miguel Pro Juárez.

Clapham, Andrew (2006) "Human Rights Obligations of Non-state Actors in Conflict Situations," *International Review of the Red Cross*, Vol. 88, No. 863, pp. 491–523.

Comisión Nacional de los Derechos Humanos (2005) *Informe especial de la Comisión Nacional de los Derechos Humanos sobre la situación de los derechos humanos en las estaciones migratorias y lugares habilitados del Instituto Nacional de Migración en la República Mexicana*, Mexico City: Comisión Nacional de los Derechos Humanos.

Comisión Nacional de los Derechos Humanos (2009) *Informe Especial de la Comisión Nacional de los Derechos Humanos sobre los casos de secuestro en contra de migrantes*, Mexico City: Comisión Nacional de los Derechos Humanos.

Comisión Nacional de los Derechos Humanos (2011) *Informe Especial sobre Secuestro de Migrantes en México*, Mexico City: Comisión Nacional de los Derechos Humanos.

El Universal (2010) "Masacre en San Fernando: Por negarse a ser sicarios los fusilaron," 26 August. (http://www.eluniversal.com.mx/primera/35447.html) (last consulted 27 December 2012).

—— (2011a) "Atacan un casino en NL; 53 muertos," National Section, 26 August. (http://www.eluniversal.com.mx/notas/788781.html) (last consulted 27 December 2012).

—— (2011b) "Veracruz: tiran a 35 ejecutados en zona turística," States Section, 21 September. (http://www.eluniversal.com.mx/primera/37768.html) (last consulted 27 December 2012).

Escalante Gonzalbo (2007) *El homicidio en México entre 1990 y 2007. Aproximación estadística*, Mexico City: El Colegio de México and Secretaría de Seguridad Pública Federal.

Escalante Gonzalbo (2011) "Homicidios 2008–2009. La muerte tiene permiso," *Nexos*, January, consulted at *Nexos en línea* (http://www.nexos.com.mx/?P=leer articulo&Article=1943189) (last consulted 20 October 2011).

Foot, Rosemary (2000) *Rights beyond Borders. The Global Community and the Struggle over Human Rights in China*, Oxford, UK: Oxford University Press.

Franklin, James C. (2008) "Shame on You: The Impact of Human Rights Criticism on Political Repression in Latin America," *International Studies Quarterly*, Vol. 52, No. 1, pp. 187–212.

Hafner-Burton, Emile M. (2008) "Sticks and Stones: Naming and Shaming the Human Rights Enforcement Problem," *International Organization*, Vol. 62, No. 4, pp. 689–716.

Harvey, Neil (1998) *The Chiapas Rebellion: The Struggle for Land and Democracy*, Durham, NC: Duke University Press.

Hawkins, Darren (2002) "Human Rights Norms and Networks in Authoritarian Chile," in Sanjeev Khagram, James V. Riker, and Kathryn Sikkink (eds.), *Restructuring World Politics: Transnational Social Movements, Networks, and Norms*, Minneapolis: University of Minnesota Press, pp. 47–70.

—— (2004) "Explaining Costly International Institutions: Persuasion and Enforceable Human Rights Norms," *International Studies Quarterly*, Vol. 48, No. 4, pp. 779–804.

Herrera Beltrán, Claudia (2010) "No se protege a *El Chapo* ni a nadie, dice Calderón," *La Jornada*, Politics Section, 25 February, p. 3

Hessbruegge, Jan Arno (2005) "Human Rights Violations Arising from Conduct of Non-state Actors," *Buffalo Human Rights Law Review*, Vol. 11, pp. 21–88.

Human Rights Watch (2010) *Paramilitaries' Heirs: The New Face of Violence in Colombia*, New York: Human Rights Watch.

—— (2011) *Neither Rights nor Security: Killings, Torture, and Disappearances in Mexico's "War on Drugs,"* New York: Human Rights Watch.

Instituto Mexicano de Derechos Humanos y Democracia (2011) "La Procuraduría Social para la Atención a Víctimas y Ofendidos, ¿Alternativa verdadera o simulación?" Press release, 29 Septembrer (http://imdhd.org/media/Op_Pria_Soc_Victimas_0911.pdf) (last consulted 20 October 2011).

Jochnick, C. (1999) "Confronting the Impunity of Non-state Actors: New Fields for the Promotion of Human Rights. *Human Rights Quarterly*, Vol. 21, No. 1, pp. 56–79.

Keck, E. Margaret, and Sikkink, Kathryn (1998) *Activists beyond Borders: Advocacy Networks in International Politics*, Ithaca, NY: Cornell University Press.

Khagram, Sanjeev, James V. Riker, and Kathryn Sikkink (2002) "From Santiago to Seattle: Transnational Advocacy Groups Restructuring World Politics," in Sanjeev Khagram, James V. Riker, and Kathryn Sikkink (eds.), *Restructuring World Politics: Transnational Social Movements, Networks, and Norms*, Minneapolis: University of Minnesota Press, pp. 3–23.

La Jornada (2011) "Preocupa a Calderón el número de desaparecidos por el crimen," Politics Section, 11 October, p. 7.

Magaloni Kerpel, Ana Laura (2007) "Arbitrariedad e ineficiencia de la procuración de justicia: dos caras de la misma moneda," Working Paper No. 26, Juridical Studies Division-CIDE, Mexico City: Centro de Investigación y Docencia Económicas.

Miroff, Nick, and Booth, William (2011) "Mass Graves in Mexico Reveal New Levels of Savagery," *Washington* Post, World Section, 24 April (http://articles.washingtonpost.com/2011-04-24/world/35231736_1_mexican-marines-cartel-state-officials) (last consulted 27 December 2012).

Movimiento por la Paz con Justicia y Dignidad (2011) "Posicionamiento de la Mesa 1: Atención a Víctimas," Public Statement, 17 October (http://movimientoporlapaz.mx/2011/10/14/posicionamiento-de-la-mesa-1-atencion-a-victimas/)(lastconsulted 20 October 2011).

Muedano, Marco (2012) "Van 47 mil muertos por narcoviolencia: PGR," *El Universal*, National Section, 12 January (http://www.eluniversal.com.mx/notas/822078.html) (last consulted 27 December 2012).

Neumayer, Erik (2005) "Do International Human Rights Treaties Improve Respect for Human Rights?" *Journal of Conflict Resolution*, Vol. 49, No. 6, pp. 925–953.

Otero, Silvia (2010) "No investigan 95% de muertes en 'guerra,'" *El Universal*, National Section, 21 June (http://www.eluniversal.com.mx/primera/35119.html) (last consulted 27 December 2012).

OUNHCHR (2011a) "El Grupo de Trabajo sobre las desapariciones forzadas o involuntarias concluye su visita a México" (http://www.ohchr.org/SP/NewsEvents/Pages/DisplayNews.aspx?NewsID=10907&LangID=S) (last consulted 22 September 2011)

—— (2011b) "Press Conference by UN High Commissioner for Human Rights, Navi Pillay, Mexico City, Mexico," 8 July (http://www.ohchr.org/EN/NewsEvents/Pages/DisplayNews.aspx?NewsID=11216&LangID=E) (last consulted 10 October 2011)

Paust, Jordan J. (1992) "The Other Side of Right: Private Duties under Human Rights Law," *Harvard Human Rights Journal*, Vol. 5, pp. 51–63.

Price, Richard (1998) "Reversing the Gun Sights: Transnational Civil Society Targets Land Mines," *International Organization*, Vol. 52, No. 3, pp. 613–644.

Ramos, Jorge (2011) "Preocupa número de desaparecidos: FCH," First Page, *El Universal*, 11 October (http://www.eluniversal.com.mx/notas/800099.html) (last consulted 27 December 2012).

Ramos, Jorge, and Gomez, Ricardo (2010) "Muerte de civiles enfrenta a poderes," *El Universal*, National Section, 17 April (http://www.eluniversal.com.mx/nacion/177082.html) (last consulted 27 December 2012).

Reveles, José (2011) *Levantones, narcofosas y falsos positivos*, Mexico City: Grijalbo.

Risse, Thomas, Stephen C. Ropp, and Kathryn Sikkink (1999) *The Power of Human Rights: International Norms and Domestic Change*, Cambridge: Cambridge University Press.

Shirk, David (2010) "Justice Reform in Mexico: Change and Challenges in the Judicial Sector," in Eric L. Olson, David A. Shirk, and Andrew Selee (eds.), *Shared Responsibility, U.S.–Mexico Policy Options for Confronting Organized Crime*, Washington, DC: Mexico Institute, Woodrow Wilson Center for International Studies and Trans-Border Institute, University of California, San Diego, pp. 205–246.

Shor, Eran (2008) "Conflict, Terrorism and the Socialization of Human Rights Norms: The Spiral Model Revisited," *Social Problems*, Vol. 55, No. 1, pp. 117–138.

Sikkink, Kathryn (1993) "Human Rights, Principled Issue: Networks and Sovereignty in Latin America," *International Organization*, Vol. 47, No. 3, pp. 411–441.

Simmons, Beth (2009) *Mobilizing for Human Rights: International Law in Domestic Politics*, Cambridge: Cambridge University Press.

Thomas, Daniel C. (2002) "Human Rights in U.S. Foreign Policy," in Sanjeev Khagram, James V. Riker, and Kathryn Sikkink (eds.), *Restructuring World Politics: Transnational Social Movements, Networks, and Norms*, Minneapolis: University of Minnesota Press, pp. 71–95.

United Nations Office on Drugs and Crime (2011) *2011 Global Study on Homicides: Trends, Context, Data*, Vienna, Austria: United Nations Office on Drugs and Crime.

Womack Jr, John (1999) *Rebellion in Chiapas: An Historical Reader*, New York: New Press.

Zepeda Lecuona, Guillermo (2003) "La investigación de los delitos y la subversión de los principios del subsistema penal en México," USMEX 2003–04 Working Papers Series, San Diego, CA: Center for U.S.-Mexican Studies.

—— (2005) "Desafíos de la seguridad ciudadana y la justicia penal en México," in Due Process of Law Foundation and National Center for State Courts, *Sociedad Civil y Reforma Judicial en América Latina*, Washington, DC: Due Process of Law Foundation and National Center for State Courts, pp. 293–300.

11 Extraordinary Laws and Torture in India in an Era of Globalization[1]

Jinee Lokaneeta

In this chapter, I analyze the implications of the globalization of antiterrorism laws for the laws and practice of torture in India. Post-9/11, the United Nations Security Council passed a number of resolutions that enabled anti-terrorism legislation in different countries. In India, however, extraordinary laws have a long history dating back to colonial times and proliferating in postcolonial times. Consequently, the effort to introduce laws such as the Prevention of Terrorism Act (POTA) in 2002 was not a new phenomenon, even though ostensibly it was a response to the Parliament attack of December 2001. The Indian state merely used the attack as an opportunity to bring in this act quickly—and in the process, the Indian state's anti-terror initiatives were recalibrated to align with a global war on terrorism. Through an analysis of Supreme Court decisions and human rights reports, I argue that the legal discourses on extraordinary laws illustrate a central tension in the protections against torture and other human rights in a postcolonial liberal state. Even though the Indian state relies on its strong safeguards against torture and other violations of rights as a marker of its liberal democratic status in the global order, and was making progress condemning routine custodial torture, India's autonomous judiciary fails to adequately contain the distinction between routine and extraordinary laws. I trace this difference to the contradictions of sovereignty, highlighted in the introduction to this volume as a critical factor conditioning the human rights impact of the globalization of law.

GLOBALIZATION AS AN IMPETUS FOR EXTRAORDINARY LAWS

Following 9/11, UN resolutions prompted many states to introduce anti-terror legislation on a fast-track basis. Resolution 1373, adopted by the United Nations Security Council immediately after 9/11, led to the Patriot Act in the United States, the Anti-Terrorism Crime and Security Act in the United Kingdom, the C36 in Canada and the Suppression of Terrorism Act in New Zealand (see Scheppele 2004). In its push for India's Protection Against Terrorism Act, the then ruling party in India, Bharatiya Janata Party (BJP), also referred to the UN Resolution. However, this use of the UN Resolution has been criticized by many scholars and activists such as Anil Kalhan, who point out that there was no effort to distinguish between the requirements for a law under the UN Resolution and the specifics of the legislation adopted by the state (Kalhan et al. 2006). Concerns within India about the impact of the proposed legislation on human rights were set aside, to use the UN Resolution as a pretext to quickly pass the anti-terror legislation desired by the government in power. The situation was worsened by the lack of effective intervention from the UN Counter Terrorism Committee to ensure that these legislations did not simultaneously undermine human rights (Kalhan et al. 2006).

The multiple initiatives in the post-9/11 context coalescing around the UN Resolution did create and strengthen a global discourse on terrorism, and scholars specifically note a strong resemblance between the provisions in POTA and the Patriot Act (see Krishnan 2004: 265–300; see Gagne 2005).[2] However, it is important to note the long history of extraordinary laws and policies that have existed since the British period (Kalhan et al. 2006). For example, the governor general during the colonial period had the ability to pronounce an emergency and use extraordinary powers at that time. Similarly, special emergency legislations such as the Defense of India Act, 1915 during World War I were introduced and continued in nonemergency periods (see Kalhan et al. 2006). In all these situations, preventive detentions and bypassing of procedural safeguards, such as lower standards of evidence and longer periods of detention, were allowed, since the defense of the colonial state overpowered the need to maintain the "rule of law" (Ruthven 1978). As Kannabiran explains, "It is evident that a legal system structured to rule colonies can never square with a constitutional scheme" (2003: 23).

The Indian Constitution makers held on to the powers of the executive to proclaim emergencies inherited from the colonial era that allowed enormous centralized powers, including the suspension of fundamental civil liberties (Haragopal and Balagopal 1998). Even though some of these extraordinary powers were introduced during emergencies, like British colonial policies they had a tendency to continue even after the crisis (Kalhan et al. 2006). The Indian Constitution also retained a provision for preventive detention in nonemergency contexts that was used to introduce laws such as the Preventive Detention Act (1950), the Maintenance of Internal Security Act (1971) and the Unlawful Activities Prevention Act (1967). Kannabiran points out that this uncritical continuation of several repressive colonial laws, ideologies and institutions directly contradicts the egalitarian visions of the Indian Constitution makers and the democratic aspirations of the Indian people.[3] Given this long tradition, TADA [Terrorism and Disruptive activities (Prevention) Act, 1985] and POTA actually follow this history of extraordinary legislations in India, and the international context becomes merely a pretext to pass particular laws.

UPHOLDING PARALLEL REGIMES OF GOVERNANCE: THE EXCEPTIONALITY OF TADA

In this section, I focus on TADA, one of the extraordinary laws that had tremendous implications for the torture debate in India. TADA was first introduced in India in 1985, one year after the assassination of then Prime Minister Indira Gandhi. The immediate impetus for TADA may have been the assassination, but it gained political support from the Congress Party (and other political parties) primarily because it simultaneously became an act to deal with the militant movements in different parts of the country, namely, Kashmir, North East, Andhra Pradesh and Punjab.[4] The response of the Indian state in all these areas of conflict was either the introduction of armed actions against the militants and/or targeting these regions with extraordinary laws.

In the case of Punjab, which was the stage for the introduction of TADA, the Indian state responded to the militant movements (that were demanding a separate state of Khalistan) by sending the army into the Golden Temple—the holy place for the Sikhs—in Operation Blue Star. As a result of the attack, alongside the Sikh militants and the members of the armed forces, a number of pilgrims were also killed, alienating the Sikhs further from the Indian state. The assassination of Indira Gandhi by her Sikh bodyguards, while tragic, was in retaliation for the brutal state repression in Punjab, particularly Operation Blue Star (Kannabiran 2003). Human rights groups documented thousands of deaths in Punjab as a result of the counterinsurgency state operations. The Indian state introduced many local laws in Punjab such as the Armed Forces (Punjab and Chandigarh) Special Powers Act, 1983, National Security Act (1984 and 1987) and also enforced the president's rule (see Human Rights Watch 1991, 2004).[5] However, the legislation having the most long-lasting impact, both in Punjab and later at the all-India level, was TADA.

Even though the introduction of extraordinary legislation was not a new phenomenon in postcolonial India, what was different about TADA was its gradual extension to most of India, and its attempt to bypass the routine criminal justice system in a radical way (see Kannabiran 2003). The law itself defined a terrorist and disruption in an extremely broad and vague manner allowing for its misuse in many instances.[6] There were several provisions in TADA that diluted the existing procedural safeguards. For example, TADA allowed for an extended duration of the detention period, extremely stringent bail provisions, and a major transformation in the routine procedure for recording of confessions (see Kalhan et al. 2006). Further, in an unprecedented move, TADA allowed senior police officials instead of magistrates to record confessions. Even though TADA was meant to introduce a parallel system of trying terrorists and "disruptionists," the Indian state ended up using it randomly against a broad section of people, often as a way of preventive detention (see Kalhan et al. 2006).

TADA was extended four times and then was allowed to lapse in 1995, due to large-scale protests (see Human Rights Watch 1991, 2004). Despite its lapsed status, TADA remains an important point of reference for the legal discourse in many ways. First, trials continued under the act even after its lapse, under a clause that allowed for the completion of proceedings initiated while the act was still in operation. As Ujjwal Singh puts it, there is a "life after death" quality of this law that allowed thousands of detainees to remain in the jails (Singh 2007: 67). Singh notes a remarkable statistic that in 2000, five years after the law lapsed, there were almost 5,000 cases where the trials had not been completed (Singh 2007). Second, despite protests by human rights activists and scholars in India and abroad against the draconian law, the Supreme Court upheld the constitutionality of TADA in *Kartar Singh v. State of Punjab* in 1994.[7] The reasoning of the court in upholding the law went a long way in legitimizing extraordinary legislation in India and, among other things, normalizing the transformation in the safeguards on recording confessions.

In the Kartar Singh case, the defense lawyers questioned the constitutionality of the TADA acts (1984, 1985 and 1987) on mainly two grounds: institutional and international.[8] First, the lawyers challenged the ability of the central government—the Indian Parliament—to pass this law since terrorism was a state subject concerning "control of public order." (*Kartar Singh v. State of Punjab* 1994: 3 SCC 569.) Second, the lawyers argued that many of the provisions of the acts were "draconian, ugly, vicious and highly reprehensible" since they were in direct violation of both the Indian Constitution and the ICCPR (International Covenant on Civil and Political Rights) that had been ratified by India in 1979 (Singh 2007: 619). The lawyers used international and national human rights reports to show that the police were using TADA to indulge in a "witch hunt against innocent people and suspects ... thereby unleash(ing) a reign of terror as an institutionalized terror perpetuated by Nazis on Jews" (Singh 2007: 619). Alongside the extra-judicial killings or encounters prevalent in the conflict areas, the de facto preventive detention regime emerged as a new form of state violence: a parallel form of governance no longer in the shadow of law.

In contrast to this stinging critique, the main position of the Indian state was that not only were the provisions constitutional, TADA was introduced by the Parliament because the existing criminal—procedural and penal—system was found inadequate to deal with the "astronomical(ly)" increase of "inhuman" terrorist actions. The state lawyers pointed to the "sense of helplessness in the citizens," created by the terrorists that had led to a loss of faith in "government's ability to protect them," and an assumption of the "impotence in government officials." The state, thus, articulated a deep-seated "crisis" in the Indian society being caused by the terrorists requiring an extraordinary response (Singh 2007: 619).

This understanding of the crisis in Indian society on the part of the state is in stark contrast with the other kinds of analyses regarding the accentuated crisis in India since the late 1960s (see Lokaneeta 2012, chapter 4). Actually, much of the violence by non-state actors emerged out of the inability of the postcolonial state to address the socioeconomic, political and cultural problems of the people in many regions and in India as a whole (see Balagopal 2000; Kannabiran 2003; and Gupta 2000). As Balagopal explains the limits of the state perspective in dealing with any form of militancy:

> Paradoxically, political militancy calls for harsh laws not because it is terror, but precisely because it is not just terror, but is a politics. It is a politics, right or wrong, with a social base of people—well guided or misguided—supporting it and its armed activity, which makes it difficult in the extreme to deal with it, if dealing with it means policing it. (2000: 2115)

According to Balagopal, the state needed to recognize that many of the armed movements—regardless of their ideology and strategy—represented politics, not "terror," and required a political solution rather than further repressive action. Thus, the crisis was mainly due to the state's inability to respond to the grievances and demands of the marginalized people, which occurred in an unrecognized global economic and political order. The crisis was further worsened by the increasing state repression on the movements in the form of "extra-judicial killings" or encounters, "disappearances" and the continual spiral of violence in many regions of India.[9] As Ujjwal Singh puts it, the state focused on these challenges as "terrorism" and "disruption" and "depoliticised identity struggles dismembering them into specific acts of violence, demanding extraordinary legal solutions, procedures and punishments" (Singh 2007: 52).

The Supreme Court, in its entry into the debate, accepted the Indian state's analysis of the crisis at face value: that the violence in Indian society was primarily due to the increase in terrorist acts and consequently upheld the right of the Parliament to impart an extraordinary response to combat the violence and protect the "Defense of India." Apart from steering clear of the underlying causes of this violence, the Court also failed to see the role of the state in perpetuating a spiral of violence. Finally, by upholding the constitutionality of the extraordinary law, the Court legitimized the notion that exceptional provisions could extend to nonemergency periods—thereby reinforcing a colonial tactic but taking refuge in specifically postcolonial state constructions. However, what is striking about this extraordinary law is also that the Court in the process of upholding the law implicitly sanctions torture.

One of the most important safeguards against torture in India has been the procedure of recording confessions that can only be performed by a judicial or metropolitan magistrate, after ensuring the voluntariness of the admission in an atmosphere free from police coercion. This protection regime, which by no means was completely effective, was directly challenged and transformed by TADA, and the change was upheld as constitutional by the Supreme Court in the Kartar Singh case. Section 15 of TADA allowed confessions to be recorded by police officials not lower in rank than a superintendent of police "either in writing or on any mechanical device like cassettes, tapes or sound tracks" (Prakash and Vashum 2002: 172). The confession could be admissible in the trial of the accused, the co-accused, abettor or conspirator. Before recording the confession, the police official had to warn the person that "he is not bound to make the confession and if he does so, it may be used as evidence" (Prakash and Vashum 2002: 172). Thus, the police may only record the confession if convinced that the confession is made voluntarily and has to certify the same (*Kartar Singh v. State of Punjab* 1994: 665).[10]

Ram Jethmalani—the defense lawyer in the Kartar Singh case—termed this particular provision as "atrocious and totally subversive of any civilized trial system" (*Kartar Singh v. State of Punjab* 1994: 665). There were two main objections. First, the new rule on confessions under TADA went against the criminal law provisions that existed precisely because the police were considered "untrustworthy." Second, the use of mechanical devices for recording was criticized since they could easily be tampered with. Thus, Section 15 of TADA was termed by the lawyers both "unjust" and "unreasonable" and a violation of Articles 14 (right to equality) and 21 (procedure established by law) of the Indian Constitution.[11]

The state counsel, however, claimed that since TADA only allowed the recording of confessions by a *superior* police officer, it served as a protection against its misuse (*Kartar Singh v. State of Punjab* 1994: 3 SCC 569). Here the state's assumption clearly is that it is only the lower-level (read poorly paid, untrained and "ignorant") police rather than the elite police (primarily civil servants from the Indian Police Service upper echelons of the bureaucracy) that indulge in misuse of power (see Baxi 1982). The class/education-based distinction between the two kinds of police officials denies the endemic nature of custodial torture noted by human rights groups that could not have continued without the participation or at the very least the sanction of higher police officials.

In response to these contending arguments, the Supreme Court, while acknowledging the significance of the safeguard especially for the right against self-incrimination, decided to uphold the constitutionality of the new rule of confessions based on two arguments: the reasonableness of the distinction and the right of the Parliament to introduce a new mode of proof. First, the Court argued that Section 15 of TADA was not a violation of the right to equality protected under Article 14. This is because Indian jurisprudence allowed "legislative classification" of distinct groups of persons for differential treatment as long as the basis of the distinction was "rational and scientific" and fulfilled the specific objective of the legislation. According to the Court, since TADA focused on a "distinct group of persons" who engaged in "aggravated and incensed ... offences," distinct from the ordinary criminals, the classification was reasonable and the different procedure did not violate Article 14 of the Indian Constitution. The Court specified that if the classification between the people had been left to the discretion of the central government, it would have been arbitrary but here the act itself made a distinction between the terrorists and "disruptionists," thus, constituted a rational reason for classification. The reasonableness of the classification also made the act compatible with Article 21 of the Indian Constitution (*Kartar Singh v. State of Punjab* 1994: 3 SCC 569). The difficulty in defining and distinguishing between a terrorist, subversive and ordinary criminal was, of course, ignored by the Court, despite the fact that the arbitrary application of TADA was a major source of contention and discrimination (*Black Laws and White Lies* 1995).[12]

Second, the Kartar Singh court decided to defer to the Parliament's right to introduce a new mode of proof in terrorism cases, despite its misgivings about the police use of torture. The Court readily acknowledged the presence of custodial deaths and torture, but upheld the constitutionality of the change by taking refuge, to an extent, in two conflicting opinions put forward by the police and the judicial commissions. The National Police Commission in its 1980 Report had noted the dissatisfaction of the police with the prevalent practice of disallowing them to record confessions based on an 1872 colonial law. The NPC Report argued that while in colonial times the police did use torture, in modern times they had greatly reduced the practice and therefore should be allowed to record confessions that could be used, at least, as supplementary evidence (*Kartar Singh v. State of Punjab* 1994: 3 SCC 569). The Court compared this report to the one submitted by the National Judicial Commission that confirmed the ongoing use of torture by the police even at the "supervisory" level (*Kartar Singh v. State of Punjab* 1994: 3 SCC 569). The discussion of conflicting reports about the continued use of torture makes the final decision of the Court with regards to recording of confessions very surprising. The Court even stated that its first instinct was to conclude that the police should not be allowed to record confessions, but the justices decided against it because they believed in the right of the legislature to introduce a new "mode of proof" in the given circumstances. The Court states,

> having regard to the legal competence of the legislature to make the law prescribing a different mode of proof, the meaningful purpose and object of the legislation, the gravity of terrorism unleashed by the terrorists and the disruptionists endangering not only the sovereignty and the integrity of the country but also the normal life of citizens and the reluctance of even the victims as well as the public in coming forward at the risk of their life, to give evidence—hold that the impugned section cannot be said to be suffering from any vice of unconstitutionality. In fact the *exigencies of certain situations* warrant such a legislation then it is constitutionally permissible as ruled in a number of decisions of this

court, provided none of the fundamental rights under chapter III of the constitution is infringed. (*Kartar Singh v. State of Punjab* 1994: 3 SCC 569: 680, emphasis added)

Thus, the Court decided that the extraordinary situation of terrorism warranted the bypassing of the usual safeguards and upheld the right of the Parliament to determine the new "mode of proof." The Court did recognize the possibility of misuse and cautioned the police officers against it but mostly found the rules for recording confessions in Section 15 of TADA to be adequate and not a violation of Articles 14 and 21 of the Indian Constitution.

Overall, thus, in the Kartar Singh case, the Supreme Court accepted the dilution of a major routine protection against torture, which in any case had not been able to effectively contain the use of custodial violence, and enabled a new mode of proof for a "different" set of people rendered easily recognizable from the others despite evidence to the contrary.[13] The Court did suggest the incorporation of additional guidelines into TADA to prevent the use of coercion, either embodying their own apprehension about the less protective regime or in response to the two strong dissents written by Justice K. Ramaswamy and Justice Sahai.[14] Prominent human rights activist and scholar K. Balagopal also criticized the Court for completely letting the Parliament determine the nature of these procedures, rather than ensuring their fairness. Thus, fairness was given an entirely new meaning in this parallel regime in terms of its absence (Balagopal 1994). In the TADA case, torture was not authorized explicitly, but as K. Balagopal puts it, the Supreme Court decision clearly did lead to the "implicit sanction of police torture" (Balagopal 1994: 2057).

Once the Indian Supreme Court upheld the constitutionality of TADA, the cases thereafter observed a further dilution of even the minimal safeguards applicable to confessions. In fact, any notion of voluntariness in confessions was completely undermined in subsequent cases, illustrating the slippery slope when procedural and substantive safeguards are radically changed. Kannabiran terms this post-TADA jurisprudence as the "weird jurisprudence of a dead act," referring to the ways in which the act continued after its death in much more dangerous ways. Yet this jurisprudence escaped much scrutiny from the legal community, even though this was the exact time that the Supreme Court was being heralded for its custody jurisprudence in the routine context.

The casualness towards the voluntariness of confessions in the TADA cases is most visible in the *Gurdeep Singh v. State (Delhi Administration)* (1999), when the Supreme Court was even willing to accept the confession of a person in handcuffs while the police were holding the chains and the armed guards were standing just outside the room (*Gurdeep Singh v. State* 1999). The counsel in the case argued that the confession could not be considered voluntary under the circumstances. The Court described the reasons behind the objections in the following way:

To substantiate this he [the counsel] refers to the facts that his [the accused] confession was recorded by S.P. Raj Shekhar Shetty, PW 13, when he was in handcuffs, there was another policeman in the same room holding the chain of his handcuff, and even outside the room, in which his confession was recorded, there were armed guards. Such set up, reveals by itself that threat perception existed which was hanging over his head, thus such confession cannot be construed to be (a) voluntary under Section 15 of the TADA Act, contended the counsel. (*Gurdeep Singh v. State* 1999)

However, despite noting the circumstances in which the confession was recorded, the Court considered it voluntary primarily because all the "formal" safeguards had been ensured by the police superintendent and "no other threat or inducement" was used in the case. The Court, in fact, stated that handcuffing and presence of guards was necessary for ensuring security and did not in any way affect the voluntariness of the confession. Pointing to the obvious contradictions in this situation, where the prisoner was subject to prolonged detention and interrogation in chains, Kannabiran writes,

> Arrest and Confinement would be coercive enough; but the denial of freedom of move, the freedom to meet people and talk to them for long periods, were sufficient to destroy both volition and will... Classifying the accused as a high-security prisoner and parading him in chains dehumanized him and destroyed his volition and will. Thereafter, nothing remained of his person that could perform a voluntary act. (Kannabiran 2003: 113)

Thus, according to Kannabiran, voluntariness in any case had very little meaning in custody, and, under TADA even less, but the process became visibly coercive in the current instance. In addition, one could argue that this case merely followed the logic upheld by the Kartar Singh Court. Once the Court agreed that under TADA, the higher-ranked police officials could record confessions despite the well-documented evidence of police abuses in routine cases, the Court demolished the very backbone of the safeguards against torture. Not surprisingly, then, the subsequent decisions did not find "minor" bypassing of safeguards as leading to involuntariness of a confession (*Wariyam Singh v. State of U.P.* 1995). In other words, the Gurdeep Singh case went a step further of "rightly" applying the logic of Kartar Singh—once a higher police official was allowed to record confession and ensure voluntariness, the handcuffing by a lower-ranked police official during the confession process was a mere extension of that logic (see *Wariyam Singh v. State of U.P.* 1995; see Kannabiran 2003: 111–113).[15]

TADA lapsed in 1995, despite the Court's intervention and attempt to uphold the constitutionality of the act. On the one hand, the end of the extraordinary law was definitely a result of the concerted campaigns by human rights groups in India and abroad. After all, under TADA (until 1994), about 76,000 were detained, 35 percent were tried, 25 percent released and 95 percent were acquitted—making the conviction rate only 1 percent (Prakash and Vashum 2002: 160). It was primarily used against the poor, marginalized and the dissenting actors in many contexts. On the other hand, the act's end may also point to an inability of the liberal state to uphold a law that was held constitutional despite its gross violation of fundamental rights, highlighting the contradiction between the routine and exceptional contexts—and it ultimately resurfaced in the following decade of globalization, just as progress was being made on routine torture.

THE IRONY: PROGRESS ON ROUTINE TORTURE

The Kartar Singh decision was even more striking because even while the Supreme Court was passing a law that would dilute the protections against torture in extraordinary laws, it was creating a parallel discourse of protections against custodial deaths as a result of torture in the routine context. Due to the rise of civil liberty groups and the power of social action litigation, the Supreme Court gave two major decisions on custodial deaths: *Nilabati Behera v. State of Orissa* in 1993 and *D. K. Basu v. State of West Bengal; Ashok K. Johri v. State of Uttar Pradesh* in 1996 (see Law Commission of India 1999, *One Hundred and Fifty Second Report on Custodial Crimes*). While most of this progress occurred within the national context, it was informed by international norms and networks, culminating in India's signing of the Convention on Torture in 1997 (even though it is still not ratified).

The Nilabati Behera case involved a twenty-two-year-old man, Suman, who was suspected of theft, picked up by the police, and whose body with multiple injuries was found the next day on the railway tracks (*Smt. Nilabati Behera v. State of Orissa* 1993). The police claimed that he had escaped from custody in the middle of the night and was hit by a passing train. The Court, however, converted a letter from the mother as a writ petition and stated that:

> The burden is, therefore, clearly on the respondents to explain how Suman Behera sustained those injuries which caused his death. Unless a plausible explanation is given by the respondents which is consistent with their innocence, the obvious inference is that the fatal injuries were inflicted to Suman Behera in police custody resulting in his death, for which the respondents are responsible and liable. (*Smt. Nilabati Behera v. State of Orissa* 1993)

The Supreme Court relied on the doctor's postmortem report that attributed the fatal injuries to "merciless beating" with a *lathi* (stick). The Court rejected a range of other improbable evidence, such as a second doctor's report and the joint inquiry by the magistrate and senior police suggesting that Suman had escaped from the police by chewing off his rope and subsequently died in a train accident.

The most significant outcome of this case is the elaboration of the right to compensation for violation of Article 21 in custodial death cases. Even the state lawyers did not deny that there was a right to compensation for a violation of Article 21, but refused to accept the death as a custodial one.[16] The Court also took a substantial and uniquely creative step in improving the safeguards against torture, by imposing the monetary burden on the state for its inability to protect the human rights of citizens. The Supreme Court stated that while there was sovereign immunity for officers in private law cases, there was no such immunity with respect to a right to compensation for violation of fundamental rights in public law (*Kasturilal Ralia Rain Jain v. the State of Uttar Pradesh* (1965).[17] An amount of 150,000 rupees was accorded to the victim Suman Behera's mother in this case, calculated according to the amount the victim Suman earned and some additional money for legal expenses. Although this was not the first case where the right to compensation was given by the Court for violation of fundamental rights or custodial deaths, the Court certainly went to great lengths to explain and justify the principle behind it.[18] Nonetheless, even in this landmark case, the Court continued to assume the general adequacy of existing procedural mechanisms to contain custodial deaths and torture.

It was not until 1996 that the Supreme Court actually addressed the procedural mechanisms required to deal with custodial deaths.[19] The Legal Aid Services in Bengal drew the Court's attention to news items about custodial deaths in lockups and asked for their letter to be treated as a writ petition to inquire into why custodial deaths were being hushed up by the police, and also to ask for developing mechanisms for compensating the victims. The Court, in turn, asked the various states of India to submit reports on custodial deaths and violence. In *D.K. Basu v. State of West Bengal*, the Court, first and foremost, acknowledged the peculiar nature of custodial violence and the "helplessness" of the victim in custody.[20] The Court, while accepting the lack of any definition of torture in the law, describes it in the following manner:

> "Torture" has not been defined in Constitution or in other penal laws. "Torture" of a human being by another human being is essentially an instrument to impose the will of the "strong" over the "weak" by suffering. The word torture today has become synonymous with the *darker side of human civilization*... "Custodial torture" is a naked violation of human dignity and degradation which destroys, to a very large extent, the individual personality. IT is a calculated assault on human dignity and *whenever human dignity is wounded, civilization takes a step backward—flag of humanity must on each such occasion fly half-mast.*

(*D. K. Basu v. State of West Bengal; Ashok K. Johri v. State of Uttar Pradesh* 1996, emphasis added)

The Court further writes, "Any form of torture or cruel, inhuman or degrading treatment would fall within the inhibition of Article 21 of the Constitution, whether it occurs during investigation, interrogation or otherwise."[21] The Court does write elsewhere that "reasonable restrictions" can be applied to the protections under Article 21, but does not clarify the nature of these restrictions.

Apart from a powerful rhetoric and enunciation of the legal safeguards against torture and custodial deaths, the D. K. Basu court was also willing to acknowledge a crisis in legitimacy being created by the widespread use of custodial violence. The Court writes:

> Experience shows that worst violations of human rights take place during the course of investigation, when the police with a view to secure evidence or confession often resorts to third degree methods including torture ... The increasing incidence of torture and death in custody has assumed such alarming proportions that it is affecting the creditability of the Rule of Law and the administration of criminal justice system. The community rightly feels perturbed. Society's cry for justice becomes louder. (*D. K. Basu v. State of West Bengal; Ashok K. Johri v. State of Uttar Pradesh* 1996, emphasis added)

Here, in noting the modus operandi of custodial violence as taking place during investigations, the Court finally recognized (without acknowledging them, of course) the findings of several human rights groups, including the People's Union for Democratic Rights, People's Union for Civil Liberties and Andhra Pradesh Civil Liberties Committee, about the methods used by the police to hide custodial deaths. The police often arrested people without any record of the arrest and subjected them to torture during interrogations. If some person died in custody, the police "disposed of the body" denying that the person was ever detained in the first place. If custody could not be denied in some cases, the police subsequently claimed that the person died after he or she was let go or escaped from the custody of the police. In order to further strengthen the custody jurisprudence, the Court reiterated the recommendation of the Law Commission asking the Indian Parliament to change the burden of proof in custodial violence cases: If a person is injured or dies in custody, the police should be presumed to be responsible for the injury (*Bhagwan Singh and Another v. State of Punjab* 1992: 3 SCC 249; *One Hundred and Thirteenth Report on Injuries in Police Custody* 1985).[22]

Finally, recognizing the need to check illegal arrests and detentions, the Court sought "transparency" and "accountability," by introducing an *arrest memo* or *custody memo* to be signed by the arrestee and a witness (relative or respectable person) during the time of arrest.[23] The arrestee was to be informed of this right, examined medically if he or she requests and the facts were to be recorded in an "inspection memo" signed by both the officer and the arrestee. The Court also required the arrestee to be examined by a recognized doctor every forty-eight hours and asserted the need for counsel during a part of the interrogation. Records of all documents were to be sent to the district magistrate and a police control room in a state or district to monitor all arrests and detention (*D. K. Basu v. State of West Bengal; Ashok K. Johri v. State of Uttar Pradesh* (1996).[24]

The Behera and Basu courts, thus, for the first time developed systematic custody jurisprudence. In this context, it may be important to note the close relationship between the domestic and international law as well. While the Indian Supreme Court referred to the provisions of the Indian Constitution in these cases, it also referred to other jurisdictions (such as England) and emphasized the international commitments towards human rights that India shared. For instance, in the D. K. Basu case, the Indian Supreme Court makes a reference to Article 5 of the Universal Declaration of Human Rights (1948) that prohibits the use of torture. In fact, the Court points to the fact that torture and custodial abuse (cruel, inhuman, and degrading treatment [CIDT]) remain a global issue of concern despite these commitments. The Court notes, "No violation of any of the human rights has been the subject of so many Conventions and Declarations as 'torture'—all aiming at total banning of it in all forms but in spite of the commitments made to eliminate torture, the fact remains that torture is more widespread now than ever before." Thus the court emphasizes the need to constantly develop ways of combating torture and CIDT. The influence of international law is also seen in the reference to how, despite the Indian government's reservation during the ratification of the ICCPR against giving compensation to persons who were subject to unlawful arrest or detention, the domestic jurisprudence had made that reservation irrelevant by providing a right to compensation under Article 21 (right to life and liberty), epitomized in cases such as Basu and Behera (*D. K. Basu v. State of West Bengal; Bhagwan Singh and Another v. State of Punjab* 1992: 3 SCC 249; *One Hundred and Thirteen Report on Injuries in Police Custody* 1985).[25]

CONNECTING THE ROUTINE AND THE EXTRAORDINARY: IMPLICATIONS FOR TORTURE AND HUMAN RIGHTS

In the 1990s, the Indian Supreme Court sent mixed signals as far as the protections against torture are concerned. On the one hand, it comes up with its most innovative understanding of custody jurisprudence in the context of deaths as a result of torture, and the Indian government signed the UN Convention Against Torture and CIDT (in 1997) and set up the National Human Rights Commission (NHRC) (in 1993) to monitor the human rights situation in India. On the other hand, the Court was willing to dilute the protections against torture by upholding the TADA that was introduced by the Indian government. This tension between the routine and the exception became further pronounced when POTA was introduced in 2002, with extraordinary provisions similar to TADA—and it was upheld by the Supreme Court once again as a necessary step to deal with terrorism. In both the Kartar Singh case and prominent POTA cases, there were references to the international protections against torture, CIDT, or self-incrimination, alongside the relevant constitutional protections that were to be taken into account—and yet the Court found ways of arguing that they could uphold these extraordinary laws.

These tensions have only increased over the years, with a growth and proliferation of extraordinary laws, and the globalization of law continues to play a contradictory role. On the one hand, the UN resolutions on terrorism contributed to further legitimizing the emergence of extraordinary legislations that focus on suspected "terrorists," or all those who dissent against the state and/or belong to targeted communities. In India, those laws have been the 2002 POTA (at the national level) that was repealed in 2004 in part due to the protests against it, the 2005 Chhatisgarh Special Public Security Act (CSPSA) in response to the Maoist movement, and the 2008 Unlawful Activities Prevention Act (UAPA—adopted after the Mumbai terrorist attacks) that is now being indiscriminately used against human rights activists and others.

On the other hand, due to the increasing role of India as an economic and political power, there is an international pressure on India to fulfill its obligations towards human rights. One of the main recommendations of the first and second Universal Periodic Review has been to ask India to pass the anti-torture bill, a crucial step in the ratification of the UN Convention Against Torture. Currently, there is such an attempt to pass an anti-torture bill in the Parliament. However, the first instantiation of the bill was thoroughly rejected by human rights activists and lawyers, due to its very narrow focus and the recommendations of the committee are currently under consideration (see the Working Group on Human Rights [2012] report on this topic). The bill, however, needs not only to address the high rates of custodial deaths due to torture in routine contexts, but also its implications for extraordinary laws and conflict-ridden contexts. After all, as the Asian Center for Human Rights (ACHR) noted using NHRC figures, the total number of custodial deaths (reported) from 1994 to 2008 has been 16,836 (or about 1,203 a year), making this a major human rights concern for India and the world.

The postcolonial Indian state continues to introduce extraordinary laws quite frequently: the 2002 POTA (at the national level), the 2005 Chhatisgarh Special Public Security Act (CSPSA) in response to the Maoist movement, and the 2008 UAPA. In recent years, the UN Security Council resolutions as well as the models and exchange of extraordinary laws in many different countries have further enabled the Indian state to hold on to these laws and try to make them a permanent feature of the Indian criminal justice system.

The mixed signals sent by the United Nations after the 9/11 attacks—to deal with terrorism at any cost, while urging the ratification of the UN Convention Against Torture in its Universal Periodic Review Reports—ironically allows the Indian state to continue maintaining the contradictory emphasis in its human rights implementation. As the critical cosmopolitan perspective introduced at the beginning of this volume suggests, the globalization of extraordinary law allows the postcolonial state to reframe globalized social crisis as security threat. Thus, unlike the pattern of Latin America where extraordinary laws are overruled, and following the trend of Israel described elsewhere in this volume, neither the globalization of law nor independent legal institutions are enough to fulfill human rights in the security crisis of a postcolonial state. As the introduction predicts, and again parallel to Israel, progress was greater on the routine domestic issues where civil liberties and democratic rights groups exercised some leverage. The future of human rights in India depends on reclaiming the full range of the rule of law, at the local and global levels, and addressing the underlying causes of the conflicts rather than treating them merely as security threats.

NOTES

1. Further elaboration of some of the themes of this chapter is in Jinee Lokaneeta, *Transnational Torture: Law, Violence, and State Power in the United States and India* (New York: New York University Press, 2012).
2. Krishnan, for instance, writes that just as the U.S. Patriot Act makes even the most "tangential" association with a "suspicious" organization the basis of punitive action, POTA also defined the association with a terrorist group very broadly and puts the onus of disproving the link with the terrorist group on the individual. The most contentious issue in both was, of course, the definition of terrorism.
3. Kannabiran points out that around 258 statutes introduced by the British were operational right up to 1960.
4. In Punjab, the insurgency was primarily due to issues of identity as Sikhs: separate personal code, quotas in military, language, question of water rights and unemployment and eventually a demand for autonomy. In Kashmir there has been a conflict between the Indian and Pakistani governments on one hand and the aspirations of the people of the state on the other since 1947. The main way in which this conflict has played out is by the use of armed state actions and extraordinary laws. In the process, there has been unprecedented violence in the region and large-scale violation of human rights on the part of both the militants and the state. The state forces, particularly the armed forces, have been involved in custodial rapes, torture, detentions and extrajudicial killings. Most of the reports also point to the lack of accountability and redress in human rights violation cases on the part of the Indian state. Even when some action is taken, it is primarily administrative disciplinary measures, not criminal liability for the rapes, torture and killings. (See *Crackdown in Kashmir* 1993; Human Rights Watch, *The Human Rights Crisis in Kashmir* 1993; and Kaur 2002: 269–300.)
5. Both these acts allowed for bypassing the usual safeguards in arrest, detention and the use of force, providing the right to use lethal force with little accountability. Once a region is declared as a disturbed area, mere warning

could allow for the officers to shoot at persons if they do not follow the law prohibiting an assembly of five persons or possess firearms.

6. The definition of a terrorist act in TADA is:

> Whoever with intent to overawe the government as by law established or to strike terror in the people ... or to alienate any section ... or to adversely affect the harmony amongst ... people using bombs, dynamite ... firearms ... as to cause ... death or injuries ... to persons ... property.... Or detains any person and threatens to injure such person in order to compel the government or any other person to do or abstain from doing any act commits a terrorist act. (Prakash and Vashum 2002: 163)

> The act stipulated punishment for both the persons who committed the act but also those who "conspire or attempts to commit, or advocates, abets, advises or incites or knowingly facilitates...." And those who harbor or attempt to harbor or conceal were to receive five years' imprisonment to life. Disruptive activity means

> any action taken, by act or by speech or through any media.... Which questions, disrupts or is intended to disrupt, whether directly or indirectly, the sovereignty and territorial integrity of India or which is intended to bring about or supports any claim, whether directly or indirectly, for the cession of any part of India from the Union. (Prakash and Vashum 2002: 164)

7. Some of the lawyers in the case were well-known civil rights activists and legal scholars of India, namely, V. M. Tarkunde, Ram Jethmalani and Rajinder Sachar.

8. The act was introduced multiple times each time with some changes. Terrorist Affected Areas (Special Courts) Act, Act 61 of 1984 allowed for speedy trials of certain offenses, the central government to declare any area as a "terrorist affected area," and special courts and judges with a right to appeal to the Supreme Court. This was allowed at the all-India level except Jammu and Kashmir. The TADA (Prevention) Act, 1985 extended these provisions to Jammu and Kashmir. This allowed for "Prevention and coping with terrorist and disruptive activities," "deterrent punishments and designated courts for speedy trials." The context was terrorist acts in Punjab and Chandigarh but also extended to other parts such as Delhi, Rajasthan, Haryana, UP. The TADA (Prevention) Act, 1987 was a renewal, and since then TADA was renewed for eight years by extending it again and again until 1995.

9. In Andhra, "encounter" killings have been a major cause of concern for human rights groups such as the Andhra Pradesh Civil Liberties Committee (APCLC). Kannabiran (2003: 9) points out that the basis of these encounters has been the operation of A. P. Suppression of Disturbances Act (1967) that was used to classify many of the tribal areas as "disturbed" and allowed the police to shoot at any party of five since it was considered unlawful under the act (*Life, Liberty and Livelihood* 1996). Amnesty International also points to the high number of disappearances in Kashmir and Punjab. In Kashmir, for instance, it quotes certain sources as putting the number of disappearances at 2,000 in the 1990s (Amnesty International 1992, 1999). In Punjab, similarly, the number of disappearances in the 1980s has been focused on by human rights groups such as the Human Rights Wing of the Akali Dal and National Human Rights Commission that have instituted an inquiry into allegations of thousands of disappearances in recent years. Kaur notes that between 1984 and 1994, human rights groups found more than 2,000 illegal cremations in just one district of Punjab (Kaur 2002: 272).

10. Rule 15 of TADA allowed the confession to be recorded in the language of the accused (or officer or the court) and played back to him and if it is in writing,

then it would be signed by the accused and also certified by the police stating that he recorded it and it was a true account. A memorandum also had to be attached to the confession confirming that the warnings were accorded to the accused and the confession voluntarily made in his presence and recorded by him and confirmed by the accused. These additional rules were similar to Section 164 of the CRPC regarding the recording of the confessions by the magistrates. The confession in case of Section 15 was then sent to the chief judicial magistrate or metropolitan magistrate who sent it to the designated court.

11. A very controversial issue in the TADA jurisprudence has been the dilution of safeguards regarding the misuse of confessions against a co-accused. Mostly in Indian jurisprudence, following Anglo American philosophy, the confession of a co-accused is considered weak evidence, requiring the confession to be taken into account only if all other evidence points towards the co-accused, and even the corroboration of confession of the accused is suggested by previous courts. Post-TADA, the confession of a co-accused became a major point of debate: The Court suggested that confession is evidence and some justices even went to the extent of stating that confession of a co-accused could be used as substantial evidence (see *State v. Nalini* 1999; and *AN Dube v. NB Bhoir* 2000). This affected the jurisprudential and statutory safeguards against relying too much on confessions.

12. Even while TADA was ostensibly selective, as the People's Union for Democratic Rights (PUDR) documented, it took in its fold people from all walks of life, advocates, judges, students, writers, artists, legislators, striking trade unionists, human rights activists and even Bollywood actor Sunjay Dutt.

13. An argument similar to Ackerman's formulation of maintaining effective sovereignty (discussed in Chapter 2) in the face of terrorism appears to be adopted by the Court for the "defense of India."

14. These guidelines included the production of the accused in front of a chief metropolitan or chief judicial magistrate to whom the confession is already sent under TADA. The magistrate was to ask the accused to sign the statement and if there was any complaint of torture to ensure that the accused was examined by a medical officer. Also, the Court cautioned that if the person asserted the right to silence during interrogation, that should be respected. The Court also suggested the constitution of review committees at the central and state levels comprising government officials to monitor the TADA cases.

15. The court goes to the extent of saying that inducements should be given to the accused in the form of reduced punishment so that he agrees to confess due to his own desire to repent and speak the truth (see *Gurdeep Singh v. State* 1999). Kannabiran writes that this leads to the idea of "effective state" and speedy trials based on confessions (2003: 111–113).

16. One area in which the Supreme Court has consistently taken a stand against officers is when the police officers attempt to defend the use of torture claiming some kind of immunity due to their authorized powers of investigation. For instance, Section 53 of the Madras/Tamil Nadu police rules asserts that there is a statute of limitations as far as possibilities of prosecution of police officers is concerned. The prosecution can be initiated only within three months of the act for actions taken under the police powers act. The Court disagreed with this interpretation of the police powers and concluded that while certain acts may be protected under this section, torture and custodial death are not since there is no "reasonable relation between the provisions of the act and the actions" (*State of Andhra Pradesh v. N. Venugopal and others* [1963]; *S. P. Vaithianathan v. K. Shanmuganathan* [1994]: 4 SCC 569). The High Court in both the cases had made the assumption that any act initiated during investigation is subject to the statute of limitations and quashed the cases, but this was not accepted by the Supreme Court, which took a strong

stand against the officers in these cases. However, the issue of sanctions under Section 197 remains to be resolved and is reiterated by human rights groups.

17. Thus, in the Kasturilal case, the Supreme Court upheld the right to sovereign immunity but that was a private tort case.

18. The precedent for the right to compensation was Rudul Sah that established the right to compensation in cases where there are violations of fundamental rights under Article 226 of the Constitution by the High Court and Article 32 of the Constitution by the Supreme Court. The Court did suggest that ordinarily the redressal for violation of fundamental rights should go back to the courts, especially when there is factual controversy. But subsequent cases have followed Rudul Sah's suggestions that compensation for violations of fundamental rights can be awarded in public law cases. This precedent was used in Saheli and Hongray (see *Saheli, A Women's Resources Centre and Others v. Commissioner of Police, Delhi Police Headquarters and Others* [1990]). The state is held responsible for the tortious acts of its employees in these cases and compensation is given (see also *Bhim Singh v. State of J&K* [1985] [4] SCC 677). Compensation for custodial violence came up in a 1989 case.

19. The Nilabati Behera as allowing for compensation for the deprivation of liberty including custodial torture and death continued to be used, for instance, in *T. C. Pathak v. State of U.P.* (1995). In this case Pathak's son, Neetu, was detained for questioning in a theft case and he was tortured, a fact confirmed by the senior superintendent of police who conducted an inquiry into the incident, though denied by the accused policemen. Even though by the time the writ came up in the Court, Neetu was free, the Court noted that this was a case of custodial torture and illegal detention based on the senior superintendent's report in violation of Article 21 and gave 10,000 rupees as compensation. This directive of the Court was not supposed to affect any other remedy in private law or prejudice any trial courts against the accused, indicating that this was just compensation under public law due to a violation of a fundamental right. *T. C. Pathak v. State of U.P* (1995) 6 SCC 357.

20. Another case was added to this Public Interest Litigation, a case of custodial death in Uttar Pradesh of Mahesh Bihari added by Ashok Johri (see *D. K. Basu v. State of West Bengal*; *Ashok K. Johri v. State of Uttar Pradesh* 1996).

21. Note that here the term is not only torture and cruel and unusual but also inhuman and degrading treatment and punishment.

22. This is an extension of the recommendation made in the case of *Bhagwan Singh v. State of Punjab* and *Shyamsunder Trivedi* that made the police responsible for explaining what happened to the person in custody. That argument was made more specific in the case of D. K. Basu in the sense of assuming the police as responsible for the death or injury if it took place in custody. This recommendation of the Court in several cases, reiterated by the Law Commission and most reports of the National Human Rights Commission (NHRC), continues to be ignored by the Indian Parliament.

23. Before the D. K. Basu case, the Supreme Court had, in an earlier case *Joginder Singh v. State of Uttar Pradesh* (1994) 3 J.T. (SC), suggested the right of the arrested person to inform a concerned person about his arrest and the Court said that he should be informed of this right. See *One Hundred and Fifty Second Report on Custodial Crimes*, Law Commission of India. If a friend/relative is not present, then the person is informed through the legal aid center telegraphically of the date, time and venue of the arrest. The arrested person had to be told of this right to inform. The identity of the arresting officers and detaining authorities also had to be properly recorded.

24. This information was to be disseminated through the police administrative channels, *doordarshan* (national television), radio and pamphlets in different

languages. The Court declared that these rules had to be followed and any violation would result in departmental action as well as contempt of court proceedings.

REFERENCES

Amnesty International (1992). *India: Torture, Rape and Deaths in Custody.* London: Amnesty International.

Amnesty International (1999). *India: "If They Are Dead, Tell Us: "Disappearances" in Jammu and Kashmir.* London, UK: Amnesty International.

Ashok K. Johri v. State of Uttar Pradesh. (1996). http://judis.nic.in/supremecourt/qrydisp.asp?tfnm=14580 (last visited June 23, 2005).

Balagopal, K. (1994)."In Defence of India: Supreme Court and Terrorism." *Economic and Political Weekly* 29: 2054–2060.

Baxi, Upendra (1982). *The Crisis of the Indian Legal System.* New Delhi: Vikas.

Balagopal, K. (2000). "Law Commission's View of Terrorism." *Economic and Political Weekly* 35: 2114–2122.

Black Laws and White Lies: A Report on TADA—1985–1995. (1995, May). Delhi: People's Union for Democratic Rights.

Crackdown in Kashmir: Torture of Detainees and Assault on the Medical Community. (1993). Boston, MA: Physicians for Human Rights and Asia Watch.

Gagne, Chris. (2005). "POTA: Lessons Learned from India's Anti-Terror Act." *Boston Third World Law Journal* 25: 261–299.

Gupta, Anirudha. (2000, March 25–31). "TADA: Hard Law for Soft State." *Economic and Political Weekly.* http://www.epw.org.in/showArticles.php?root=2000&leaf=03&filename=1122&filetype=html (last visited January 26, 2006).

Gurdeep Singh v. State. (1999). Delhi Administration. http://judis.nic.in/supremecourt/qrydisp.asp?tfnm=16663 (last visited June 23, 2005).

Haragopal, G., and K. Balagopal. (1998). "Civil Liberties Movement and the State in India." In *People's Rights: Social Movement and the State in the Third World,* eds. Manoranjan Mohanty, Partha Nath Mukherji, and Olle Tornquist. New Delhi: Sage.

Human Rights Watch. (1991). *Punjab in Crisis: Human Rights in India.* New York: Human Rights Watch.

Human Rights Watch. (1993). *The Human Rights Crisis in Kashmir: A Pattern of Impunity.* New York: Human Rights Watch.

Human Rights Watch. (2004). *Dead Silence: The Legacy of Abuses in Punjab.* New York: Human Rights Watch.

Kalhan, Anil, Gerald P. Conroy, Mamta Kaushal, Sam Scott Miller, and Jed S. Rakoff. (2006). "Colonial Continuities: Human Rights, Terrorism, and Security Laws in India." *Columbia Journal of Asian Law* 20(1): 93–234.

Kannabiran, K. G. (2003). *The Wages of Impunity: Power, Justice and Human Rights.* New Delhi: Orient Longman.

Kaur, Jaskaran. (2002). "A Judicial Blackout: Judicial Impunity for Disappearances in Punjab." *Harvard Human Rights Journal* 15: 269–300.

Krishnan, Jayanth K. (2004). "India's 'Patriot Act': POTA and the Impact on Civil Liberties in the World's Largest Democracy." *Law and Inequality* 22: 265–300.

Law Commission of India. (1999). *One Hundred and Fifty Second Report on Custodial Crimes.* Delhi: Printed by the Govt. of India Press for the Controller of Publications.

Life, Liberty and Livelihood: Civil Liberties in Andhra Pradesh Vol. 1 (1996). *(Fact Finding Committee Reports 1978–84).* Hyderabad: Andhra Pradesh Civil Liberties Committee.

Lokaneeta, Jinee. (2012). *Transnational Torture: Law, Violence, and State Power in the United States and India*. New York: New York University Press.

One Hundred and Thirteenth Report on Injuries in Police Custody. (1985). Delhi: Law Commission of India.

Prakash, Louis, and R. Vashum. Eds. (2002). *Extraordinary Laws in India*. New Delhi: Indian Social Institute.

Ruthven, Malise. (1978). *Torture: The Grand Conspiracy*. London: Weidenfeld and Nicholson.

Saheli, A Women's Resources Centre and Others v. Commissioner of Police, Delhi Police Headquarters and Others. (1990). http://indiankanoon.org/doc/467223/ (last consulted December 27, 2012).

Scheppele, Kim. (2004). "Other People's Patriot Acts: Europe's Response to September 11." *Loyola Law Review* 50: 89–148.

Singh, Ujjwal Kumar. (2007). *The State, Democracy and Anti-Terror Laws in India*. New Delhi: Sage.

State v. Nalini. (1999). http://judis.nic.in/supremecourt/qrydisp.asp?tfnm=16831 (last visited August 5, 2005).

State of Andhra Pradesh v. N. Venugopal and others. (1963). http://judis.nic.in/supremecourt/qrydisp.asp?tfnm=3492 (last visited September 6, 2005).

Wariyam Singh v. State of U.P. (1995). http://judis.nic.in/supremecourt/qrydisp.asp?tfnm=10505 (last visited August 5, 2005).

Working Group on Human Rights. (2012). http://www.wghr.org/pdf/Assessment%20of%20implementation%20of%20UPR1%20recommendations.pdf (last visited December 27, 2012).

Index

References to tables and figures are indicated with an italic *t* and *f*.

For Product Safety Concerns and Information please contact our EU
representative GPSR@taylorandfrancis.com
Taylor & Francis Verlag GmbH, Kaufingerstraße 24, 80331 München, Germany